Counseling Students

in Levels 2 and 3

Counseling Students

in Levels 2 and 3

A PBIS/RTI Guide

Jon M. Shepard
Jeffrey D. Shahidullah
John S. Carlson

CORWIN
A SAGE Company

CORWIN
A SAGE Company

FOR INFORMATION:

Corwin

A SAGE Company

2455 Teller Road

Thousand Oaks, California 91320

(800) 233-9936

www.corwin.com

SAGE Publications Ltd.

1 Oliver's Yard

55 City Road

London EC1Y 1SP

United Kingdom

SAGE Publications India Pvt. Ltd.

B 1/I 1 Mohan Cooperative Industrial Area

Mathura Road, New Delhi 110 044

India

SAGE Publications Asia-Pacific Pte. Ltd.

3 Church Street

#10-04 Samsung Hub

Singapore 049483

Acquisitions Editor: Jessica Allan

Associate Editor: Kimberly Greenberg

Editorial Assistant: Heidi Arndt

Permissions Editor: Karen Ehrmann

Project Editor: Veronica Stapleton Hooper

Copy Editor: Terri Lee Paulsen

Typesetter: C&M Digitals (P) Ltd.

Proofreader: Dennis W. Webb

Indexer: Karen Wiley

Cover Designer: Anupama Krishnan

Copyright © 2013 by Corwin

Printed in the United States of America

A catalog record of this book is available from the Library of Congress.

ISBN: 9781452255644

This book is printed on acid-free paper.

SUSTAINABLE FORESTRY INITIATIVE

Certified Chain of Custody
Promoting Sustainable Forestry
www.sfiprogram.org
SFI-01268

SFI label applies to text stock

13 14 15 17 10 9 8 7 6 5 4 3 2 1

Contents

Preface

In recent years, research and legislation has increasingly sought to improve students' learning and socialization by seeking ways to improve mental health services in schools. There are a variety of evidence-based interventions and programs available for school practitioners at the universal (i.e., service to all or many), selected (i.e., service to some), and indicated (i.e., service to few) prevention levels. This book focuses on utilizing counseling as an intervention for students who require extensive support within the secondary (i.e., selected) and tertiary (i.e., indicated) prevention levels of Positive Behavioral Interventions and Supports (PBIS) and Response to Intervention (RTI). Only a cursory view of school-based counseling at the universal or primary level of prevention is included. There are other sources (referred to in this book) that provide in-depth coverage of primary prevention approaches to school-based mental health services.

Our major aim is to explore the role of counseling within *integrated school mental health programming* based on *best practices* in current research and practice. From the perspective of comprehensive school mental health service delivery, we apply PBIS/RTI as an organizing framework from which to provide integrative school mental health programming. Within this context, we focus specifically on utilizing counseling as an intervention for students who require extensive support.

This book is most relevant for school mental health professionals, such as counselors, school psychologists, and social workers, who provide counseling and psychological services. It is also intended to be a useful resource for school administrators; special education directors; psychological service directors; clinical supervisors; school mental health liaisons; university faculty who teach coursework in counseling, psychology, and/or special education; students being trained in the fields of counseling, psychology, and/or special education; and other stakeholders who are interested in developing and improving school-based mental health service delivery.

Progressive service delivery models require data-based outcomes for those children who are experiencing social-emotional-behavioral challenges in school. This book provides guidance for school mental health professionals to adapt their practices to the changing landscape associated with effective educational outcomes and accountability. Special attention is given to practical and useful techniques that can be carried out as intended and with high levels of acceptability by providers and stakeholders. Additionally, this book expounds on professional growth and development as a counselor during a time when outcomes and accountability must be examined and documented within school-based practice.

This book is divided into two major parts. In Part I, we examine the role of responsive school-based counseling in PBIS/RTI. We emphasize collaborative approaches and view PBIS/RTI as a joint initiative of general education and special education. RTI is designed to help students be successful in the general education curriculum. As such, RTI should increase the accuracy of special education referrals. We intend for Part I to serve as a guide for school practitioners who provide evidence-based counseling services within PBIS/RTI. We examine considerations for service delivery for students in both general education and special education. Part II focuses on related topics, including advancing one's clinical skills in counseling, professional development, and emerging models for difficult service delivery areas in school mental health.

Discussion questions are provided for each chapter. In the Resources section we have included sample forms (e.g., "Intervention Planning Form"), lists of further resources—such as a list of books and websites for counselors, students, and parents—and a counselor self-evaluation survey and professional growth plan form. We hope this book provides a useful and accessible guidebook for counselors, school psychologists, other mental health professionals, and other school personnel who work tirelessly to meet the social, emotional, and behavioral needs of their students.

Acknowledgments

We wish to thank our acquisitions editor, Jessica Allan, for her work, insightful considerations, and support in bringing this book to reality. We also wish to acknowledge the contribution of our advisory board. Their input was exceedingly helpful in improving the content, organization, and usefulness of chapters. Finally, we thank all of the children and families that each of us has worked with in the past. Those experiences helped to motivate us to write this book for our colleagues working in the field.

PUBLISHER'S ACKNOWLEDGMENTS

Corwin wishes to acknowledge the following peer reviewers for their editorial insight and guidance.

Jennifer Betters
School Counselor
Verona Area School District
Verona, Wisconsin

Janet Slowman Chee
School Psychologist and Chief of Planning
Tsehootsoi Medical Center
Fort Defiance, Arizona

Karen M. Joseph
School Counselor
Roberto Clemente Middle School,
Montgomery County Public Schools, Maryland
Germantown, Maryland

Diana Joyce
Psychologist, Associate Scholar
University of Florida
Gainesville, Florida

Neil MacNeill
Principal
Ellenbrook Primary School
Ellenbrook, Western Australia, Australia

Katy Olweiler
Counselor
Lakeside School
Seattle, Washington

Diane P. Smith
School Counselor
Smethport Area School District
Smethport, Pennsylvania

About the Authors

Jon M. Shepard, PhD, LSSP, is a licensed psychologist and licensed specialist in school psychology in Texas, currently a practicing school psychologist in Denton, Texas. He has worked in school districts in the Dallas–Fort Worth, Texas, area and in Oklahoma. Dr. Shepard also maintains a part-time private practice working with children, adolescents, and adults. After receiving his master's degree in counseling at Harding School of Theology, he worked for Youth Villages in Tennessee, providing in-home family counseling to assist at-risk and juvenile offending youth. He received training and supervision in using Multi-Systemic Therapy (MST) while working there. Dr. Shepard received his PhD in educational psychology at Oklahoma State University. He completed his predoctoral internship at the Oklahoma Health Consortium with rotations in the Oklahoma City Public Schools, Norman Child Guidance Clinic, and Jim Thorpe Rehabilitation Hospital.

Jeffrey D. Shahidullah, EdS, NCSP, is a school psychology PhD student at Michigan State University. He holds a BA degree in psychology and an EdS degree in school psychology from Baylor University. He is a nationally certified school psychologist (NCSP) and has practiced in multiple public school districts in Central Texas, as well as the Methodist Children's Home, a residential program for at-risk youth. Jeff has experience working within PBIS and RTI frameworks to provide general education social skills and group counseling services, as well as special education counseling services. Additionally, Jeff has experience providing counseling services to children and families within a medical setting as a child behavioral health consultant at the University of Michigan Health System–C. S. Mott Children's Hospital, Ann Arbor. His research and professional interests pertain to the prevention and intervention of academic and behavior problems and pediatric school psychology.

 **John S. Carlson, PhD, NCSP,** is an associate professor and director of clinical training of the School Psychology Program within the nationally renowned College of Education at Michigan State University. He is both a nationally certified school psychologist and a licensed psychologist (Michigan). In addition to his faculty work at MSU, Dr. Carlson provides mental health services and consultation to children, families, and schools within his private practice, Child and Adolescent Psychological Services, PLC, in East Lansing, Michigan. He holds a BS degree in child psychology from the University of Minnesota and his MA and PhD in school psychology from the University of Wisconsin–Madison. He completed his predoctoral internship at Primary Children's Medical Center, Department of Psychiatry, in Salt Lake City, Utah. His research and clinical interests pertain to evidence-based interventions for children's mental health issues.

Part I

The Role of Responsive School-Based Counseling in PBIS/RTI

Part I comprises the central focus of this book—the role of responsive school-based counseling in PBIS/RTI. Chapter 1 reviews the national problem of children's and adolescents' mental health and then provides a rationale for schools using an integrative mental health service delivery framework. In Chapter 2, we begin to describe the role of counseling within the framework of PBIS/RTI and explore the potential benefits and limitations of utilizing responsive school-based counseling as an intervention. Chapter 3 delves further into the counselor's role at the secondary and tertiary prevention levels in PBIS/RTI. We specifically focus on coordinating with the RTI team utilizing a problem-solving method in this chapter. Chapter 4 examines the role of counseling within special education. Of course, the goal of RTI is to promote student success in the general education curriculum; nevertheless, there will be some students who do require special education supports. Utilizing PBIS/RTI within special education can help assure students are being educated in the *least restrictive environment* (LRE). Also, knowledge in special education law and how certain disabilities can impact students can facilitate appropriate and effective service delivery. In Chapter 5, we review three approaches to counseling (Psychoeducational Approaches, Cognitive-Behavioral Therapy, and Solution-Focused Therapy) that fit well into the types of services that allow for data-based decisions

● 1

about a student's response to intervention across multiple levels of service delivery. Chapter 6 explores two definitions for evidence-based counseling and provides examples of evidence-based counseling interventions in Levels 1–3. This chapter also reviews considerations for group counseling, play therapy, counseling young children, and cultural counseling. Chapter 7 discusses assessment of students' needs, measuring levels of performance, developing relevant and measurable goals for counseling, and measuring progress toward those goals. Finally, in Chapter 8 we provide case studies to illustrate principles discussed in this book.

1 Integrated School Mental Health Programming

INTRODUCTION

There has been a rise in mental health problems in children and adolescents in recent years. The proportion of pediatric patients seen in primary care who present with psychosocial problems has nearly tripled over the past 20 years (Kelleher et al., 2000). Results from a recent national study found that over one in five children (or 22.2%) have a mental disorder severe enough to disrupt their daily living (Merikangas et al., 2010). When left untreated, mental health problems in children and adolescents may lead to increases in suicide, school failure, juvenile and criminal justice involvement, and health care utilization (National Alliance on Mental Illness, 2011). Improvements in children's and adolescents' mental health will require a collaborative effort from families, communities, health care providers, and schools.

The public school system is the primary setting for identifying mental health problems and providing mental health services for youth in the United States (American Academy of Pediatrics, 2004; Farmer, Burns, Phillips, Angold, & Costello, 2003; Foster et al., 2005). The demands of school often necessitate specialized assistance for children with learning, behavioral, social, or emotional problems. Of course, the nature and severity of the problem as well as the child's resources, both internally and environmentally, influence the kinds of support the child may require.

This chapter provides a comprehensive overview of school-based mental health services. First, we discuss mental health needs of children and adolescents followed by a review of legislation that enables schools to provide mental health support for students. Then, we discuss the importance of providing comprehensive and collaborative services through the use of an integrative service delivery model. The specific focus of this book, responsive school-based counseling, is framed within an integrative service delivery model in this chapter.

EDUCATING STUDENTS WITH MENTAL HEALTH ISSUES

Mental Health Needs of Students

Children's social-emotional functioning is a critical factor in their academic achievement. Children with significant social, emotional, and/or behavioral problems place not only themselves at greater risk for academic failure, but their problems can also interfere with the learning of others. Research and legislation has increasingly sought to improve student's learning and socialization by seeking ways to improve mental health in schools.

The first and only (to date) nationwide study of school mental health services, School Mental Health Services in the United States, 2002–2003 (Foster et al., 2005), was released by the Substance Abuse and Mental Health Services Administration (SAMHSA) in 2005. The study found that 20% of students received some form of individualized mental health service due to a mental health concern. The greatest mental health concern as ranked by schools was social, interpersonal, or family problems for both males and females. The second and third most frequently cited concerns were different for male and female students—aggression or disruptive behavior and behavior problems associated with neurological disorders for males and anxiety and adjustment issues for females. The areas of concern also changed by school level; for example, for males and females, depression and substance use/abuse were reported more frequently for high school students.

Survey results from the 2005 SAMHSA study of school mental health services also revealed that certain types of services were more or less difficult to deliver. Individual and group counseling, behavior management, and crisis intervention were most frequently ranked as "not difficult" or "somewhat difficult," while family support services, medication management, and substance abuse counseling were ranked as "difficult" or "very difficult." Barriers to effective service delivery included financial constraints of families, insufficient school and community-based resources, competing priorities for use of funds, difficulties with transportation, and linguistic and insurance barriers (see Foster et al., 2005).

Providing mental health services in schools is beneficial, and even necessary, to provide students (1) a safe learning and social environment,

(2) an opportunity to grow and develop socially and academically, and (3) access to mental health services for some children who would otherwise not receive it. The school setting, too, is ideal for linking ecologically valid assessment, intervention, and progress monitoring. Multiple, ongoing formal and informal assessments of student progress are already built into educational programs.

Understanding and Supporting Students With Unique Needs

Because of the high expectations for achievement in school and the natural comparison group with same-age peers, a child may first be identified as at risk in school. These students may require additional support in order to make adequate progress in school. The individualized support a student receives in school can serve as a protective factor. Using the stress-diathesis model (Zubin & Spring, 1977), later reformulated as the stress-vulnerability-protective factors model, a student's ability to successfully manage the demands of school depends on the interaction of the student's individual characteristics, the standards in which the student is expected to perform, and the degree of supportiveness of the student's environment. Some students are able to manage the demands of school with relatively limited support. Others, with some additional assistance, are able to develop new skills to begin to manage school expectations with less support over time. Then, there are a small percentage of students who require extensive, ongoing support in order to progress in school.

Many students who require additional support qualify for special education services. The school dropout rate is significantly higher for students in special education, and students labeled with an emotional disturbance have the highest dropout rate by disability, approximately 50%, within special education (Jans, Stoddard, & Kraus, 2004; U.S. Government Accounting Office, 2003). School dropout is associated with increased rates of unemployment, underemployment, and involvement in the corrections system. Schools that are committed to creating supportive school climates have demonstrated a decrease in the special education dropout rate over time. For example, in the state of Michigan, with the implementation of the *Michigan Merit Curriculum* that emphasizes relationships, relevance, and rigor, the special education dropout rate steadily declined from 58.3% to 23.5% between the years 1998 and 2005 (Michigan Department of Education [Annual Performance Report, 2005–06], 2011). Progress on key indicators at district and state levels requires well-coordinated and systemically implemented evidence-based models, programs, and practices. Trained educators and counselors can help facilitate a supportive environment for students with significant emotional problems by seeking greater understanding of students' unique strengths and interests, assisting students in communicating effectively and building positive relationships with others, and working collaboratively with teachers, school staff, parents, and the community to promote student success.

School Mental Health Legislation

Legislation has led to greater levels of assistance for students with mental health issues. The groundbreaking legislation Public Law 94–142, or the Education for All Handicapped Children Act of 1975, required schools to provide a free and appropriate public education (FAPE) to all children with disabilities in order to receive federal funds. The disability category, serious emotional disturbance (SED), was defined by this legislation. With the re-authorization of PL 94–142 in 1997 and 2004, now referred to as the Individuals with Disabilities Education Act (IDEA), school mental health services were expanded further. Through IDEA, federal funds are available for early intervention services, counseling services for all students with disabilities, and counseling for parents to assist them in better understanding their child's disability and with the implementation of their child's Individualized Education Plan (IEP) or Individualized Family Service Plan (IFSP). IDEA also authorizes positive behavioral intervention and support to facilitate inclusion of children with disabilities in the general education curriculum and in school activities with nondisabled peers.

The No Child Left Behind Act (NCLB) of 2001 enables schools to provide greater coverage in meeting the mental health needs of students who do not require special education services. NCLB authorizes grants for integrating schools and mental health systems and for programming for early childhood emotional and social development. The Consortium for Citizens with Disabilities Education Task Force advocates that "NCLB must continue to build on IDEA's strengths" and, as a part of this emphasis, urges the following regarding students' social and emotional needs:

> *Schools should create a climate that is conducive to learning and that addresses the social/emotional health of all students. Strategies such as positive behavior supports, response to intervention or other scientifically-based interventions should be implemented in schools to identify struggling learners or students with mental health issues or other issues that affect learning as early as possible and to provide targeted instruction and appropriate behavior supports for such students.* (Consortium for Citizens with Disabilities, 2006, p. 1)

Prevention and Early Intervention

With a greater emphasis on schoolwide prevention and early intervention, it is hoped that the high need for intensive individualized services will decrease. Funding to promote children's mental health in schools through prevention and early intervention has come through the Safe Schools Healthy Students Initiative, Drug-Free Schools and Community Act (DFSCA), Centers for Disease Control (CDC) and Prevention's Division of Adolescent and School Health (DASH), U.S. Department of Education, and IDEA, as well as from Medicaid and state and local funding. Based on a large and growing body of research, school-based universal prevention and early intervention efforts have shown to be effective in improving student outcomes in several areas, including decreasing school violence, improving academic performance, increasing children's social competence, reducing school dropout, and increasing school attendance (e.g., Beets et al., 2009; Durlak, Weissberg, Dymnicki, Taylor, & Schellinger, 2011; Gottfredson & Wilson, 2003; Gottfredson, Wilson, & Najaka, 2002; Hahn et al., 2007; Ialongo, Poduska, Werthamer, & Kellam, 2001; Tobler & Stratton, 1997). Various prevention models, including Caring School Community (CSC) programs, Responsive Classroom programs, social and emotional learning (SEL) programs, character education, and Positive Behavioral Interventions and Supports (PBIS), have been influential in promoting children's social, emotional, and behavioral competencies through universal prevention (see Bear, 2008). Doll and Cummings (2008) provide a comprehensive review of universal prevention in schools.

Comprehensive Mental Health Services in Schools

The focus of this book is on secondary (i.e., service to some) and tertiary (i.e., service to few) prevention, but each level of prevention—primary (i.e., universal; service to all), secondary, and tertiary—is critical and contributes to the success of the others. For example, primary prevention sets the stage for effective secondary and tertiary prevention. Likewise, effective secondary and tertiary prevention contributes to the school's optimal functioning at the universal level. Collaboration within and between levels of prevention can result in synergy and positive feedback loops. Implementation of an integrative service delivery model can help set this into motion.

MODELS OF SCHOOL MENTAL HEALTH PROGRAMMING

Collaborative approaches to mental health are generally more effective than isolated approaches. Integrated school mental health programming holds that: (1) a guiding model that clearly defines goals and objectives within and between levels of care facilitates cohesion and continuity; (2) the exact nature of services will depend on contextual factors, including the school and community's indigenous resources, the prioritized mental health needs within a population, and the individual needs of students; (3) clearly defined professional roles facilitates resource efficiency (including personnel efficiency); and (4) collaboration within and between multiple systems in the child's ecology benefits the whole child through enhancing protective factors, addressing risk factors, and promoting intervention consistency across settings (see Atkins, Hoagwood, Kutash, & Seidman, 2010; Stormshak et al., 2011). Examples of mental health programming models that promote integrative services include varieties of schoolwide programs that coordinate with parents and the community, PBIS, and the Ecological Approach to Family Intervention and Treatment (EcoFIT).

The ASCA Model

The ASCA Model, published by the American School Counselor Association (2003), was developed to guide school counselors in implementing comprehensive school counseling programs. The ASCA Model's delivery system is comprised of four components: (1) guidance curriculum, (2) individual student planning (e.g., planning and monitoring academic growth and development, educational and career/vocational planning), (3) responsive services (e.g., individual and group counseling, crisis response, referral, consultation, and peer mediation), and (4) systems support (e.g., implementation of a comprehensive guidance program, professional development, collaboration, teaming, program management, and program evaluation). The ASCA Model also exemplifies integrated school mental health programming.

PBIS

The PBIS model (also sometimes referred to as Positive Behavioral Supports [PBS]) delineates intervention levels in school mental health services. PBIS is a multilevel approach that focuses on prevention by creating a positive school environment. Within the PBIS model, all students receive support at the universal or primary level that involves schoolwide and classroom systems. Examples include positive school climate programs, systematic schoolwide screenings, and guidance lessons. Students who are identified as needing additional support beyond what is provided at the schoolwide level receive more intensive support at the secondary level that involves small-group and intense individualized plans. Students who continue to struggle behaviorally, socially, or emotionally despite "targeted" interventions require the most intensive level of support at the tertiary level. According to a position statement by the National Association of School

Psychologists (NASP; 2009), Level 3 supports may require services from specialized individuals, functional analyses of behavior, behavior intervention planning, multisystemic interventions, progress monitoring, special education services, and a highly individualized education plan. Different types of interventions within and between multiple systems are often necessary to promote positive coping and pro-social development. A team approach helps to ensure that a comprehensive, individualized intervention plan is developed and that specific strategies are implemented consistently across settings. Furthermore, the intervention components, such as academic modifications and accommodations, behavioral support strategies, peer supports, tutoring, home-school collaboration, counseling and community supports, should be implemented with integrity.

PBIS and RTI

PBIS provides a *Response to Intervention* (RTI) function that seeks to identify struggling students based on their performance level, implement interventions, and assess student progress. Students who do not progress despite supportive interventions may be identified as requiring more intensive interventions or multidisciplinary evaluation for special education support. Comprehensive information, resources, and support about PBIS is provided through the Office of Special Education Programs (OSEP) and through the National Technical Assistance Center on PBIS. The National Education Association (NEA) views RTI and PBIS as general education initiatives, though the impetus for both was derived from the special education law IDEA (NEA, 2012).

Common Goals of NCLB, ASCA, IDEA, and PBIS/RTI

A concentrated effort to promote universal or primary prevention helps ensure a positive school environment that sets the stage for effective and coordinated services for students who may require targeted or intensive, individualized support. The ASCA Model, NCLB, and IDEA each have somewhat different emphases, but they all support high expectations for student success as well as equal access to a quality education, and they all can be conceptualized within an integrative framework, such as the PBIS model (see Figure 1.1). Kutash, Duchnowski, and Lynn (2006) conclude that "the early results of PBIS interventions implemented at the indicated level, and the growing body of support for implementation at the universal and selective levels for children who have emotional/behavioral problems is very promising" (p. 32) and that "administrators have a preponderance of evidence to support their exploration of PBIS as a viable model for School-based Mental Health programs" (p. 33). Further, Fixsen, Blase, Duda,

Figure 1.1 Common Goals of NCLB, IDEA, and the ASCA Model Within the PBIS Model and RTI

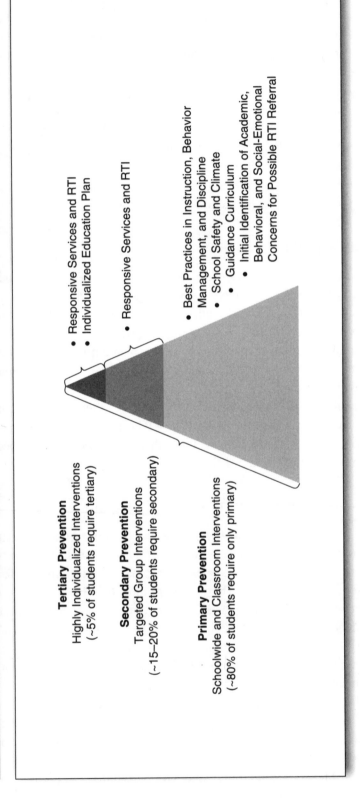

Naoom, and Van Dyke (2010), in their discussion of implementation of evidence-based treatments for children and adolescents, spotlight school-wide PBIS as an example of a well-implemented evidence-based program.

SCHOOL MENTAL HEALTH COMPETENCIES

Recognizing the importance of integrative mental health services, school mental health providers and educators can become increasingly effective as they acquire knowledge and develop competencies in core areas, including normal child and adolescent development, principles of learning and behavior, effective team problem solving, evidence-based interventions, effective service delivery, and mental health systems of care. A foundation of interdisciplinary competencies will promote effective communication, problem solving, and collaborative interventions. Teachers and school support staff work "in the trenches" every day with students, so mental health professionals should provide consultative support that can assist teachers in the most useful ways possible.

Various types of interventions may be implemented to promote positive student mental health and learning (see Figure 1.2). Comprehensive, integrative intervention planning recognizes the potential benefits of different types of intervention strategies as well as their synergistic effects. Intervention team members (e.g., general education teacher, special education teacher, administrator, counselor, psychologist, speech therapist, occupational therapist, teacher aide, social worker, community intervention support member, or parent) have different roles, specializations, vantage points, and perspectives that contribute to the overall intervention plan. School mental health services are increasingly efficient and effective as intervention team members understand each other's roles and how intervention components are interrelated. Implementation of a comprehensive, integrated approach can help services flow more productively.

ROLES AND RESPONSIBILITIES OF SCHOOL MENTAL HEALTH PROFESSIONALS

The roles and responsibilities, as well as professional backgrounds and competencies, of school mental health providers, including school counselors, school psychologists, school social workers, and pupil personnel workers, can vary significantly. This book is about providing counseling interventions at the *secondary* and *tertiary* prevention levels within an integrative mental health framework. The amount of time a service provider can devote to responsive counseling services depends on one's roles, responsibilities, and resources.

Figure 1.2 Types of School-Based Mental Health Interventions

- Schoolwide Universal Prevention
- Comprehensive Schoolwide Positive Reinforcement Systems
- After-School Programs, Social Clubs, Peer Mentoring
- School Counseling Programs
- Early Childhood Intervention
- Parent Collaboration
- Behavioral Consultation
- Individual and Group Counseling/Therapy
- Social Skills Training
- Crisis Management
- Psychological Assessment
- Functional Behavioral Assessment
- Behavior Management Plan
- In-Class Teacher Support
- Educational Supports (e.g., academic accommodations and modifications, related services)
- Change of Placement (e.g., specialized classroom settings)
- Discipline and Manifestation Determination Review
- Training for School Personnel
- Family Support Services (e.g., parent training, family counseling)
- Medication Management and Health Services
- Collaboration With Community Mental Health Providers
- Community Referral and Resource Information for Parents
- Transition Planning

From a systems perspective, while the implementation of research-based comprehensive and integrative prevention models in schools (e.g., PBIS) does require resources (e.g., time, personnel, and money), research is demonstrating the cost effectiveness of these kinds of prevention models (see Horner et al., 2012; Kutash et al., 2006; Simonsen et al., 2012). Furthermore, effective planning, organization, leadership, and collaboration can enable schools to implement effective prevention programming even with limited resources.

Our goal in writing this book is to provide research-based material that is readily accessible and useable for school mental health professionals. We hope this book will not only provide a conceptual framework, but also spark creativity and enthusiasm in school mental health service providers to provide high-quality services for children and adolescents.

CONCLUSION

Recent laws, new initiatives, and contemporary guidelines from the ASCA, NEA, NCLB, and IDEA clearly expect school personnel to use best practices in meeting the needs of all students. In order to address children's and adolescents' mental health problems effectively, there must be collaboration between multiple systems, with schools playing a significant role.

Research suggests that providing comprehensive and integrative mental health services in schools is efficacious. Broadly speaking, the implementation of integrative mental health services can result in synergistic effects. In other words, the effects from the interconnected intervention parts are greater than the sum of the individual intervention parts. In sum, Chapter 1 provides a framework for responsive school-based counseling—integrated mental health services. In the following chapters, we focus more specifically on school-based counseling as an intervention. In Chapter 2, we discuss the potential benefits and limitations of school-based counseling.

DISCUSSION QUESTIONS

1. Approximately 1 in 5 children and adolescents have some type of mental health problem. What kinds of mental health problems do children and adolescents most commonly display? How does mental health impact school performance?

2. What kinds of mental health services are most needed in schools today?

3. Who is competent to provide mental health services in schools?

4. Define integrated school mental health programming.

5. What are some potential barriers to implementing integrated school mental health programming and services? How might these barriers be addressed effectively?

6. What might be some effective ways of enhancing mental health competencies across all professional roles (e.g., teachers, administrators, mental health providers) within a school or school district in order to promote integrative mental health services?

2 The Need for Mental Health Counseling in Schools

A s reviewed in the previous chapter, there is clearly a need for mental health services in schools for children and adolescents. We also discussed the importance of an integrative framework in the provision of school-based mental health services. In this chapter we focus on counseling as an intervention. Individual and group counseling is considered one of the least difficult types of school mental health services to provide. More important questions, though, are whether responsive school-based counseling is relevant and effective. In this chapter, we begin to answer these questions by considering the potential benefits and limitations of school-based counseling (Chapter 6 reviews the current empirical evidence of school-based counseling outcomes). We begin this chapter by framing the role of counseling within an integrative framework. Next, we discuss the potential benefits and limitations of responsive school-based counseling and then conclude the chapter with practical considerations in planning for counseling services.

SCHOOL-BASED COUNSELING WITHIN AN INTEGRATIVE FRAMEWORK

There is a definite interrelationship between students' social-emotional development, academic performance, and career development. The goal of school mental health counseling is to help students achieve academic success. Social, emotional, and behavioral problems are all too common barriers impeding students' academic progress.

This book is about counseling students with emerging or persistent social, emotional, or behavioral problems—students who require secondary or tertiary intervention support. Many of these students either have been diagnosed with a disorder or disability or are suspected as having one. Some of these students may require temporary support due to stressful circumstances or a primordial or emerging problem. Along a continuum of mental health illness, these students' level of functioning may range from mildly to significantly impaired.

While this book focuses specifically on counseling or psychotherapy, the broad collection of interventions, support services, and key stakeholders (parents, teachers, administrators, support staff, and community partners) working collaboratively cannot be emphasized enough. An integrative approach utilizing *best practice* interventions in different areas, which may include educational accommodations, behavior management, medical management, and other support services (e.g., counseling, speech therapy, peer tutoring, home-school collaboration, parent support groups, after-school programs) is recommended. Because of the multiple factors that impact children's development (see Figure 2.1), interventions are most effective when they target the interaction of these multiple factors and systems rather than the individual, disconnected parts. The role of counseling can greatly assist with the integration of various interventions and services. Counseling is viewed here as an oftentimes integral piece of an interrelated, comprehensive intervention plan.

BENEFITS OF SCHOOL-BASED COUNSELING

Meta-analytic research of counseling has demonstrated positive outcomes in children and adolescents for a variety of conditions (see Chapter 6). But why should responsive (i.e., *secondary* and *tertiary* level) counseling be provided in schools? This is a philosophical question that may be considered from the perspective of public health, civil rights, ethics, sociology, economics, or standards-based education. Whatever the fundamental reasons for this specialized service, there appears to be practical benefits of responsive school-based counseling, including that *many barriers to mental health service delivery for children are addressed.* For example, services are provided at no cost to the parent, transportation is not required because the student is already present at school, problems can be identified early, a multidisciplinary team approach can be implemented, and progress can be observed directly in the school environment.

Another benefit of responsive school-based counseling is that it *provides students an opportunity to manage difficult emotions so they can focus on learning.* Students who have difficulties managing their emotions may require a safe place where they can express their emotions, process their thoughts and feelings, and regain their composure before returning to class. Moreover, students can learn strategies for managing their emotions in healthy ways that can be generalized to natural settings such as the classroom. For students who internalize fears or worries, counseling can provide them a safe environment to express their concerns. Basic counseling processes and strategies, such as unconditional positive regard and warmth, normalizing concerns, reframing the situation, challenging cognitive distortions, and problem solving, can provide reassurance and help to empower students. Counseling can be useful in defusing crises, assessing student risk, and accessing additional supports when needed.

Third, *counseling provides students individualized or small-group support for skill development,* particularly in problem solving, organization, emotional coping, developing replacement behaviors, and social skills. A small-group setting is ideal for teaching, modeling, and practicing

Figure 2.1   Interacting Systems and Children's Social-Emotional Development

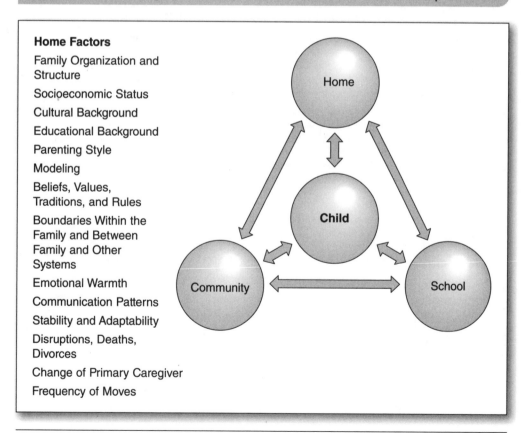

Home Factors

Family Organization and Structure

Socioeconomic Status

Cultural Background

Educational Background

Parenting Style

Modeling

Beliefs, Values, Traditions, and Rules

Boundaries Within the Family and Between Family and Other Systems

Emotional Warmth

Communication Patterns

Stability and Adaptability

Disruptions, Deaths, Divorces

Change of Primary Caregiver

Frequency of Moves

(Continued)

Figure 2.1 (Continued)

Child Factors	Medical and Health Care	Focus on Academic Achievement
Biology	Employment Opportunities	Family Involvement
Physical Characteristics	Organizations, Clubs, and Faith-Based Communities	Socioeconomic Intake
Cognitive System	Support of Life Cycles	Diversity
Emotional System	Peer and Social Influences	Community Linkages
Personality and Temperament	Recreation	Student, Teacher, and Staff Relationships
Beliefs, Assumptions, and Attributions	Diversity	Peer Relationships
Internalized Experiences and Learning	Other Resources	School Rules and Discipline
Unique Characteristics	**School Factors**	Prevention and Early Intervention
Community Factors	Safety	Individualized Support
Safety	School Climate and Morale	Physical, Educational, and Personnel Resources

Adapted from Bronfenbrenner's bioecological model (see Urie Bronfenbrenner's book, *Making Human Beings Human: Bioecological Perspectives on Human Development* (2005), for a thorough explanation of the bioecological theory of human development and its practical implications), general systems theory (Bertalanffy, 1968), and multisystemic treatment (Henggeler, Schoenwald, Borduin, Rowland, & Cunningham, 1998).

targeted skills. Generalization of targeted skills to the student's natural environment can be fostered through goal setting, teaching self-monitoring, problem solving with students to overcome potential barriers, and involving parents, teachers, and other school personnel in helping the student transfer the skill to natural settings. Collaboration between the counselor and classroom teacher is often necessary for generalization to occur.

A fourth benefit of responsive school-based counseling is that *it provides an opportunity for the student to receive individualized attention and build a positive relationship with an adult.* Research on children's resilience has shown that students are much more likely to achieve when they have at least one positive, meaningful relationship with an adult at school (Benard, 1991; Garbarino, 1995; Werner & Smith, 1992). Students with social, emotional, and/or behavioral problems often have difficulty establishing positive relationships with their teachers and peers. These students can benefit from the support of a counselor who expresses interest in them, accepts them for who they are, and is "on their side." The positive relationship experience they receive with their counselor can also help them build the confidence and skills to develop positive relationships with others.

Fifth, *counseling can provide students a voice.* Struggling students may have difficulty communicating effectively with others regarding their needs or special circumstances. At times, their behaviors are misinterpreted due to poor communication skills, unknown context factors (e.g., changes in the home, medication changes, peer conflicts, cognitive distortions), or not adequately expressing their interests, such as what motivates them, their hidden talents, or future aspirations. Counselors can facilitate the student's communication by providing a safe interaction environment, showing interest, and asking questions. As a result, counseling can help resolve misunderstandings, assist students in articulating personal goals, and open a door for meaningful home-school collaboration. As students' needs are better clarified, parents and supportive adults can be provided information regarding relevant school and community resources. While maintaining the appropriate limits of confidentiality, the information gained in counseling can *assist the multidisciplinary team in developing an integrative intervention plan that is relevant to the student's needs.* Beyond advocating *for* students, counselors can teach students self-advocacy skills.

Sixth, *counseling can help students develop greater self-awareness.* Depending on the student's developmental level and maturity, a child or adolescent may benefit from gaining a better understanding of how her or his behavior patterns may be influenced by various factors, such as a disability, health or medical condition, learned behaviors, environmental demands, or available support systems. This knowledge can empower students to problem-solve more effectively, make better decisions, and self-advocate. For example, students can benefit from discussing health habits, such as the importance of sleep, diet, and exercise.

Discovery of personal strengths, talents, and abilities is especially important. While self-awareness about one's needs may be important to target skill development or replacement behaviors, it can be demoralizing for students when the focus is always on where they fall short. It is important to praise students for their positive habits as well as positive exceptions to their poor choices or habits. A positive, strengths-based approach can facilitate positive momentum.

Further, *counseling can provide a source of hope for students*. Research on "common factors" related to successful psychotherapeutic outcomes suggests that "hope factors," such as positive expectancy, placebo effects, anticipation of change, and inspired motivation, account for about 15% of successful therapeutic outcomes (Asay & Lambert, 1999; Lambert, 2003; Murphy, 2008). Hopefulness may be cultivated through various therapeutic factors or conditions, such as positive relationship factors with the counselor, identifying personal strengths, problem solving, goal setting, focusing on solutions, and defining reachable steps toward goal attainment. Murphy (2008) points out the merits of brief solution-focused counseling (BSFC) for young people with school problems as it is a research-supported approach that incorporates the four "common factors" that have been empirically shown to account for positive psychotherapy outcomes—client factors, relationship factors, hope factors, and model/technique factors (see Chapter 9 for further discussion on "common factors" in psychotherapy).

Finally, *research suggests that effective psychotherapy may result in changes in the structures and processes of the brain*. We have learned through brain research about *neuroplasticity* or how our brains have the ability to adapt and grow through reorganizing and strengthening neural pathways, pruning (or eliminating) weakened and unused pathways, and creating new neural pathways. Counseling or psychotherapy can help clients learn new ways of thinking and to develop strategies and skills that can influence or possibly change their neural circuitry.

In fact, studies utilizing imaging techniques such as positron emission technology (PET) and functional magnetic resonance imaging (fMRI) show that effective psychotherapy impacts specific brain structures, including the hippocampus, cingulate gyrus, amygdala, temporal lobe, prefrontal cortex, and other cortical regions (Brody et al., 2001; Goldapple et al., 2004; Schnell & Herpertz, 2007). Brain imaging studies have shown that psychotherapy and pharmacotherapy impact overlapping as well as distinct brain areas (Goldapple et al., 2004; Kennedy et al., 2007; Lehto et al., 2008; Siegle, Carter, & Thase, 2006). Liggan and Kay (1999) explain that different psychotherapeutic approaches involve different brain structures. For example, *behavioral psychotherapy* targets learning, memory, and related motor behavior that involves the amygdala, basal ganglia, and hippocampus, whereas *cognitive psychotherapy* attempts to help clients identify maladaptive thought processes and modify thinking patterns that involves the neocortex and frontal cortex. Therapy can potentially impact the child at a biological level resulting in lasting changes in the child's developmental trajectory.

LIMITATIONS OF SCHOOL-BASED COUNSELING

School-based counseling services also pose potential drawbacks, including that *counseling can be potentially harmful to students.* Nicholson, Foote, and Grigerick (2009) point out there are few studies that discover harmful effects of counseling and psychotherapy because undesirable research findings are often unpublished. Nonetheless, they summarize research findings regarding deleterious effects of psychotherapy and counseling in the schools. For example, research suggests that group interventions involving a higher percentage of antisocial or delinquent youth are related to increased incidences of aggressive or antisocial behavior in the group (Kazdin, 1997). Along with the potential harmful effects related to the actual counseling process itself, counselors need to be sensitive to how students perceive counseling and how it may impact their self-esteem. For example, some students may feel singled out when they are asked to leave the classroom to attend a counseling session. Counselors should use methods that protect students' privacy as much as possible. A student may also feel embarrassed or self-conscious when placed in a group with students who have significant social deficits. When forming groups, counselors should be sensitive to each student's needs, perceptions, and wishes. In some students, counseling could potentially trigger negative self-evaluation, or thoughts that there is something wrong with them.

Second, *skills learned in counseling do not always generalize outside the counseling session.* The transfer of skills learned in counseling often requires collaboration with parents, teachers, and other personnel who can facilitate the generalization process through practicing the new behavior with the child, structuring the environment, prompting, and using positive reinforcement. Furthermore, counseling sessions may have limited impact when there are significant negative contributing factors in outside settings, such as peer, community, or family systems, that are left unaddressed. In some cases, even when interventions are implemented with integrity across settings, progress toward targeted goals may be negligible or slow-going due to other factors, such as the severity of the individual's mental health challenges.

Third, *counseling sessions can take time away from academic instruction.* Consequently, the student may have less time to master new academic concepts, develop academic skills, or organize and complete assignments. Alternatively, students may not receive counseling frequently enough or in a consistent fashion, resulting in minimal effects. This may be due to poor planning by the counselor, large caseloads, or the counselor not wanting to pull students away from their academic instruction time. Service providers should schedule sessions that best meet each student's individual needs. This often requires seeking feedback from teachers, parents, and the student regarding scheduling of sessions. Counselors should continuously assess the productivity and effectiveness of sessions as well as whether a student may be using sessions to gain attention or to avoid academic engagement.

Another potential drawback of counseling services is that *the student may not be invested in counseling.* The student might not think they have a problem, they may respond apathetically or resent being "made to go" to counseling, they may wish to keep personal matters private, or they may feel embarrassed if their peers find out that they are getting special support. It is important to be sensitive to the student's values, perceptions, preferences, and individuality. A student's readiness for change and investment in counseling is important to assess across time. Motivational interviewing (MI), a counseling approach developed by Miller and Rollnick (2002; Rollnick & Miller, 1995), recognizes that clients enter therapy at different levels of readiness for change. MI was designed to promote a client's willingness to engage in counseling and seek change. While there are many factors that may influence a student's willingness to receive counseling, the development of a positive client-therapist relationship is a significant factor. Ultimately, though, it is the student's choice whether he or she will participate in counseling. Sometimes students and families may not be interested in school counseling but may welcome information regarding private counselors or other community resources. Counselors should be careful not to personalize "therapeutic failures" as there are many possible variables that impact a client's readiness for therapy. When a counselor consistently experiences problems building therapeutic relationships with students, the counselor should critically evaluate his or her practices.

Finally, *the skills and attributes of the counselor influence counseling outcomes.* There is not necessarily a prototypical counselor—different personalities and styles can be beneficial (Zinn, 1996), but it is necessary that a counselor be able to facilitate the development of a therapeutic relationship with clients. Counselors who lack basic skills, hold skeptical attitudes about counseling or their own counseling abilities, or have significant unresolved personal issues are unlikely to see many positive results, and may even cause harm to the client. Effective counselors are able to establish a therapeutic relationship, establish clear boundaries with their clients, utilize a guiding therapy model, be flexible and adaptable in their approaches, be perceptive to the client's underlying motivations, self-monitor their own motivations and biases as a counselor, and have realistic expectations. Beyond foundational training and supervision, ongoing professional development can help counselors sharpen previously learned skills, develop new competencies, develop areas of specialization, and stay updated on current topics. Wampold (2001), in his comprehensive quantitative review of studies on psychotherapy's effectiveness, found that the therapist accounted for greater variance in outcomes of psychotherapy than did the chosen treatment model. Jørgensen

(2004) also points to the primary role of the therapist's attributes in effecting change:

> *The individual therapist's ability to catalyze the common mechanisms of change depends on his (her) having been part of—and having internalized central elements of—a good therapeutic culture. Factors such as good clinical judgment, empathy, social intelligence, relational competence, ability to handle interpersonal conflicts in a sensible and growth enhancing way, and ability to articulate, organize, and legitimize the patient's subjective experience—all of which are important elements in good psychotherapeutic practice—are unlikely to be developed significantly by formal technical training alone. Provided that the person training to become a therapist is not himself (herself) severely disturbed, practical clinical training and competent supervision will make it possible for him (her) to internalize these qualities and integrate them as parts of his (her) personality. (p. 536)*

PLANNING FOR COUNSELING SERVICES

To be most effective, school-based counseling involves more than conducting therapy sessions. School-based counseling involves planning and preparing for all components of counseling, including provision of individual and group counseling, consulting with others to help facilitate the generalization of skills to the student's natural settings, coordination with school programs, and collaboration with parents and the community (see Figure 2.2).

Service planning may be viewed from a broad perspective, such as districtwide or department-wide, as well as from a more narrow view, such as service plans for an elementary school or middle school or by an individual service provider. Some key planning questions that program supervisors and practitioners should consider include the following:

- Are efforts concentrated in the areas of greatest need?
- Are service providers trained and competent? How is this determined?
- Are the ratios of service providers to students appropriate?
- Are the responsibilities and tasks of the service providers clear? Do campus administrators, teachers, and staff understand the roles and tasks of the service providers?
- Is collaboration between service providers, school personnel, parents, and community partners effective?
- Are the services or programs relevant, efficient, and effective?

- Are the services evidence based?
- Are the services developmentally and culturally appropriate?
- Are there adequate counseling resources (e.g., space, materials, funding, support, supervision, training)?
- How are the services/programs evaluated?

A formal or informal *needs assessment* can be used to identify current mental health service needs (i.e., specific populations, behaviors, programming, resources, training) across *primary, secondary,* and *tertiary* prevention levels. Steps used to conduct a needs assessment include defining the purpose and objective of the assessment, determining the target audience that data will be collected from, establishing methods for data collection (e.g., sampling procedures, techniques, instruments), analyzing the collected data, prioritizing needs, developing goals and plans, implementation, and re-evaluation. Table 2.1 outlines basic considerations in planning for responsive school-based counseling services across all of these areas.

Adelman and Taylor (2010) contend that current policy and reform practices contribute to school services and student support programs that are categorical and fragmented. For example, programs often focus on one issue or type of service (e.g., academic competence, drug prevention, anti-bullying, peer mentoring, after-school programs) and lack cohesion with other programs. As

Figure 2.2 Collaborative Counseling

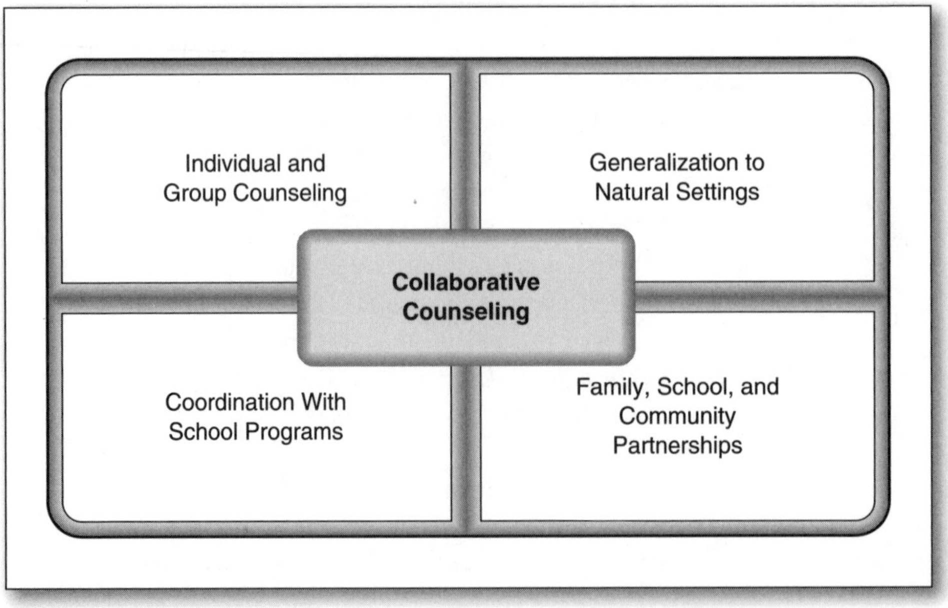

Table 2.1 Planning for Intensive School-Based Counseling Services

Individual and Group Counseling	Generalization to Natural Settings	Coordination With School Programs	Family and Community Partnerships
Physical Resources: Plan for counseling space, décor, atmosphere, privacy, safety; access counseling resources, manuals, games, props, supplies (see Resource C for information on counseling resources)	*Knowledge:* Identify areas of concern; learn about the student's academic demands, social context, behavioral expectations, setting variables; utilize best practice interventions; monitor progress	*Knowledge:* Identify available supports and programs in the student's home campus and school district (social clubs, tutoring, peer supports, service learning and volunteer opportunities, innovative programs); identify program coordinators	*Knowledge:* Identify available supports and programs in the community (after-school programs and activities, mental health services)
Caseload: Identify ages, grade levels, capabilities, disabilities; review background information, functional behavioral assessments (FBA), and counseling goals	*Communication:* Establish relationships; clarify goals and expectations of teachers, school staff, parents, and the student; use a positive, team approach; be flexible to communication preferences (time, modes of communication, frequency, consultation styles); use efficient data collection methods; provide intervention support (explain, simplify, model, provide feedback) to facilitate generalization; promote self-advocacy	*Communication:* Establish relationships with program coordinators	*Communication:* Establish relationships with parents and community members; develop a resource list of mental health providers and other community support programs
Time and Scheduling: Access students' class schedules; determine frequency and length of sessions			
Counselor Preparation: Plan counseling sessions, devise systems for progress monitoring and case notes; seek consultation and professional development			

a result, educators and interventionists focus on individual program goals and fail to recognize overlapping goals and interdependent functions of various support structures and programs. Adelman and Taylor (2010) recommend focusing instead on service planning that is "comprehensive, multifaceted, and integrated" that will more effectively address "the many overlapping barriers to learning, development, and teaching" (p. 31). Comprehensive, integrated services can be effectively realized when service providers identify the unique needs of students and work collaboratively with all team members in actively developing and coordinating an individualized plan. This requires thoughtful planning.

Because school-based counseling is embedded in the school environment, this affords counselors the opportunity to know the student's school environment well, to communicate efficiently and effectively with teachers and school staff, and to facilitate communication between the student, school, home, and community. An overarching goal of school-based counseling is to guide and support students in developing independence so they can experience success in life. To help make this happen, school-based counselors must often take on the role of both therapist and consultant concurrently. Sometimes extensive consultation and intervention support in the student's natural setting is necessary for generalization to occur, while in other cases the student can apply what he or she learns in counseling with relatively limited intervention support from others. It is important for students to develop personal responsibility and learn to advocate for themselves appropriately. Supportive adults can assist students in developing effective coping skills and self-confidence so they can become increasingly independent and successful.

CONCLUSION

In this chapter we reviewed the benefits and limitations of responsive school-based counseling as an intervention. School-based counseling can potentially provide the following benefits:

- A practical service delivery setting that is accessible to all students
- A "safe place" for students
- An appropriate setting for students to learn to express and manage their emotions
- Individualized or small-group support for skill development
- An opportunity for students to receive individualized attention and build a positive relationship with an adult
- A "voice" or an opportunity for students to share about their strengths and interests as well as their concerns

- Assistance in developing an integrative intervention plan that is relevant to the student's needs
- Support in developing self-advocacy skills
- An opportunity for students to develop greater self-awareness
- A source of hope (e.g., positive expectancy, placebo effect, anticipation of change, and inspired motivation)
- Changes in the structures and processes of the brain.

Potential limitations of school-based counseling include the following:

- Negative effects on the counselee, such as developing learned behaviors that are counterproductive from members in a group and lowered self-esteem
- Generalization of learned skills from the counseling session to other settings may be poor
- Counseling sessions can interfere with academic instruction
- Students may not be invested in counseling
- The skills and attributes of the counselor may impact outcomes

Some of these limitations may be easily addressed, while others may be more difficult. Systemic issues can be the most challenging to overcome. For example, limited funds and resources may lead to counselors having large caseloads, or powerful negative influences in the child or adolescent's social ecology may mitigate the influence of counseling.

Strategic planning can help address barriers to providing effective and efficient counseling services, both from a large systems perspective (e.g., counseling services for a school district) as well as by individual counselors (e.g., developing a plan that meets each student's needs and is based on an integrative or collaborative model of service delivery).

In Chapter 3, we examine the role of counseling services within the framework of RTI at the *secondary* and *tertiary* prevention levels.

DISCUSSION QUESTIONS

1. In what ways do you think school-based counseling can be most beneficial? Are there other ways counseling as an intervention may be beneficial other than what was already discussed in Chapter 2?

2. In what ways do you think school-based counseling can be most problematic? Are there other ways counseling can be problematic other than what was already discussed in Chapter 2?

3. What does planning for counseling services encompass? In what ways can planning be helpful?

4. What are your personal views on utilizing counseling as an intervention in schools?

5. How can you determine the effectiveness of counseling? How does counseling within an integrative or collaborative framework make causality more difficult to determine?

3 Counseling Students Within the Secondary and Tertiary Prevention Levels

Recent trends in educational practice emphasize proactive approaches to identifying and remediating students' academic, behavioral, and socio-emotional needs. Federal initiatives to close student achievement gaps (e.g., No Child Left Behind Act [NCLB] of 2001) have established expectations for increased accountability requirements in the educational system (Pub. L. No. 107–110). With these accountability requirements, education systems are expected to ensure that students have access to high-quality learning environments and become proficient in basic skills as demonstrated by progress-monitoring data (Tilly, 2008). Accountability requirements have also led to less emphasis on the use of cognitive discrepancies within special education eligibility decision making and more emphasis on student response to high-quality instruction and intervention (Fletcher & Vaughn, 2009). The use of Response to Intervention (RTI) (or response to instruction) and Positive Behavioral Interventions and Supports (PBIS) to lessen social, emotional, and behavioral deficits may involve the provision of school-based counseling services for those individual or small group of students who are not benefiting from class or schoolwide preventative approaches to promoting school functioning. These interventions that fail to meet these unique individual needs might include school or classwide curriculum (e.g., bullying prevention, character building). Examples of resource- and time-intensive services that are necessary for those who do not respond to other preventative approaches implemented in schools might include small-group interventions (e.g., social skills, dealing with transition/loss) and/or individual approaches to counseling (e.g., self-monitoring, solution-focused interventions). These more individualized and intrusive approaches to change in students' behavior are a necessary part of the PBIS/RTI service delivery system.

This chapter delves further into specific, pertinent issues related to counseling children and adolescents with social, emotional, and/or behavioral problems who do not respond to universal interventions provided to all students (e.g., Schoolwide Positive Behavioral Interventions and Support). First, we provide a brief overview of RTI by reviewing the three levels of prevention services within its hierarchical framework. Then, we discuss the role of the counselor within service provision at the secondary and tertiary prevention levels of an RTI framework. As discussed in Chapters 1 and 2, we frame *counseling as an intervention* as a piece of the comprehensive, integrated intervention plan as school mental health providers play a role in both the planning and delivery of the comprehensive intervention plan as well as in delivering specific counseling services within that plan.

THE ROLE OF RTI IN THE PROVISION OF COUNSELING SERVICES

Traditionally, school districts have utilized a discrepancy model of learning disability identification, whereby an established point discrepancy between intellectual ability and academic achievement scores were used (e.g., 16 points or scores differing by more than 1.5 standard deviations). Only students meeting this rigid criterion received needed additional support, generally in the form of special education services. Many in the field of education (e.g., IRIS Center, 2007; Siegel, 1988; Speece, Molloy, & Case, 2003) have argued against this method of determination, dismissing it as a "wait-to-fail" or reactionary approach. More recently, school districts have begun to utilize preventative approaches that identify academic, behavioral, social, and emotional deficits long before qualifying for special education services. These methods aim to ultimately decrease the number of students in special education by identifying early risks and intervening.

The fields of school psychology and education have increasingly emphasized the use of data-based decision making within a preventative approach to applied practice. The passage of the No Child Left Behind Act in 2001 emphasized the use of early intervention, high-quality instruction, and data-based decision making in addressing various obstacles that inhibit student success (Fletcher & Vaughn, 2009). Through early intervention, school practitioners are more likely to identify children not making adequate progress and at risk for future failure. These initiatives have advocated for greater accountability in demonstrating that specific practices have a measurable impact on student performance.

Currently, another hallmark of the prevention initiative is the widespread implementation of RTI in schools. RTI came into practice under the 2004 Individuals with Disabilities Education Act reauthorization (IDEA; U.S. Department of Education, 2004) as an approach to early and efficient identification of children at risk for special education services. IDEA 2004 regulations no longer required states to use the discrepancy model of special education assessment. Rather, they were free to use an RTI process to identify needs based on a child's responsiveness to empirically based interventions (Fletcher & Vaughn, 2009). Part of RTI progress monitoring involves comparing current performance to baseline levels, benchmarks, or normative standards. Linking assessment with intervention highlights the dual emphasis that RTI promotes. The National Center on Response to Intervention (NCRTI, 2010) defines RTI as an

> *integration of assessment and intervention within a multi-level prevention system to maximize student achievement and reduce behavioral problems. With RTI, schools use data to identify students at-risk for poor learning outcomes, monitor student progress, provide evidence-based interventions and adjust the intensity and nature of those interventions depending on a student's responsiveness, and identify students with learning disabilities or other disabilities.* (p. 2)

While RTI implementation initiatives have typically focused on academic domains, its multilevel framework is also tailored to social-behavioral domains within schoolwide PBIS programs (Sugai, Horner, & McIntosh, 2008). These multilevel service delivery systems can be implemented on a schoolwide or broad scale basis. Student progress in academic, behavioral, and mental health domains is continually assessed by trained teams. As student needs increase, the intensity of services increases accordingly through a multilevel prevention framework.

THREE LEVELS OF PREVENTION

Recently, there has been a change in nomenclature regarding the distinction between "levels" and "tiers." Traditionally, the RTI framework was classified as a three-tier system of prevention. However, the NCRTI has now adopted the use of a three-level system of prevention. Within this system, each "level" consists of one or more "tiers" of specific interventions. While levels of prevention should remain constant, tiers of intervention may likely vary by school and district. No strict requirement exists regarding the number of tiers a level must have, but the more tiers of support a level offers, the more comprehensive the preventative effort becomes. When a student fails to respond to prevention levels and specific intervention tiers within levels, increased intensity of evidence-based support and more individualized support is used. The following sections provide a brief introduction to the three levels of prevention within RTI.

Primary prevention services (Level 1) include the use of empirically validated social-behavioral core curriculums implemented across classrooms. These schoolwide curricula (e.g., PBIS; see http://pbis.org/) are implemented within the general education classroom (NCRTI, 2010) and aim to foster basic social-behavioral skills within all students. Primary prevention also includes the use of universal screening for strategic monitoring of these students to identify those who are not responsive to this core curriculum. These brief screening assessments are administered at the start of the school year with subsequent monitoring (for a review of research-based screening tools, see http://RTI4success.org). This level of primary prevention will generally meet the needs of most children (i.e., 80–95%) (NASDSE, 2007).

Secondary prevention services (Level 2) (i.e., targeted group intervention, resource and time-limited individual intervention) may be provided to students failing to respond to primary social-behavior supports. Generally, 5–15% of students will require these moderate-intensity interventions (NASDSE, 2007). These Level 2 services are provided in addition to Level 1 supports and may include interventions such as small-group instruction provided by trained personnel (e.g., classroom teachers, interventionists, school counselors, school psychologists, and other paraprofessionals). Strategic monitoring allows for Level 2 interventions to be targeted to specific deficiencies in student performance (Hunley & McNamara, 2010). If Level 2 supports demonstrate to be effective, the student can return to Level 1 primary prevention services. If extensive Level 2 supports are documented to be ineffective, the student may require tertiary prevention services.

Tertiary prevention services (Level 3) (i.e., intensive and more intrusive individualized intervention) are provided to students showing minimal response to primary (Level 1) and secondary (Level 2) support. Generally, up to 5% of students will require these individualized services (NASDSE, 2007). At this level, additional in-depth assessment methods are typically utilized (e.g., functional behavioral assessment [FBA]) to quantify skill deficits and determine needs. Also, intensive assessment may be conducted to rule out the possibility of an alternative diagnosis (e.g., intellectual disability, emotional disturbance) (Fuchs & Fuchs, 2005). Hunley and McNamara (2010) divide this level between 3A and 3B, whereby 3A involves a systematic problem-solving case study to develop specific interventions that have not been utilized at Levels 1 or 2. Level 3B includes a comprehensive evaluation for special education services. At this level in the continuum, enough evidence would likely exist suggestive of a disability that requires specialized services through special education (Hunley & McNamara, 2010).

THE COUNSELOR'S ROLE AT THE SECONDARY AND TERTIARY PREVENTION LEVEL

Position statements of both the ASCA and National Association of School Psychologists (NASP) posit that the provision of behavioral, social, and emotional supports within an RTI framework aligns with each association's goals of improving student achievement (ASCA, 2008; NASP, 2009). Professional school counselors and school psychologists design and implement school counseling or social-behavior interventions and supports aimed at providing early intervention to students either at risk for future problems or those already demonstrating severe and profound needs. The aim of this section is to provide a brief overview of the school counselor's roles in coordinating efficiently with a team that shares the common goal of enhancing student success at the secondary and tertiary levels of prevention. We focus specifically on the roles of the counselor or school mental health professionals who provide counseling as intervention, as these practitioners play a role in both the planning and delivery of the comprehensive intervention plan as well as in delivering specific counseling services within that plan. With this narrowed focus on school mental health providers, the reader is also encouraged to explore other sources of information (e.g., Appelbaum, 2009; Lane, Kalberg, & Menzies, 2009; Martella, Nelson, Marchand-Martella, & O'Reilly, 2012; Mellard & Johnson, 2008; Wheeler & Richey, 2010) that provide a more expansive discussion of the PBIS/RTI process and focus more specifically on its implementation.

Coordinating With an RTI Team

Contrary to common perception, RTI is not just a special education initiative, but rather a collaborative effort from general and special education (Fletcher & Vaughn, 2009). Practitioners within general education provide their prevention-focused curriculum to all students. Practitioners with expertise in special education use their knowledge of evidence-based assessment and intervention for students with disabilities to work within general education to intervene early with students at risk for future problems. This collaborative effort is needed to create a seamless transition throughout the hierarchical framework of RTI while relying on the expertise and skill sets of other stakeholders as well. These stakeholders include families, general and special education teachers, school administrators, counselors, school psychologists, and other related services personnel. We will refer to this group as the RTI team. Proper RTI implementation and fidelity relies on input from all team members as each typically works with students in a different capacity and has unique perspectives to offer.

The RTI team essentially functions as a "problem-solving" team. The team meets regularly to discuss student progress in response to a system of universal social-behavior supports. If students are unresponsive to a level of supports, the problem-solving process is initiated. Steps within the problem-solving process are driven by data analysis and can take many forms. One practical and widely used approach in the field of education is Bransford and Stein's (1984) IDEAL problem-solving method, which consists of five steps: (1) *I*dentifying the problem to be solved, (2) *D*efining the problem, (3) *E*xploring possible solutions, (4) *A*cting on the chosen solution, and (5) *L*ooking back and evaluating the effects. This framework is easily adapted for use within RTI teams for the purposes of data-based decision making (see Figure 3.1 for a diagram of this data-based decision-making process). The counselor's roles in collaborating amongst the RTI team in the problem-solving process are highlighted in the following sections.

Phase 1: Identifying and Assessing At-Risk Students

Bransford and Stein (1984) refer to this initial step within the problem-solving process as "problem identification." Counselors function as part of the RTI team to determine whether a problem really exists. Many schools that have an RTI system in place will have separate grade-level teams, each consisting of all the grade-specific teachers. These grade-level teams meet regularly to assess data (typically in conjunction with the RTI team) from universal behavior screening tools (e.g., Behavior Assessment System for Children–Behavioral and Emotional Screening System, 2nd ed.; Conners' Rating Scales–Revised; Devereux Early Childhood Assessment) and discipline data (e.g., office referral and suspension reports) to identify students who struggle to meet established behavior expectations. They can compare actual student progress to expected progress based on comparison to other students in their classroom, students in other classrooms, or established

Figure 3.1 Data-Based Problem-Solving Process

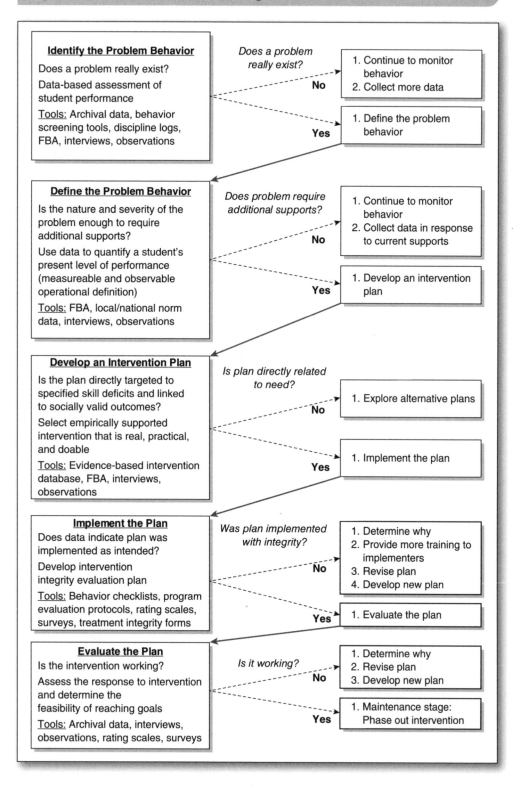

benchmarks or grade-level norms (local or national). Students not making effective progress may need additional support. The RTI team can assist these grade-level teams by closely examining progress-monitoring data with the goal of determining which students may need more individualized interventions at the secondary or tertiary levels.

Specifically, the counselor's role in the problem identification phase varies depending on where a particular student's needs fall within the hierarchy of the RTI framework. Typically, counselors use their knowledge of mental health and evidence-based assessment to work within a consultative capacity. These professionals provide oversight of the implementation of the core behavioral skills curriculum at the universal level. Additionally, they may develop screening and assessment procedures to track student progress and train others in how to use them. Students who show a lack of progress given the universal behavior supports are then provided targeted behavior supports. At the secondary level, counselors are still relied on for their expertise in screening, assessment, and progress monitoring. Their assessment focus is on selecting the best targeted interventions (moderate intensity) that may be effective for a group of two to eight students. If data suggest a student is still unresponsive to these supports, it may be necessary to select an intervention that is provided on a more intense and individualized basis (tertiary support) (Hawken, Adolphson, MacLeod, & Schumann, 2009).

The importance of the counselor's role in identifying and assessing students who may be at risk socially, emotionally, or behaviorally is consistent within all levels of RTI. Progress monitoring drives treatment decision making, assists in the selection of appropriate intervention methods, and increases the success rate of those interventions (Deno, 2005). However, the assessment approach for counselors at secondary and tertiary levels includes more individualized assessment methods (e.g., FBA) used to base interventions and/or develop Behavior Intervention Plans (BIP) or Behavior Support Plans (BSP) (McKevitt & Braaksma, 2008).

Phase 2: Defining the Problem Behavior

At the next phase of the problem-solving process, the counselor works with the RTI team to assess the nature and severity of the identified problem. The use of data to quantify a student's present levels of performance (PLP) aids the team in developing a problem definition. This problem definition is based on assessment of the student's behavior or functional performance in comparison to peers or established expectations and includes indicators of the severity of the problem, noting its frequency, intensity, duration, latency, and topography (Hunley & McNamara, 2010). Noting these features of the behavior allows the team to develop a quantified problem definition that is both observable and measurable. This is important for tracking progress as it allows the team to understand the severity of the problem and dictate the intensity of supports needed.

Counselors' background in mental health and evaluation make them likely to play active roles within this process of assessing a student's social, emotional, and behavioral deficits. They may be relied on to develop the assessment procedures and observation and interview protocols used to collect data to quantify the extent of a problem behavior. They likely have the expertise to assess the nature and severity of a problem behavior to determine if it requires further supports or would likely resolve on its own. This evaluation of the nature and severity of the behavior needs to be shared with all stakeholders involved (e.g., students, families, teachers, school staff) as these individuals will be integral in the next phase of developing an intervention plan and establishing common goals and expectations.

Phase 3: Exploring Possible Solutions and Developing an Intervention Plan

At this phase within the problem-solving framework, the nature and severity of a behavioral deficit has been identified and the RTI team likely has a quantifiable understanding of the gap between a student's current and expected levels of performance. The next step is to develop an intervention plan that aims to close the gap between current and expected levels of performance. Interventions such as direct instruction of specific skills and positive behavior interventions and supports need to be targeted to the development of a skill that ultimately has academic, functional, behavioral, and social relevance. For example, students identified as having a specified number of office discipline referrals or suspensions may be provided with special instruction in conflict resolution or social skills. These skills allow the student to decrease their number of office discipline referrals, provide them more time in the classroom, and work effectively with others in society after they finish school. These interventions target not only academic, functional, and behavioral outcomes, but also ones that are socially valid.

Counselors work collaboratively with the RTI team to develop group or individual behavior intervention plans. The development of any intervention plan is a multifaceted process with numerous components to consider. Wheeler and Richey (2010) highlight some of the key considerations in developing a plan:

- What intervention will be used?
- How will the intervention be implemented?
- Is the intervention plan real, practical, and doable?

- What type of coordination and collaboration is needed across multiple settings (i.e., school, home, community)?
- Are the intervention techniques developmentally appropriate?
- What is the time frame for the intervention?
- Who will be involved?
- How will progress-monitoring data be collected?
- How often will progress-monitoring data be collected?
- When do we modify the plan if insufficient progress is made?
- At what point do we say the intervention was successful?

Given these various considerations in developing intervention plans, it is critical that a collaborative team approach is used. The entire RTI team, as well as the target student and their family, needs to provide input. Involving the target student in the planning process may help them feel invested in the plan and motivated to participate.

Phase 4: Acting on the Chosen Solution (Implementing the Counseling Solution)

Once the RTI team has identified and developed the appropriate secondary or tertiary intervention (e.g., counseling) to be used with either a group or an individual student, they can then implement that plan. Whether a counselor or other staff member is responsible for conducting the counseling intervention, they must work with the premise that behavior is functionally related to the student's learning environment (Stormont, Lewis, Beckner, & Johnson, 2008). This means that the goals of the intervention must align with the outcomes obtained from the FBA. The specific problem behaviors that have been identified as taking place because of a lack of environmental supports should be addressed. The goal of short-term, solution-focused counseling approaches is to use an organized and systematic approach to provide the support to develop the skills the student needs to better access and benefit from the school's learning environment.

While only an individual or small group of staff members will undertake the duty of working directly with a target student or group of students, there is, ultimately, a team of staff members involved in the implementation of that intervention plan. Brown-Chidsey and Steege (2010) identify two vital roles for team members to undertake at the intervention implementation phase: (1) monitoring that the intervention is carried out as designed (i.e., treatment integrity) and (2) monitoring the student's response to that intervention.

The importance of carrying out an intervention plan in exactly the intended manner (i.e., intervention integrity) cannot be understated. Without strict adherence to the intervention plan the RTI team can never accurately assess whether the intervention was truly effective (Brown-Chidsey & Steege, 2010). Treatment integrity can be evaluated using self- or observer-reported behavior checklists/rating scales (Lane, Kalberg, & Menzies, 2009) or evaluation tools such as the School-Wide Evaluation Tool Version 2.1 (SET; Sugai, Lewis-Palmer, Todd, & Horner, 2001). Results from these evaluation protocols should be shared with individuals involved in the intervention plan (e.g., counselors, teachers, and support staff) and the RTI team. Counselors may be needed to not only collect and share these evaluation outcomes, but also provide ongoing performance feedback and consultative support to the staff involved in directly providing the intervention (Brown-Chidsey & Steege, 2010). See Figure 3.2 for an example of a completed treatment integrity checklist. Also, see Resource A for a blank treatment integrity checklist form.

Phase 5: Looking Back and Evaluating the Effects (Progress Monitoring)

Once a counseling intervention is implemented, the ongoing collection of data regarding a student's response to that intervention allows the RTI team to determine if the intervention is working. The data obtained in this phase of the problem-solving process help the RTI team make important decisions. If the intervention has demonstrated success, the team may take the next steps to possibly build upon it by developing new goals and objectives to meet or may implement a behavior maintenance plan to sustain the behavior change as the supports are phased out. If data indicate that some progress has been made, but slower than expected, it may be necessary to adjust the frequency, duration, or intensity of the current intervention plan. If the plan has not demonstrated success, then the RTI team may elect to either rework the plan or develop an alternative plan based upon further data collection. Ultimately, the problem-solving framework is designed to be used in an ongoing and dynamic process as it allows for flexibility in thinking and emphasizes intervention selection that caters to various levels of indicated need.

This section provided a brief overview of what the steps in the problem-solving process entail for counselors working as part of an RTI team at the secondary or tertiary levels of prevention. See Resource B for an example of an Intervention Planning Form that RTI teams can use to document progress through the five steps of the problem-solving method. Specific procedures used in data collection and individual evaluation (e.g., single-case research design) of an intervention can be found in Chapter 7. Computerized data management systems can assist with behavioral progress monitoring at group (Levels 1 and 2) and individual (Levels 2 and 3) levels. For example,

Figure 3.2 Treatment Integrity Checklist (Completed Example)

Intervention Implementer: John Smith, School Counselor   School: Success Elementary

Date: 6/5/12   Time: 2:30-3:00   Evaluator: John Smith, School Counselor

Intervention: *Fairy Tale Conflict Resolution Group* (grades 3-5). The small group discusses common fairy tales that contain scenarios involving conflict (*The Frog Prince, The Spirit in the Bottle*, etc.) and ways the characters might resolve their conflicts using healthier means.

Evaluator Directions: Either the person implementing the intervention or an observer completes this form at the end of each day that the intervention is conducted.

Intervention Tasks	Completed		Comments
	Yes	No	
1. Ask the group what they think "conflict" means	X		
2. Pass out student materials (fairy tale story and conflict analysis worksheets)	X		
3. Tell all students to read story either silently or aloud	X		
4. Explain to group that they will use the worksheet to identify possible solutions that would help characters solve their problems in healthier ways	X		
5. Ask group to answer worksheet questions (What's the conflict? Characters? Feelings about conflict? Wants and needs? Possible solutions?)	X		
6. Ask each student to share their answers aloud to the group	X		
7. Provide immediate positive feedback to each student after they share		X	I did not get a chance to provide immediate feedback to Chris
8. Ask each student to think of one conflict that they have seen at school	X		
9. Ask each student to tell the group how that conflict was handled		X	Anthony and Austin did not go because we ran out of time
10. Ask students if there might have been a healthier way to handle that conflict	X		

Total Number of Tasks Completed (Yes) = __8__ / __10__ (Out of Total Number of Tasks Required)

= __80__ % Total Effective Treatment Integrity

the *Behavior Intervention Monitoring Assessment System* (BIMAS; McDougal, Bardos, & Meier, 2011) is a multi-informant measure useful for behavioral universal screening, progress monitoring, outcome assessment, and program evaluation within the RTI framework. The BIMAS provides assessment reports, progress reports, and comparative reports at the individual and group levels and demographic reports at the group level.

CONCLUSION

School-based counseling services must be outcome focused. Prevention, early intervention, and tertiary intervention require that behavioral targets for change be identified early within the process and be frequently monitored for progress and growth. In sum, data-based problem solving is a prerequisite for counseling services within RTI as it allows for the RTI team to determine if a student is responsive to evidence-based counseling interventions. By intervening early and ensuring that multiple Functional Behavior Assessment (FBA)–indicated interventions are implemented, the RTI team serves to prevent students from requiring special education supports and services at Level 3B. However, some students will not demonstrate adequate progress in response to general education prevention supports and will require more intrusive interventions within special education. The following chapter discusses the process of qualifying for more intense counseling interventions within special education.

DISCUSSION QUESTIONS

1. Why are counseling services important to consider at Levels 1 and 2 given that traditional counseling interventions have been more closely aligned with Level 3 services or those targeted at individual children with chronic and treatment-resistant challenges?

2. Why is data collection and progress monitoring such an important part of PBIS/RTI?

3. What does it mean when the chapter says that the RTI team must work with the premise that a student's behavior is functionally related to the student's learning environment?

4. What does it mean when the chapter refers to the problem-solving framework as a "dynamic" process?

4 Counseling Students Within Special Education

I n the previous chapter we discussed the role of counseling within Levels 2 and 3 in the RTI framework. Well-designed and implemented prevention support services provided at Levels 1–3 should result in decreased referrals for special education. Nevertheless, some students will require special education services in order to be successful in school. Hunley and McNamara (2010) explain that Level 3 is conceptualized as part of the problem-solving process in RTI regardless whether the setting is in general or special education. Specifically, Level 3 is conceptualized as a case study procedure that is highly individualized for the specific needs of the student.

In this chapter we address the role of counseling within special education. Just as Levels1–3 in RTI employ a preventative focus, special education may also be viewed as preventative. After all, students who receive a special education will either: (1) develop competencies over time so that they no longer require a special education, (2) continue to require the support of special services in order to make educational progress, or (3) regress further, leading to significant impairment in functioning.

Much of this chapter also deals with mental health diagnostic considerations as this has important implications for counseling. Students in Levels 1–3 may have a formal diagnosis outside the school setting, so understanding diagnostic implications can be important at the pre-referral levels; however, a student's disability is formally recognized in schools when a student is identified as requiring special education services or receives a Section 504 plan due to a diagnosed disability. We begin this chapter with an overview of special educational programming.

EDUCATIONAL PROGRAMMING FOR SPECIAL EDUCATION STUDENTS

The Role of School Counselors and Mental Health Professionals

Collaboration between team members (i.e., general education teachers, special education staff, school counselors, administrators) who serve students receiving special education services is essential. Isolated or disconnected practices that discourage collaboration between all team members result in diminished benefits of special education services. The goal of special education services is to assist the student in becoming proficient academically and within the general education setting, as much as possible. A seamless coordination between general and special education can be difficult to achieve. Fitting a student's Individualized Education Plan into a general education setting requires adequate resources, flexibility, and sometimes a high degree of ingenuity. The expertise and support of counselors and other school mental health professionals are not only valuable resources for students with disabilities, but are also welcomed resources for teachers who feel pressure to "make it work."

Marshak , Dandeneau, Prezant, and L'Amoreaux (2010) in their book *The School Counselor's Guide to Helping Students With Disabilities* discuss the role school counselors provide in working with students with disabilities. They emphasize the school counselor's role in promoting inclusion, protecting the rights of students with disabilities, fostering resilience in students, and helping students to achieve intrapersonally, interpersonally, academically, and occupationally. They reference ASCA's position statement, *The Professional School Counselor and Students with Special Needs* (for more information see http://www.schoolcounselor.org/files/PS_SpecialNeeds. pdf), as "the best starting point for gaining clarity and understanding the role of school counselors with students with disabilities" (p. 7). Trolley, Haas, and Patti's (2009) book *The School Counselor's Guide to Special Education* is another useful resource for understanding the school counselor's role with students with disabilities as well as for accessing foundational information about special education.

It is important that the primary roles that school mental health professionals fulfill are communicated effectively to school personnel and parents. In general, roles that school mental health professionals may provide in supporting students who receive a special education include:

- Serving as a member of the multidisciplinary evaluation team
- Collaborating in the development of a student's IEP related to academic, behavioral, and/or career goals

- Assisting in the development and implementation of accommodations and modifications and behavior management plans
- Providing consultative support to teachers, school personnel, and parents
- Providing individual and group counseling
- Providing family counseling and parent training
- Collaborating with school and community specialists
- Providing referrals and information about school and community resources
- Assisting with grade-level transitions and career planning
- Advocating for students with special needs and providing information about students' needs

Many of these interventions are shared by school counselors, school psychologists, school social workers, or other school mental health providers. However, some interventions may be a primary responsibility of a specific professional depending on a district's approach to an integrated service delivery model.

Direct and Indirect Influences of Interventions

As already discussed in Chapter 2, there is a definite interrelationship between students' social-emotional development, academic performance, and career development. Specific areas of concern may seem unrelated to one another on the surface. In actuality, there is oftentimes a reciprocal interaction between one area (e.g., social, emotional, or behavioral functioning) and another area (e.g., learning or academic performance). Thus, interventions that specifically target one area (e.g., academics) may indirectly influence another area (e.g., behavior) and vice versa. Figure 4.1 depicts how special education interventions may have both direct and indirect influences on multiple problem areas. We must keep in mind, though, that special education services are only a part of the child's or adolescent's bioecology that contributes to student outcomes (see Figure 4.1).

Educating in the Least Restrictive Environment

In regard to special education programming, a topic that warrants special attention involves decision making regarding *change of placement* and educating students in the *least restrictive environment* (LRE). As a general rule, interventions should facilitate a student's ability to access the general education curriculum in the mainstream environment and to socialize with his or

Figure 4.1 Direct and Indirect Influences of Special Education Interventions

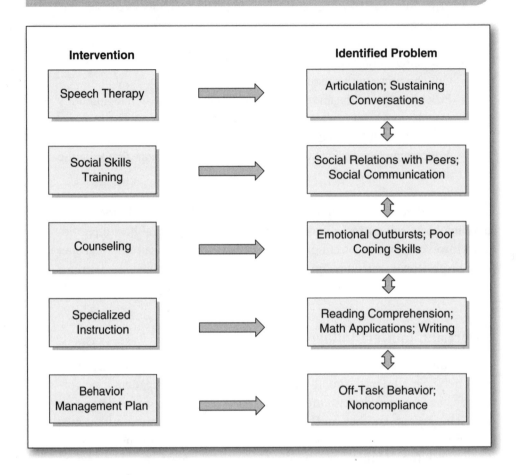

her general education peers as much as possible. In some instances, general education teachers may lack the time, specialized knowledge, or resources to implement individualized interventions adequately (e.g., academic accommodations and modifications, specialized instruction, behavioral support strategies). In order to improve service delivery in the LRE, training and support for teachers, aides, paraprofessionals, and other staff may be needed to bolster their capacity to respond to students' needs. Further, team problem solving (e.g., grade-level teams, RTI teams, etc.) can help to assure that interventions have been implemented with integrity in the LRE. Inclusion teachers and support staff play a vital role in assessment, intervention, and monitoring outcomes. Regarding behavioral support, positive behavioral support strategies may be specified in a student's *behavior intervention plan* (BIP) that can assist teachers and school personnel in implementing strategies or interventions that target specific behaviors based on a *functional behavioral assessment* (FBA).

Students who do not respond favorably to lesser restrictive interventions (e.g., in the regular mainstream setting) may require placement in a self-contained classroom to remediate significant and persistent social, emotional, and/or behavioral problems. As with all levels of intervention, the goal is to remediate the areas of concern so the student can be successful in the LRE. Some school districts may provide self-contained classrooms for students with significant social-emotional problems in each school campus while other districts may select only a few schools or other locations to provide this service. A significant advantage of offering the program in the student's home campus is that it allows for continuity of services and flexibility in providing a gradual integration back into the mainstream. However, if the population is small, particularly in elementary schools, then it may not be feasible to have a campus-based program on site. The self-contained classroom provides a more structured setting for the student to receive instruction in core subjects. Additionally, social skills lessons and behavior management are incorporated into the class. Teachers who educate students with emotional problems in a self-contained classroom are responsible for providing structure, teaching academics and social skills, providing positive reinforcement, setting limits and enforcing consequences, monitoring progress, conferencing with students, and consulting with teachers, school staff, and caregivers.

The additional supports afforded by special education services may help to ameliorate social, emotional, and/or behavioral problems. With this increased structure and support in place students may be better situated to learn and apply new coping skills.

COUNSELING AS A RELATED SERVICE

Within special education, counseling may be included in the student's IEP as a *related service*. Students who require counseling as a related service demonstrate some form of social, emotional, or behavioral concern that significantly impedes their educational performance. For example, these students may display difficulty focusing on schoolwork, poor social skills, impulsivity, isolating or withdrawing from others, school avoidance, somatic or physical complaints, inappropriate attention-seeking behaviors, verbal or physical aggression, emotional instability, self-injury, or conduct problems. Of the 13 disability categories defined by IDEA, students who receive counseling as a related service are most often identified within one of the following categories: Emotional Disturbance (ED), Autism (AU), Other Health

Impairment (OHI) that includes Attention-Deficit/Hyperactivity (ADHD), and Specific Learning Disability (SLD).

The Code of Federal Regulations (CFR) defines the purpose of related services, such as audiology services, speech therapy, physical and occupational therapy, medical and health services, and counseling services, in special education. Title 34, Section 300.320 (a) (4) in the CFR (Definition of Individualized Education Program, 2007) states:

> *(4) A statement of the special education and related services and supplementary aids and services, based on peer-reviewed research to the extent practicable, to be provided to the child, or on behalf of the child, and a statement of the program modifications or supports for school personnel that will be provided to enable the child—(i) To advance appropriately toward attaining the annual goals;(ii) To be involved in and make progress in the general education curriculum in accordance with paragraph (a)(1) of this section, and to participate in extracurricular and other nonacademic activities; and (iii) To be educated and participate with other children with disabilities and nondisabled children in the activities described in this section.*

The purpose of a related service, such as counseling, is to support students who require a service in order to benefit from their education, progress in the general education curriculum, and participate with their peers in school activities. The goals and objectives of counseling may be specified in a Counseling IEP or based on a BIP. Counseling goals and objectives are operationally defined, or developed to be observable and measurable, and are based on multiple measures of formal and informal assessments. A baseline measure of the student's *present levels of performance* for the target behavior(s) provides a starting point to develop goals and objectives and monitor progress. See Chapter 7 for additional discussion and examples of developing goals and monitoring progress across all levels of a PBIS/RTI service delivery model.

MENTAL HEALTH DIAGNOSTIC CONSIDERATIONS

Students must meet criteria for a disability category in order to receive an IEP. IDEA defines the disability categories used for qualification for special education services in schools and includes the following: autism, deaf-blindness, developmental delay (ages 3 to 9 years), emotional disturbance, hearing impairment (including deafness), intellectual disability, multiple disabilities, orthopedic impairment, other health impairment, specific learning disability, speech or language impairment, traumatic brain injury, and visual impairment (including blindness). See the Code of Federal Regulations, Title 34, Section 300.8, for definitions of disability terms. Students with disabilities can also receive special assistance through Section 504 of the 1973 Rehabilitation Act.

The term *disability* may be viewed along a continuum as a medical/physical reality on one end of a continuum to a social construction on the other end. As Smart and Smart (1997) point out, "Disability is not caused by disease and injury alone, but is also related to the way in which institutions define and diagnose disability" (p. 12). Nonetheless, educationally defined disabilities related to deficits in social, emotional, and/or behavioral functioning generally involve a neurobiological component.

Neurobiological Factors

The cause of a child's disability may be due to multiple factors that include a neurobiological component. Abnormal neurological development may cause disturbances in thinking, feeling, or relating at varying levels of severity. Examples of neurobiological disorders include developmental disabilities, autism, attention deficit disorder (with or without hyperactivity), learning disabilities, Tourette's syndrome, sleep disorders, bipolar disorder, major depression, schizophrenia, obsessive-compulsive disorder (OCD), anxiety disorders, fetal alcohol syndrome, brain tumors, tuberous sclerosis complex, and traumatic brain injury. Some of these disorders are driven primarily, or almost entirely, by a neurobiological cause (e.g., autism, Tourette's syndrome, or the effects of a brain injury), while other disorders may involve gene-environment interactions (e.g., mood disorders, anxiety disorders, eating disorders, or impulse control disorders). Also, the etiology of some diagnosable emotional and behavioral disorders may be substantially related to having experienced or been exposed to some form of trauma or abuse. For example, Cicchetti and Barnett (1991) found that 80% of abused or maltreated infants exhibited attachment disorder symptoms. K. E. Fletcher (2003) reported that in a meta-analysis of 34 studies, on average, 27% of adolescents, 33% of school-aged children, and 39% of preschool children exposed to traumatic events were diagnosed with posttraumatic stress disorder (PTSD). Furthermore, research studies have demonstrated specific brain abnormalities in children associated with childhood abuse and PTSD, including smaller corpus callosum and frontal lobes, hippocampal volumetric differences becoming apparent in adulthood, limbic irritability, deficient development and differentiation of the left hemisphere, deficient left-right hemispheric integration, and abnormal activity in the cerebellar vermis (Karl et al., 2006; Teicher, 2000). Outcomes were moderated by MRI methodology, PTSD severity, medication, age, and gender (Karl et al., 2006). Alterations in these areas of the brain enhance the risk for developing depression, anxiety disorders, PTSD, hypervigilance, dissociative symptoms, memory impairments, and impulsivity (Teicher, 2000).

Advantages and Disadvantages of Diagnostic Labels

There are various types of disabilities, including physical, sensory, cognitive, mental health, and health related. This section deals primarily with issues related to mental health diagnoses. Service providers should keep in mind the advantages and disadvantages of diagnostic labels, as these understandings will guide decision making regarding interventions. First of all, access to highly individualized supports and interventions, such as special education services, may require a formal diagnosis. Another advantage of labels is that they can provide a general conceptual framework for understanding and describing an individual's symptoms, behavioral characteristics, and learning style. This can facilitate ease of communication between professionals and provide direction regarding evidence-based instructional, behavioral, or medical interventions. Diagnostic labels, too, can provide relief and hope to both the parents and child or adolescent as they may feel like they have a better grasp and more control over choices and directions in dealing with the disability and its consequences. When a disability is identified this may also relieve feelings of guilt or blame regarding the cause of the symptoms. Obtaining an accurate diagnosis can help the child receive the most effective interventions, supports, and services.

Regarding disadvantages of diagnostic labels, they can potentially result in stereotyping, differential treatment, and self-fulfilling prophecies because of labeling biases (e.g., Pygmalion effect or Rosenthal effect). The diagnosed child or adolescent may be at risk for giving the label too much power, resulting in learned helplessness. Labels, too, are not always accurate due to unreliable or invalid assessments, alternative or multiple etiologies for a child's symptoms, or the possibility that symptoms are due to a mismatch between the child and his or her environment rather than an inherent disability. Sometimes the child may be unfairly labeled as "the problem" or the "identified patient" in a dysfunctional social environment. Furthermore, even when diagnoses are accurate, the child should never be viewed solely within the confines of a disability—every individual is uniquely complex, and the symptom presentation and severity as well as the other traits of an individual can be quite variable.

In regard to Asperger's syndrome (AS) or high-functioning autism (HFA), Baron-Cohen (2000) points out that autism is commonly viewed as a "disorder," "disability," or "impairment," but that the less severe AS/HFA might be more fairly characterized as a *different* cognitive style. In other words, individuals with AS/HFA display a unique profile in regard to their cognitive and social characteristics, but that does not mean there is something "wrong" with them. He reviews two cognitive models, the *folk psychology–folk physics model* and the *central coherence model,* which characterize the cognitive differences in individuals with AS/HFA. The folk psychology–folk physics model offers that individuals with AS/HFA display inherent weaknesses in folk psychology, involving understanding complex emotions, pretense, and other's mental states, while they show superior abilities in folk physics, involving understanding mechanistic functions and physical systems. The central coherence model poses that individuals with AS/HFA display a cognitive style that involves greater attention to local details relative to more global information (or weak central coherence). Baron-Cohen (2000) concedes that the term "disability" may need to be maintained for AS/HFA due to the current legal requirements that financial and other supports may be provided only to individuals with disabilities. In the *Diagnostic and Statistical Manual of Mental Disorders, Fifth Edition,* Asperger's syndrome is no longer recognized as a separate disability; however, individuals who meet the diagnostic criteria for Asperger's syndrome will meet criteria under the all-encompassing label Autism Spectrum Disorder.

Avoiding Generalizations and Assumptions About a Child's Diagnosis

Mental health concerns can be particularly difficult to diagnose as symptoms may change over time and multiple causes may contribute to the presenting concerns. The special education disability category *emotional disturbance* may be viewed as a "catch-all" for a wide range of emotional or behavioral problems. Students who are labeled with an emotional disturbance under IDEA guidelines may or may not be formally diagnosed with a mental disorder as defined by the *Diagnostic and Statistical Manual of Mental Disorders, 5th Edition* (DSM-V). The definition of an emotional disturbance by IDEA does not require identifying the cause of the emotional disturbance, though it states that the term does not apply to children who are *socially maladjusted,* unless it is determined that they also have an emotional disturbance. Title 34, Section 300.8 (c) (4) in the CFR (Child with a disability, 2007) defines emotional disturbance:

> *(4) (i) Emotional disturbance means a condition exhibiting one or more of the following characteristics over a long period of time and to a marked degree that adversely affects a child's educational performance:*
>
> > *(A) An inability to learn that cannot be explained by intellectual, sensory, or health factors.*
> >
> > *(B) An inability to build or maintain satisfactory interpersonal relationships with peers and teachers.*
> >
> > *(C) Inappropriate types of behavior or feelings under normal circumstances.*
> >
> > *(D) A general pervasive mood of unhappiness or depression.*
> >
> > *(E) A tendency to develop physical symptoms or fears associated with personal or school problems.*
>
> *(ii) Emotional disturbance includes schizophrenia. The term does not apply to children who are socially maladjusted, unless it is determined that they have an emotional disturbance under paragraph (c)(4)(i) of this section . . . [§300.8 (c) (4)]*

Stakeholders should be careful not to make assumptions about the etiology or contributing factors of the child's symptoms based on his or her label, especially one that is broadly defined as is *emotional disturbance.* The child's emotional and behavioral problems may be substantially related to poor parenting or other problems in the family, or the symptoms may be largely biologically based. The problem behaviors may be related to a constellation of known and/or unknown biological and environmental factors such as genetic or biological characteristics, an undisclosed trauma the child experienced such as abuse, complications during the pregnancy, or other factors. In many cases, environmental risk factors (e.g., poor parenting, stressful life events) may precipitate symptoms in individuals who have a predisposition toward a mental illness or emotional-behavioral disturbance. Generally speaking, when there is a sustained problematic situation with a student, it is advisable for practitioners to consider possible stress and trauma roots before attributing the student's problems or symptoms to specific clinical pathology.

Within the individual child's context, professionals should also be careful not to predict a negative prognosis based on a child's diagnosis or disability category. There are innumerable factors that may influence a child's developmental trajectory toward dimensions of mental health/ mental illness, including changes in the family, risk and protective mechanisms, maturation, and brain development. Children are particularly resilient yielding less predictable prognoses compared to adults. The child's developmental history and cultural context should also be taken fully into account when attempting to understand the child's behaviors (Zalaquett, Fuerth, Stein, Ivey, & Ivey, 2008).

In sum regarding diagnostic labels, the interaction between the diagnostic presentation (e.g., symptoms, comorbidities, etiologic factors, cultural and contextual factors, degree of diagnostic certainty) and the beliefs held by the child, family, school personnel, mental health professionals, and others about the disability will influence intervention planning and educational decision making. Mental health professionals, including counselors, should be keenly aware of the advantages and disadvantages of diagnostic labels to assist all stakeholders in understanding these diagnostic issues and related decisions.

Talking to Parents, Children, and Adolescents About a Diagnostic Label or Disability

Parents may question how best to reveal to their child about his or her mental health diagnosis or developmental disability or whether to reveal the diagnostic label at all. It is advisable that parents meet with their child's physician, psychologist, or other related child specialists to become fully informed about the disability before they share with their child about a formal diagnosis or disability. Taking into account the child's cognitive and developmental levels, personality, and other unique characteristics, it is recommended that parents be open with their child about the nature of his or her difficulties. Young children may not understand diagnostic terms, so supporting the child in learning and practicing skills that may be challenging, such as friendship skills, as well as emphasizing the child's unique strengths is recommended. Older children and teens typically have the cognitive capabilities to better understand the nature of their problem, and they may be acutely aware of their problems and how they might be different from their peers.

Teens are increasingly responsible for personal decision making, so openness about a diagnosis through supportive conversations is recommended. Some children or adolescents may wish to learn more about their disability or disorder through books or other resources (see Resource C for books and resources available for children and adolescents of all ages). By high school, students usually participate in their own IEP meetings and become increasingly active in advocating for themselves.

Mental health professionals should be self-aware regarding their views on diagnosed disabilities and how this impacts how they talk with students and parents about disabilities. Professionals may ask themselves the following questions:

- What is my level of competency in diagnosing disabilities or providing diagnostic impressions?
- Do I understand the complexities of children's development as it relates to diagnosing a disability?
- Do I recognize the possibility that alternative explanations may explain a child's behavior?
- Do I tend to ignore diagnostic labels?
- Do I tend to view a student's disability status as static or dynamic?

COUNSELING CHILDREN AND ADOLESCENTS WITH DISABILITIES

Knowledge about a student's diagnosis can assist in understanding what might be driving the student's behavior and what forms of intervention may be indicated. Table 4.1 presents counseling goals and interventions for students in relation to diagnostic categories. While diagnostic considerations can facilitate intervention planning, counseling goals and interventions should be individualized for each student.

In counseling students with special needs, the specific goals targeted in counseling may be viewed within the context of the broader goals of facilitating inclusion, protecting the student's rights, fostering resilience, and helping the student to develop (see Marshak et al., 2010). There is a balance in protecting students' rights that may include providing special accommodations while at the same time working toward inclusion in the LRE. This requires ongoing assessment of students' progress and scaffolding goals based on present levels of performance.

At some point in their education, many students question how math or history class will help them reach their future goals in life. This may be especially true for students who experience learning challenges or who are overwhelmed with social-emotional concerns. Counseling provides an opportunity to help students understand the relevance of their education and how it may fit in with their own dreams for the future. When a therapeutic relationship is established, students may begin to not only share their interests and goals, but identify current barriers to attaining their goals and engage in problem solving and skill building.

CONCLUSION

Students who receive special education services demonstrate chronic problems related to an identified disability that significantly interferes with

Table 4.1 Counseling Goals and Interventions for Students With Specific Disabilities

Diagnosis/Disability	Targeted Goals for School Success	Counseling Interventions

ADHD and Learning Disabilities
 	
DSM-V Categories
 	
(ADHD Combined Type, Predominantly Inattentive Type, Predominantly Hyperactive-Impulsive Type); Learning Disorders (Cognitive Disorders, includes Traumatic Brain Injury)
	• Increase time on task
	• Organize assignments and materials
	• Increase work completion
	• Initiate assigned tasks independently
	• Ask for assistance when needed and utilize academic supports
	• Increase response inhibition or self-control
	• Develop positive self-concept
	• Demonstrate positive social interactions with peers and school staff
		• Teach, demonstrate, practice:
		  – Organizational and self-monitoring strategies
		  – Managing impulsivity
		  – Problem solving
		  – Assertiveness skills
		• Psychoeducation regarding ADHD (or other disability):
		  – How disability may influence educational performance
		  – Health and prevention
		• Strengths-based, solution-focused counseling; Cognitive-Behavioral Therapy; social skills counseling

Disruptive Behavior Disorders **DSM-V Categories** Conduct Disorder; Oppositional Defiant Disorder; Disruptive Behavior Disorder NOS; Adjustment Disorder with Disturbance of Conduct	• Increase time on task • Comply with teacher's requests • Increase positive social interactions with others/decrease verbal or physical aggression • Follow school rules • Increase educational motivation • Increase self-control/decrease responding impulsively • Resolve conflicts appropriately	• Individual and family counseling • Parent training and collaborative problem solving • Behavioral therapy; conjoint behavioral consultation • Multisystemic therapy • Cognitive problem solving • Social skills counseling • Anger management

(Continued)

Table 4.1 (Continued)

Diagnosis/Disability	Targeted Goals for School Success	Counseling Interventions
Anxiety Disorders **DSM-V Categories** Acute Stress Disorder; Agoraphobia; Generalized Anxiety Disorder; Obsessive-Compulsive Disorder; Panic Disorder; Posttraumatic Stress Disorder; Selective Mutism; Separation Anxiety Disorder; Social Phobia; Specific Phobia	• Increase active participation in learning and socialization • Use positive coping skills when experiencing stress • Increase self-confidence and assertiveness • Increase positive, goal-directed behaviors/decrease somatic complaints, social withdrawal, fearfulness, obsessions and compulsions, etc.	• Cognitive-Behavioral Therapy; supportive counseling • Relaxation training; systematic desensitization; graded exposure therapy • Social skills and assertiveness counseling • Psychoeducation; stress management; health and prevention
Mood Disorders **DSM-V Categories** Adjustment Disorders; Bipolar Disorders; Depressive Disorders	• Increase active participation in learning and socialization • Increase positive, goal-directed behaviors/decrease somatic complaints, social withdrawal, etc. • Use positive coping skills to manage difficult emotions • Increase self-confidence and assertiveness • Demonstrate positive social interactions with peers and school staff	• Individual and group therapies, including Cognitive-Behavioral Therapy; Solution-Focused Brief Therapy; Dialectical Behavioral Therapy; supportive/expressive therapies • Social skills and assertiveness counseling; social support • Health and prevention
Autism **DSM-V Categories** Autism Spectrum Disorder	• Increase positive social interactions, including initiating and maintaining conversations, expressing interest in other's ideas or interests, engaging in conversational turn-taking, expressing oneself through nonverbal communication, etc. • Utilize positive coping strategies when experiencing stress (e.g., changes in routine, sensory stimulation, etc.) • Identify emotional states in self and others	• Social stories; comic strip conversations; social scripts • Social skills groups; role play • Video-tape modeling; use of video, technology, computer software to teach social skills, recognizing emotions, understanding nonverbal communication, etc. • Psychoeducation to teach positive coping strategies

their educational performance. The highly individualized supports within special education can propel students to develop the requisite coping strategies to manage greater levels of independence and responsibility over time in the LRE.

The role of counseling is essentially the same in Levels 2 and 3 and in special education: to assist in remediating students' social, emotional, and/or behavioral problems that interfere with their educational progress. Counseling in Level 3, whether it is in the general or special education setting, is more individualized and intensive and resource dependent than in Level 2. Students in special education are identified with a diagnostic label and may receive counseling as a *related service* as a part of their IEP. Much of this chapter examined diagnostic considerations. Knowledge about a student's diagnosis or disability can assist counselors in designing appropriate evidence-based interventions. The clinical impressions held by the counselor or school mental health professional about a student's diagnosis will influence the problem-solving and decision-making processes of the RTI team. Effective interventions are preceded by sound assessments that inform clinical impressions.

In utilizing counseling, school-based mental health practitioners should use evidence-based practices as set forth through standards-based educational initiatives and laws as well as through professional governing bodies. In regard to developing student IEPs, 34 CFR §300.320 (a)(4) (2007) states that services provided to the child or on behalf of the child be "based on peer-reviewed research to the extent practicable." The next chapter hones in on three specific counseling approaches that may be used at Level 2 or 3 and allow for data-based decisions to determine a student's responsiveness to the intervention.

DISCUSSION QUESTIONS

1. What are some examples of how special education services may indirectly impact a student's social-emotional functioning?

2. Why should a student be educated in the LRE as much as possible? Can a student receive too much support? If so, what are the potential consequences? How can the appropriate amount of support be determined (e.g., not too little, not too much)?

3. What are some ways collaboration can be fostered between professionals who work primarily with special education students and school professionals who work substantially with a large number of general education students?

4. How can expertise in diagnostic considerations facilitate counseling?

5. Should students be told they have a disability? Why or why not? If so, what are some general parameters to consider?

6. What is the purpose of counseling as a *related service* in special education?

5 Effective and Efficient Counseling Approaches for School Settings

Around the time that the PBIS/RTI movement was gaining momentum within schools, a national panel report in school counseling highlighted the need to focus the profession on evidence-based approaches (Carey, Dimmitt, Hatch, Lapan, & Whiston, 2008). Prior to that time, school counseling services were criticized for embracing the role of gate keeping and failing to focus on outcomes (Hart & Jacobi, 1992). Prior to RTI, the goals of school-based counseling approaches for students identified as in need of improved personal and social development might have progressed through the following stages: development of rapport, a focus on establishing a trusting and open relationship, and engagement in regular communications (daily or weekly) about challenges and stressors facing the student. Such an approach would yield an undetermined end point, and specific goals for counseling may have been limited to relationship building and trust. The point at which counseling was concluded and determined successful or unsuccessful was not a natural part of the services provided. Data-based problem solving (i.e., problem identification, problem analysis, intervention planning and implementation, and progress monitoring) was limited and explicit focus on changes in achievement or improved skill development typically absent.

The constraints of the school setting and the emphasis on learning and access to educational curriculum requires counseling services to be time limited and goal directed within a PBIS/RTI service approach. Progress monitoring and promoting students' success within the school setting is now and must be in the future an underlying foundation of school-based counseling approaches. With a primary focus on students' response to intervention, it is a prerequisite that the counseling services provided to students involve measureable goals within a highly transparent service delivery format. Techniques used within counseling approaches in schools must meet higher standards for accountability to assist in decision making regarding the level of services necessary to meet the unique needs of the child. Goal development and monitoring approaches within the counseling process are necessary to support the effectiveness of services provided as well as to justify the costs of services rendered.

Three approaches to counseling (psychoeducational approaches, Cognitive-Behavioral Therapy, and solution-focused therapy) are identified from the literature that fit well into the types of services that allow for data-based decisions about a student's response to intervention across multiple levels of service delivery. This focus on evidence-based practices involves a clear delineation of the purpose, goals, and outcomes at the onset of the counseling services. Each of these approaches is relatively easy to implement, is short in duration, remains focused on positive and adaptive changes, and is flexible in its delivery to meet students' diverse needs. Each of these approaches assumes that students are competent and able to implement positive change on their own or with support.

PSYCHOEDUCATIONAL APPROACHES

Psychoeducational approaches to counseling focus on students' knowledge of their own mental health challenges and teaches them to use this knowledge to make improvements in their own functioning. The primary purpose of this approach is to help the student learn improved ways of functioning in an effort to prevent or intervene efficiently when faced with new and challenging situations and circumstances. Self-help techniques are often the target of this approach. This involves teaching students to critically problem solve, including how to identify, select, and monitor possible solutions to their difficulties. Promoting self-efficacy through the documentation of improvement and challenges is a positive outcome of psychoeducational counseling approaches. Moreover, this approach is efficient as students can be taught how to generalize this self-help approach to other difficulties and challenges they may have in the future. Psychoeducational counseling approaches allow counselors the opportunity to use their services to meet the needs of numerous students as this approach is time limited, goal directed, and can be completed in either individual or group formats. Examples of group psychoeducational counseling may include those targeted at social skills and competencies, adjustment to major life changes, problem solving, conflict resolution, or anger management. Cognitive-Behavioral Therapy, which we will discuss next, can be used as a psychoeducational approach; for example, teaching students anxiety management techniques using cognitive-behavioral strategies.

Psychoeducational approaches target students' deficits through teaching and modeling skills when there is a *knowledge deficit,* using role play and feedback to develop skills when the student demonstrates a *performance deficit,* and using repeated practice when there is a *fluency* deficit. The following scenario illustrates how the potential usefulness of a Level 2 psychoeducational approach may be identified in a counseling session.

Managing Academic Frustration: An Individualized Session With a Sixth-Grade Boy

Counselor: Last week you brought up some frustrations you were having in class. How are things going now?

Student: (shrugs shoulders in a way suggesting things might not be better)

Counselor: Are things better?

Student: No.

Counselor: What's the problem?

Student: My teachers are rushing me. Every time I'm trying to finish an assignment they tell me to stop working on it because we're starting a new one.

Counselor: That sounds frustrating. Why do you think your teachers are rushing you?

Student: I don't know.

Counselor: Maybe they just want you to be able to hear the new lesson so you will understand how to complete the next assignment? What do you think?

Student: I guess.

Counselor: What do you do with the work you have not finished yet . . . the assignments they tell you to stop working on?

Student: I put it in the back of my binder with my other junk.

Counselor: Your other junk? (laughing with student) Like your homework or other assignments you have not finished yet?

Student: Yes. (student smiles back)

Counselor: So you know when you put those assignments in the back of your binder they will still be there later . . . they aren't going anywhere, right?

Student: Right.

Counselor: Sometimes I feel frustrated too when I'm working on something and then have to stop because something else comes up. I've learned some strategies that have helped me get better at it though. You know, juggling several tasks at the same time. Or, really, learning to organize my tasks; for example, putting unfinished work in a certain place on my desk, making a list of what I need to accomplish, and then checking off the tasks that I complete. Does that make sense?

Student: Yeah.

Counselor: It sounds like you are already using an organizational system by putting your incomplete assignments at the back of your binder . . . that's good. Learning how to organize multiple tasks requires practice for it to become a habit. I am starting a group with a few other sixth-graders where we will learn and practice some specific organizational strategies that can be helpful for students in middle school. Would you be interested in joining our group?

Student: OK; will we get to play some games too?

Counselor: Yes, we will have fun too (smiling). Typically we practice organizational strategies the first part of group, then we play a game at the end. Sound OK?

Student: Sure. (smiling)

Discussion Questions

1. In the above scenario, what type of deficit is this student most likely demonstrating?

2. What are some specific organizational strategies the counselor might introduce in the group? How might the counselor teach these strategies?

3. Role-play another possible avenue the counselor might have taken with the student in the session (e.g., exploring the student's use of stress management techniques, exploring how he communicates with his teachers about his frustrations, etc.).

4. If stress management or communicating his feelings to teachers was identified as a need in counseling, how might the counselor proceed?

5. What other intervention strategies could be tried to facilitate the generalization of skills taught in counseling sessions?

Recommended Sources for Further Information About Psychoeducational Approaches in Schools

DeLucia-Waack, J. (2006). *Leading psychoeducational groups for children and adolescents.* Thousand Oaks, CA: Sage.

Mobley, J., & Fort, S. (2007). *Planning psychoeducational groups for schools.* Retrieved from http://counselingoutfitters.com/vistas/vistas07/Mobley.pdf

COGNITIVE-BEHAVIORAL THERAPY

Cognitive-Behavioral Therapy (CBT) is well-suited for school settings as this approach can effectively and efficiently address academic-related concerns by targeting students' motivation, their beliefs about their ability to perform tasks, and their ability to control and redirect their emotional responses to tasks, as well as to help reduce students' levels of stress and anxiety (Zyromski & Edwards-Joseph, 2008). CBT focuses on the directional influence of one's thoughts on their behaviors in targeting improvement in functioning at home and school. With respect to exploring one's cognitions or thoughts, the key to this approach is to help students better understand their lens or view of life events. This includes a close look at the perceptions and interpretations that typify one's day-to-day interactions with people and events.

Understanding possible errors in thoughts and beliefs is the primary focus of cognitive-behavioral approaches (see Figure 5.1 for common distorted thinking patterns). The identification of problematic thinking is directly targeted in counseling sessions. This approach allows students to be better problem solvers, become more adept in coping with stress and challenges, regulate affect and emotion, improve interpersonal skills, and increase engagement in goal-directed behaviors. Changing one's thoughts and beliefs is viewed as a prerequisite for improvement in the student's actions and behaviors.

Figure 5.1 Common Distorted Thinking Patterns

1. *All-or-nothing thinking:* Seeing things in "black or white"; expecting perfection from yourself or others; failure to see "shades of gray"

2. *Overgeneralization:* Creating a negative generalized view based on a single event or situation

3. *Mental filter:* Seeing things from a narrow view; not paying attention to all the evidence

4. *Disqualifying the positive:* Discounting or filtering out the positive evidence about our performance or a situation

5. *Jumping to conclusions:* Assuming the worst; including *mind reading* (e.g., assuming what others think about yourself, "he doesn't like me, etc.) and *fortune telling* (e.g., predicting a negative outcome)

6. *Magnification or minimization:* Exaggerating or minimizing a memory of a situation

7. *Emotional reasoning:* Assuming that emotions reflect reality

8. *Should statements:* Having a fixed idea of how others or oneself should behave

9. *Labeling and mislabeling:* Labeling yourself or others (e.g., "I'm dumb," "she's evil," etc.)

10. *Personalization/Blame:* Personalization is a tendency to hold yourself responsible for events that were out of your control; blame is a tendency to not take responsibility for events and to blame others

Source: Adapted from Burns (1999).

School counselors can easily adapt cognitive-behavioral interventions, such as teaching self-awareness and self-monitoring, rational analysis, cognitive restructuring, self-talk, relaxation training, imagery, and exposure/experiential methods, into practical and brief adaptations to address many types of student needs. CBT interventions may be applied in a very individualized way, such as using the A-B-C-D-E method (**A**ctivating Event, **B**elief, **C**onsequence of belief, **D**ispute negative thoughts, and **E**xplore alternative ways of thinking) at an opportune time during an individualized session, or CBT interventions may be included in a manualized treatment program. The following example shows how a school district selected a CBT school-based program to assist students who were exposed to traumatic events.

Implementation of a CBT School-Based Program in a Large Urban School District

A planning committee was formed in a large urban school district with the task of analyzing district needs regarding service delivery of mental health services. One of the priorities identified was to address the mental health needs of students who had experienced some type of trauma. A significant number of students throughout the district were experiencing or had experienced traumatic events that impacted their day-to-day functioning. These events included witnessing violence at home or in the community, experiencing physical or sexual abuse, or experiencing unexpected events (e.g., a serious injury or death of a friend of family member, a suicide, witnessing a car accident).

A school social worker and counselor within the district developed a districtwide intervention plan to address the identified need. By searching the *SAMHSA's National Registry of Evidence-Based Programs and Practices* (see Resource D) they found the Cognitive Behavioral Intervention for Trauma in Schools (CBITS) program (n.d.; see http://cbitsprogram.org/). The social worker and counselor both took the CBITS online training course and utilized the available resources to prepare for presenting a detailed plan on how to implement the program in their district. The planning committee accepted the plan and then information was provided to the school counselors, social workers, and school-level administrators about the program (see Figure 5.2 for a condensed summary of the CBITS program).

Full support was obtained from the school principal of each participating school within the district before any of the CBITS program was initiated at the campus level. Students were identified through a screening process, and group or individualized sessions were provided at the students' school at an ideal time for both the students and school. The sessions were led by counselors, social workers, or school psychologists who had received training. It was determined that it was neither feasible nor practical for all school mental health professionals in the district to be trained or be expected to provide this intervention.

Components of the CBITS program include educating students about trauma and common symptoms, changing disruptive/unhelpful thoughts, teaching them relaxation techniques and use of the fear thermometer, and improving problem solving. Skills were taught through drawings, talking in groups and individualized sessions, and between session assignments. The students completed a follow-up survey at the end of the program to track their progress. This vignette illustrates a districtwide implementation of an evidence-based program (the CBITS program) targeting a specific mental health need at Levels 2 and 3. Next, we discuss how CBT interventions can be adapted to the specific needs of students within school settings.

Figure 5.2 CBITS Program Summary

- The goal of CBITS is to alleviate symptoms of posttraumatic stress disorder (PTSD), depression, and general anxiety for children exposed to trauma
- CBITS is a small-group intervention for students in grades 6–9 consisting of 10 weekly hour-long sessions
- Emphasis is on skill building: relaxation skills, challenging upsetting thoughts, social problem solving, and processing traumatic memories and grief
- Parent and teacher education sessions are included
- Pre- and post-assessment measures are used (e.g., Life Events Scale, Child PTSD Symptom Scale, and Children's Depression Inventory)
- CBITS provides training guidelines to use the program
- CBITS has been implemented effectively on a wide range of racially and ethnically diverse children
- Parent materials are available in Spanish and English

Source: http://cbitsprogram.org/.

IMPLEMENTING CBT INTERVENTIONS PRAGMATICALLY IN SCHOOLS

Just as there are various CBT interventions (e.g., challenging distorted thinking; exposure; self-monitoring of thoughts, emotions, physiological responses, and/or behavior; developing adaptive coping mechanisms, such as "thought-stopping," motivational self-talk, imagery, relaxation, mindfulness, and acceptance), there are also different ways to implement CBT interventions. For example, CBT interventions can be presented formally by teaching, modeling, role-playing, and discussing skills or strategies during a group intervention or counseling session. Alternatively, CBT interventions can be implemented casually in a naturalistic setting such as through shaping desired interactions in a classroom, during lunch, or at recess. The student's age, developmental level, personality, preferences, and readiness for intervention, as well as the intensity of the student's behavior, can influence how the counselor or teacher may choose to implement the intervention. The following example illustrates how CBT interventions can be adapted for maximum impact.

Managing Difficult Emotions: CBT With a First-Grade Boy

Troy is social and intelligent, and he thoroughly likes school—a typical first-grade boy. He is also very competitive, usually the first student to raise his hand to answer questions and volunteer to lead the class line out of the classroom.

His eagerness to lead, though, soon became agitating to many of his classmates as evidenced by arguing and pushing. Troy's misbehavior persisted despite his teacher providing structure, specific instructions regarding procedures, social lessons about taking turns and respecting other's feelings, and positive reinforcement and consequences. He was actually becoming increasingly frustrated and aggressive with his peers despite these interventions.

Troy's teacher expressed her concern about his behavior with both Troy's mother and the school counselor. His mother was also concerned and shared that Troy had been having problems at home too. She explained that the family was dealing with a recent separation and divorce between herself and Troy's father. The school counselor proposed to his mother that Troy could participate in a small group with other students who were also dealing with their own parents' divorce. After they discussed the potential benefits and harmful effects of Troy participating in the group, Troy's mother expressed interest in trying this intervention.

The school counselor utilized lessons and materials from Sylvia Margolin's (1996) *Complete Group Counseling Program for Children of Divorce: Ready-to-Use Plans & Materials for Small & Large Groups, Grades 1–6* in a small group with Troy and three other first-graders. Troy actively participated in the group and often took the lead during activities and discussions. The counselor utilized the group session to not only target the students' thoughts and emotions to better cope with their parents' divorce, but also used the small-group format to shape interactions between the students. For example, the counselor facilitated turn-taking, waiting and listening, demonstrating respect and empathy, and the students' relating to shared experiences between themselves. Troy responded positively to the group intervention, and he also began to generalize what he learned in the group to the classroom with continued support from the teacher.

Discussion Questions

1. How might Troy's parents' divorce be impacting his behavior at school? What other factors might explain his problematic behaviors?

2. How might CBT be used in a natural setting (e.g., at recess, lunch, or in the classroom)? When might it be most appropriate to utilize CBT in natural settings? When might it be most appropriate to use CBT in an individualized or group format as opposed to a more natural environment?

3. Conceptually speaking, how does Cognitive-Behavioral Therapy improve functioning at school?

Recommended Sources for Further Information About CBT in Schools

Mayer, M., Van Acker, R., Lochman, J., & Gresham, F. (2009). *Cognitive-behavioral interventions for emotional and behavioral disorders: School-based practice.* New York, NY: Guilford.

Mennuti, R., Christner, R., & Freeman, C. (2012). *Cognitive-behavioral interventions in educational settings: A handbook for practice* (2nd ed.). New York, NY: Routledge.

SOLUTION-FOCUSED BRIEF THERAPY

Solution-focused approaches are by nature aimed at solving problems and promoting one's functioning and success. Identifying the replacement or adaptive behaviors that may improve a student's functioning is the first step within this approach. By the very nature of these services, they are very brief given the focus on a rapid resolution of problems. The basic premise is to do more of what works and less of what does not work. This approach is primarily focused on strengths as opposed to focusing on students' problems. Similar to psychoeducational counseling, students construct their visions and goals for change.

Solution-Focused Brief Therapy (SFBT) involves a conversation between the counselor and student that includes three major ingredients or processes: (1) the counselor focusing on the student's concerns (e.g., what is important to the student, what the student's preferred future looks like), (2) the counselor and student co-constructing altered or new meanings for the student, and (3) the counselor using specific questioning and responding techniques to facilitate co-construction of a vision of a preferred future and drawing on the student's strengths to help make the vision a reality (Trepper et al., 2008). Greenberg, Ganshorn, and Danilkewic (2001) present the acronym MECSTAT—standing for Miracle questions, Exception questions, Coping questions, Scaling questions, Time-out, Accolades, and Task—for recalling the basic strategies used in SFBT.

The *miracle question* elicits the student to envision how the future will be different when the problem is no longer present. The counselor can use follow-up questions to further assist the student in expanding on how things will be different. The initial miracle question might be phrased something like this: "Imagine you wake up tomorrow morning and a miracle happens where the problem no longer exists. What might you first notice that will show you the problem is gone?" Follow-up questions might include questions such as "What would be different between the two of you?" or "When would this occur?" The student's responses to these questions then lead to concrete goals for counseling.

Looking for *exceptions to the problem* can help students understand what they might be doing differently when the problem is not occurring.

Examples of exception questions might include "Can you remember a time when you were able to prevent an anger outburst?," "What percentage of the time do you feel comfortable volunteering in class?," or "What is different about the times when the problem is not happening?" The goal is to help students repeat strategies that have worked for them in the past.

The use of *coping questions* can assist students in identifying their personal resources, particularly when they are losing hope and energy to do something about their problems. Examples of coping questions might include "How do you manage to deal with such difficult circumstances?," "It's admirable that you are able to do so well under these circumstances. How are you doing it?," or "What keeps you going?" Coping questions can help reenergize students to use their personal resources/coping strategies to work toward solutions.

Scaling questions can help students quantify their perceptions regarding the severity of the problem, rate their level of motivation or confidence, and track their progress. Examples of scaling questions might include "On a scale from 1 to 10, with 10 representing the problem is solved, where would you rate the problem today?," or "You say the problem is a 5 today in terms of the problem being solved. What do you need to do to get to a 6?"

Incorporating *time-out* or a break from the session to allow the counselor an opportunity to reflect on the conversation or dialogue with colleagues about the session before providing accolades and a therapeutic message to the client may not be practical in many practice settings, such as schools. Instead, the counselor can be observant and reflective throughout the session to assess the student's readiness for change and prepare for potential tasks for the student.

Accolades (or compliments and cheerleading) can be used to validate the student's progress and strengths. Using accolades can help build the student's confidence as well as help to strengthen the counselor-client relationship.

At the end of the session the counselor can suggest a *task* or homework assignment. The task may be phrased as an "experiment" the student might consider trying between sessions. The task might involve the student doing more of what has already worked in the past or trying something new that he or she may have thought of and wants to try.

In SFBT, follow-up sessions typically begin with the counselor asking the student what is better, even if it is small, since the last session. The counselor assists the student in noticing details about the positive changes. If the problem has maintained or gotten worse, the counselor can use *coping questions* to ask the student what they did to keep the problem from getting even worse. The following is an example of a counselor using SFBT with a high school student.

SFBT With an Adolescent Female With Depressive Symptoms

Amy, a junior in high school, sought assistance from her school counselor due to feelings of depression, crying spells, low self-esteem, and interpersonal problems. During the initial session the counselor began by asking basic questions to better understand Amy's presenting concerns and assess potential contributing factors to her problems. Amy stated that she had felt depressed for quite a while and that it was getting worse. She shared that she was not taking medication for depression or seeing a private therapist. Amy had difficulty identifying what might be causing her to feel depressed. She made some general negative self-comments, such as "I don't like the way I look," "I'm not that smart," and "Most people ignore me."

The counselor began by taking an SFBT approach by asking Amy a *miracle question,* "Let's pretend you went to bed tonight and when you woke up your problems disappeared. What would you first notice that would make you think, 'Wow, my problems are gone!'?" A conversation ensued between Amy and the counselor in which Amy formulated specific goals for counseling. She wanted to take pride in her appearance while at the same time accepting herself and not judging herself so harshly. She wanted to develop better study habits. She also wanted to increase her involvement in social activities with her peers. The counselor then used *scaling questions* to establish a baseline of how she felt presently about her goals (10 = feeling completely well and her goal has been achieved; 0 = the moment she felt her worst). She scored herself a 3, 5, and 4 on her goals, respectively. The counselor then engaged Amy in conversation where she identified *exceptions* to her problems; for example, times when she felt good about her appearance, felt intelligent, and engaged in a confident interaction with a peer. She provided several exceptions, including a time she participated in a volunteer program, keeping up a healthy diet and exercise program, having a "makeover," making a high grade on an algebra test, cooking a surprise dinner for her mother, and helping her friend through tough times. The counselor complimented Amy for taking the initiative to seek assistance and for being able to clearly define specific goals for herself. The counselor and Amy agreed to meet again for a follow-up session. The counselor encouraged her to look for opportunities between sessions to continue to build on her strengths.

The counselor began the second session by asking Amy, "What have you noticed that is better?" Amy shared that she had been exercising after school almost every day and she was on top of her studies. She rated herself a 7, 7, and 4 on her goals, respectively. The counselor asked Amy how she managed to make so much progress after one session and also prompted her to describe in detail what she noticed that she was doing differently. Amy felt good about her progress, but she did not feel she was making progress toward her interpersonal goal. The counselor engaged her in conversation about her resources that led in to her generating some ideas about how she could get to know more people, such as through considering joining a club or an organization where she can do positive things for others. The counselor and Amy met for several more sessions. During that time, Amy became a peer tutor for underclassmen who were taking Algebra I and took a lot of pride in this role. The final session the counselor complimented her on her progress and asked her how she was going to celebrate.

Discussion Questions

1. In the example with Amy, what strategies did the counselor use to help Amy construct a vision of a preferred future?

2. Compare and contrast SFBT with psychoeducational counseling and CBT.

Recommended Sources for Further Information About SFBT in Schools

Kelly, M., Kim, J., & Franklin, C. (2008). *Solution-focused brief therapy in schools: A 360-degree view of research and practice.* Oxford, UK: Oxford University Press.

Murphy, J. J. (2008). *Solution-focused counseling in schools* (2nd ed.). Alexandria, VA: American Counseling Association.

CONCLUSION

Psychoeducational approaches, cognitive-behavioral counseling, and solution-focused counseling all fit well within Level 2 (i.e., time-limited individual or small-group approach) or Level 3 (i.e., intensive support) services within an RTI model. Each of these approaches facilitates evidence-based counseling as they promote a clear delineation of the purpose, goals, and outcomes of counseling services. They are also efficient and adaptable for school settings. Chapter 6 looks more closely at evidence-based counseling as well as reviews considerations for group counseling, play therapy, counseling young children, and cultural counseling.

6 Evidence-Based Counseling in Schools

T his chapter highlights two definitions of *"evidence-based counseling in schools."* A user-friendly table to highlight evidence-based counseling approaches, including those reviewed in Chapter 5 (psychoeducational, cognitive-behavioral, and solution-focused techniques), is presented below in Table 6.1. A set of easy-to-navigate websites is presented (see Resource D) to help clinicians find programs that target specific mental health challenges faced within their district. In addition, examples of specific counseling techniques with strong empirical evidence for their use at Level 1, Level 2, and/or Level 3 within a PBIS/RTI service delivery model in schools are reviewed later in the chapter within Table 6.2. The chapter concludes with a brief review of special topics in school-based counseling including group counseling, play therapy, counseling young children, and addressing the needs of our nation's diverse students within the counseling relationship. We first review current research findings regarding the effectiveness of counseling as an intervention for children and adolescents in schools.

EFFECTIVENESS OF COUNSELING IN SCHOOLS

Research is showing that school counseling interventions are effective. Wilson, Lipsey, and Derzon (2003), in a meta-analysis that included 200 studies involving nearly 56,000 students on the effects of school-based programs on aggressive behavior, found that violence prevention programs effectively reduced violent and disruptive behavior. The intervention modalities included social competence training with and without cognitive-behavioral components, classroom management techniques, counseling, social skills programs, peer mediation, academic interventions, and multimodal approaches using various combinations of the preceding. The programs were categorized as universal (delivered in a classroom setting targeting all students), selected/indicated (delivered outside of the classroom to small groups or individuals), comprehensive (included multiple treatment components and formats), and special schools/classes (delivered in a special class outside of the mainstream setting for students with significant behavioral problems). The results from Wilson and colleagues' (2003) study found that violence prevention programs in schools were effective, especially programs that provided small-group or individualized services for selected students (effect size = .29). Using statistics from the Centers for Disease Control and Prevention that approximately 15% of school children get into a fight at school each year, Wilson and Lipsey (2005) translate the treatment effect size of .29 for selected/individual interventions into practical terms: "If 15% of students who received no violence prevention programming were getting into fights before intervention, only about 6% of children in selected/indicated programs were getting into fights" (p. 25).

In a 2007 meta-analysis of 117 studies, Whiston and Quinby (2009) found that students who participated in school counseling interventions improved close to a third of a standard deviation (effect size = .30) on various outcomes compared to those who did not receive interventions. Upon examination of school counseling outcome research by intervention components (guidance curriculum, individual planning, responsive services, and program management), the meta-analysis revealed that guidance curriculum and responsive services produced the largest weighted effect sizes, .35 for each. Responsive services included individual counseling, group counseling, referral, consultation, and peer assistance programs. The meta-analysis further revealed that group counseling was often evaluated and also produced an effect size of .35. In comparing the effectiveness of individual counseling with group counseling in schools, Whiston and Quinby (2009) conclude that research findings are mixed. They also found that there were surprisingly few studies evaluating the effectiveness of individual counseling in schools.

While there are relatively few studies evaluating the effectiveness of SFBT in schools, studies have found SFBT to be effective in reducing classroom-related behavioral problems (Franklin, Biever, Moore, Clemons, & Scamardo, 2001; Franklin, Moore, & Hopson, 2008; LaFountain & Garner, 1996) and students' internalizing behaviors (Franklin et al., 2008). In their study, Franklin and colleagues (2008) utilized a combination of individual sessions of SFBT with students, teacher training, consultations, and collaborative meetings. Students received five to seven sessions lasting 30 to 45 minutes weekly. In other studies, three brief individual counseling approaches were effective in alleviating high school students' concerns about problems, facilitating advancement toward their goals, and reducing negative feelings related to their problems (Littrell, Malia, & Vanderwood, 1995) and brief counseling approaches were effective with students with learning disabilities (Thompson & Littrell, 1998).

Overall, research is showing that school counseling interventions, including time-limited approaches, are effective. Next, we examine two definitions of evidence-based counseling: techniques grounded in theory and techniques grounded in theory and practice.

TECHNIQUES GROUNDED IN THEORY

Evidence-based counseling in schools typically has one of two meanings. The first is a more traditional meaning of evidence-based counseling: namely, the use of counseling techniques, grounded in theory, that allows for data or information gathering regarding the effectiveness of that technique on the specific student or students receiving treatment. These treatments typically have theoretical support for their use within school-aged populations and are widely discussed within the literature. There are literally hundreds of therapy and counseling approaches appearing in the literature that are rooted in theory. Some (i.e., cognitive-behavioral techniques, social skills training, teacher consultation) also have a long history of empirical support when used within schools to treat children's social, behavioral, and emotional problems (Hoagwood & Erwin, 1997). Cognitive-Behavioral Therapy, for example as a Level 2/3 service, has been found to be effective in improving locus of control, symptoms of depression, attendance, and substance use when implemented in schools.

A common characteristic that cuts across all counseling techniques is the importance of the counselor-student relationship. This relationship demonstrates trust, care, and support. Active listening, showing respect and understanding, and responding effectively within the counseling relationship are essential features of the counseling relationship. The range and assortment of counseling approaches that allow for this relationship to develop effectively is important to recognize. There is general agreement that counselors must be well trained in numerous approaches to develop an adequate counseling technique "toolbox" from which they may select an intervention that is most likely to succeed given the presenting needs of the student or students being provided services. In sum, school counselors must be well trained in a number of different techniques so that they can effectively and efficiently adapt their interventions to meet the individual and group needs of a diverse student population.

Table 6.1 provides examples of a theoretically diverse array of counseling strategies typically used in schools and firmly grounded in theory. An

Table 6.1 Frequently Used Counseling Techniques With Children and Adolescents

Theoretical Perspective	Technique	Goals/Targets
Brief Counseling or Solution-Focused	**Co-construct the Problem/Goal** Identifying/Amplifying Exceptions Scaling Exceptions Journaling Problem-Free Talk Strength Based Crystal Ball Technique Miracle Question Flagging the Minefield Focus on Goals	**Goal Directed, Focused on Change and Improvement** Define problems on a continuum Find previous exceptions to students' problem Keeping track of exceptions to the problem Focus on positive talk, problem-free talk Highlight students' resources and strengths Think of being problem-free in the future Consider a miracle cure for the problem Identifying (flag) barriers (minefield) to change
Adlerian	**Focus on What/Why** I-Position/I-Messages Immediacy Encouragement Acting As If Spitting in the Soup Mutual Storytelling Paradoxical Intention Socratic Questioning Focus on Understanding	**Identify, Explore, and Challenge One's Beliefs** Reduce negativity when confronting others Focus on feelings in the moment Use strengths to build motivation to change Presume what it is like to fix the problem Make negative behaviors less attractive/desired Generate more adaptive ways to interact Focus on needing to feel sorry for self Leading to a solution through questioning
Gestalt	**Self-Awareness, Insight** Internal Dialogue Empty Chair/Chairwork Body Movement/Exaggeration Role Reversal	**Align Intentions and Actions Positively** Role play internal conflicts Role playing focused on self-exploration Use movement to express problems

Theoretical Perspective	Technique	Goals/Targets
	Making the Rounds	Take others' perspective
	Focus on Personal Responsibility	Express concerns to others
Social Learning	**Learning to Change From Others**	**Action-Oriented Approach to Change Interactions**
	Modeling	Observational learning, imitating role model
	Behavioral Rehearsal	Feedback with behavioral practice
	Role Playing	Practice solutions in real-life situations
	Reinforcing Imitation	Positively responding to attempts at imitation
	Social Skills Training	
	Assertiveness Training	Developing social competence via practice
	Focus on Observation/ Imitation	Develop social initiative via role playing
Cognitive	**Changes in Thinking/ Cognitions**	**Alter Thoughts to Improve Functioning**
	Self-Talk	Talking oneself successfully through a problem
	Visual-Guided Imagery	Imagining a successful resolution
	Reframing	Shift negative thoughts to neutral/positive
	Thought Stopping	Eliminate self-defeating or illogical thinking
	Cognitive Restructuring	
	Focus on Thinking Differently	Replace illogical thoughts with realistic ones
Behavioral	**Changes in Doing**	**Change Behavior to Improve Functioning**
	Premack Principle	Pair negative-positive: peas before ice cream
	Behavioral Charting	Visible display of goals and progress
	Token Economy	Reinforcement and response cost combined
	Behavioral Contracting	
	Redirection	Reinforce contingent on behavior
	Extinction	Shift attention away from undesired behavior
	Time-Out	
	Response Cost	Take away reinforcement for a negative behavior
	Overcorrection/Positive Practice	Removing from a reinforcing setting
	Focus on Behaving Differently	Removal of a privilege
		Restore and improve on the desired behavior

(Continued)

Table 6.1 (Continued)

Theoretical Perspective	Technique	Goals/Targets
Cognitive-Behavioral	**Changing Thoughts and Behaviors**	**Reduce Problematic Actions and Thoughts**
	Cognitive Restructuring	Changing thinking patterns to activate behaviors
	Behavioral Activation	
	Bibliotherapy	Overcome obstacles to engage in fun activities
	Deep Breathing	Using books and self-help resources
	Progressive Muscle Relaxation	Calming down the body and mind
	Systematic Desensitization	Reducing physiological/psychological tension
	Stress Inoculation Training	Gradual getting comfortable with fearful event
	Focus on Thoughts-Behavior Link	Reducing/preventing negative response to stress

Source: Adapted from Erford, Eaves, Bryant, & Young (2010).

overview of these techniques for use within individual or group counseling sessions and related goals/targets associated with each technique is presented. Additional information about a number of these techniques also can be found in Table 9.1.

The evidence-based techniques presented in Table 6.1 are primarily intended for delivery in small groups of at-risk students (Level 2), to individual students who may be at risk (Level 2), to groups or individuals diagnosed with a mental health condition who may not be receiving special education services (Level 3a), or to those individuals who are receiving special education services for their disability (Level 3b). It is important to point out that many of the behavioral techniques presented are associated with effective classroom management techniques and integrate effectively and efficiently into Level 1 services (i.e., all children). These techniques are typically translated into practice by teachers who have developed these skills through preservice or in-service training and/or through consultation with mental health counselors. These Level 1 services when provided to all students can result in the prevention of behavioral problems and reduce the need for more intensive and time-consuming Level 2 and 3 services. Given the limited mental health resources that may exist within schools, these approaches provide a cost-effective and resource-limited approach to mental health prevention and early intervention. The existence and documentation of these effective techniques within classrooms is an essential first step for counselors to address within a problem-solving approach.

This next section of Chapter 6 calls attention to five specific Level 1 ecological-behavioral techniques that are associated with the mental health approaches presented in Table 6.1. These five have been identified as evidence based through a critical review of the literature conducted and reported by the Department of Education's What Works Clearinghouse (WWC; see Resource D). Each approach, when implemented by classroom teachers as intended, has demonstrated at least "Moderate" support for their effectiveness according to a practice guide titled "Reducing Behavior Problems in the Elementary School Classroom" (Epstein, Atkins, Cullinan, Kutash, & Weaver, 2008) published on the WWC website. Increasing students' engagement in learning activities and reducing behavioral distractions and problems within the classroom are at the core of each of the following five techniques:

1. *Modify the classroom learning environment to promote desired, adaptive behaviors and to reduce problem behavior* (**Strong Support**). This is accomplished by removing factors that trigger negative behaviors and establishing a positive fit between the classroom and the student. Clear behavioral expectations for students, arranging the environment and demands to match the student's needs, and adapting instruction to match student skill level are three specific strategies leading to improved classroom behavior. The use of clearly defined structure, routine, and transitions can effectively reduce problematic behavior. Making changes to the environment as opposed to making changes in a single child may have profound implications on altering the behavior of many students.

2. *Teach specific skills that may be new to the students to help them to demonstrate adaptive classroom behavior and to promote a positive classroom climate* (**Strong Support**). Disorders like ADHD are sometimes best conceptualized as a developmental delay. For example, children with ADHD may be developmentally delayed in reacting effectively to social cues in their environment when compared to their same-aged peer. These skill deficits must be remediated through teaching discrete social skills and effective use of behavioral reinforcement. Students must be taught how to use these skills, when to apply them, and under which conditions these skills should be used. Teaching all students these adaptive skills helps to establish the importance of the behaviors within the classroom while limiting the spotlight that might be inadvertently placed on a student who has particular deficits.

3. *Identify the antecedent and consequential conditions that prompt and reinforce problem behavior* (**Moderate Support**). The ABCs approach (i.e., Antecedent, Behavior, Consequence) to improving students' behavior is an important classroom-wide technique for teachers to employ. Through consultation, teachers can be taught how to carefully observe for the conditions under which both positive (adaptive) and negative (maladaptive) behaviors are being demonstrated. Appropriately responding to these behaviors has the ability to increase those that are desired (e.g., via reinforcement) and diminishing those behaviors that are problematic to classroom functioning (e.g., via ignoring).

4. *Work collaboratively across home and school settings to support students' successful functioning at school* (**Moderate Support**). Helping teachers to find allies who can work collaboratively to address problem behaviors is a crucial component of a well-defined classroom management strategy. Looking to create consistency in responding to problematic behavior and promoting adaptive behaviors across settings can be a powerful management technique. Problem behavior that is consistent across settings may represent global issues with adaptability or signify pervasive problems or issues within the person-environment fit. Insights from other settings, alternative strategies that may be effective, and support from others in dealing with the challenging behavior has the potential to improve a student's behavior across multiple settings and contexts.

5. *Adopt schoolwide strategies and supports that have been shown to reduce negative behaviors and increase positive interactions across the district* (**Moderate Support**). Working collaboratively with teachers and school administrators, mental health counselors can assess the need and effectiveness of districtwide approaches to improving students' behavioral functioning. Not only is it important to establish consistent guidelines for classroom functioning, a strong preventative approach is to uniformly implement buildingwide or districtwide expectations for students' behavior. This systemic approach (e.g., PBIS) requires the buy-in and implementation support of district administrators who then work with all school personnel to effectively implement these practices within their building(s).

Establishing documentation that provides evidence that school personnel are implementing these five evidence-based techniques with integrity is essential. Gathering the data necessary to clearly demonstrate students are failing to respond to these services should be considered a prerequisite to implementing Level 2/3 services within a tiered service delivery model. Use of these techniques by teachers serving all students (i.e., set clear expectations for behavior combined with reinforcement for appropriate behavior, ignore or withhold attention for inappropriate behavior, punish or remove the student for classroom rule violations) promotes successful academic and behavioral outcomes in schools. The costs and resources required within Level 2 and 3 services can be considerably conserved by making sure strong supports for promoting positive behavior are at play within a district's Level 1 services.

The majority of the counseling techniques presented in Table 6.1 are developmentally appropriate for children and adolescents who present with the ability for introspection, open communication, and a willingness to change. Techniques for young children, who may present to counseling having not met these developmental assumptions, require greater reliance on behavioral treatments where clear expectations for appropriate behavior is articulated frequently and often by those within the child's environment. Often adults, including teachers, parents, and other school personnel, are necessary and active members of the counseling intervention given their role in helping to monitor, provide feedback, and reinforce desired behaviors. This means that child management classes for parents or classroom management support via consultation to teachers like those highlighted by the WWC need to be implemented in an effort to promote developmentally appropriate behavior in young children.

TECHNIQUES GROUNDED IN THEORY AND PRACTICE

The second meaning of "evidence-based counseling in schools" has a more political and societal influence reflective of the accountability movement found within contemporary health care and education systems. Specifically, this second definition focuses on the idea that the counseling technique being used by counselors has been previously deemed evidence based, through prior research (e.g., randomized controlled trials) that demonstrated effective change within a specific population of children and adolescents. The attention on programs and interventions meeting the criteria of rigorous research methods has been the target of mental health researchers for many decades (e.g., Hoagwood & Erwin, 1997).

Examples of treatment programs and packages that can be utilized within an evidence-based approach to school counseling are presented in Table 6.2. This table provides an overview of only a handful of all of those that have been identified as evidence-based counseling programs at the elementary, middle school, and high school levels. An example of an evidence-based program specifically tailored for each of these developmental periods is featured for each level of a tiered service delivery approach. Specifics pertaining to the empirical support for each program can be explored in greater detail through the National Center for Mental Health Promotion and Violence Prevention website (http://www.promoteprevent.org/), the Promising Practices Network (http://www.promisingpractices.net/default.asp), and additional resources appearing in Resource D. Table 6.2 highlights the nature of the research setting in which support has been documented, as well as providing information about the goals of the program and factors related to transportability.

A wide variety of treatment programs was selected from the dozens highlighted within resources found in Resource D. There is an assumption that those receiving Level 3b services as highlighted in Table 6.2 would be receiving special education services. Yet, this assumption may not hold true for some students who may have a clearly defined mental health diagnosis but not meet the threshold for meeting criteria leading to eligibility for receiving special education services. Aside from this nuance of the tiered approach, these programs highlight the importance of training and experience when matching the needs of a population identified in the schools and the corresponding treatment approach. Specifically, attention needs to be placed on the intended target population for each treatment. For example, when age criteria or availability of resources doesn't match those linked to the evidence-based program, possible adaptations are necessary. Such changes then warrant the use of progress monitoring techniques to help determine the appropriateness of that treatment for the intended purpose.

CONTRASTING THE DEFINITIONS OF EVIDENCE-BASED COUNSELING

The difference in the meanings behind these two definitions of evidence-based counseling pertains to the point at which the treatment is deemed effective. Is it at the point of conclusion of services or prior to the onset of services? Ideally, as described in this book, it must be both. Counseling techniques that work for specific groups of children and adolescents need to be widely disseminated, understood, and applied to populations of children that are likely to benefit. In addition, given the limitations inherent within the research on those interventions, the individual impact that the selected evidence-based counseling technique has on the student must be documented and clearly communicated within a tiered system of mental health service delivery. We note that there are dozens of other programs highlighted

Table 6.2 Examples of Evidence-Based Counseling Interventions at Level 1/2/3a/3b

Examples of Evidence-Based Programs by Level	Nature of the Program and Research Support	Transportability and Dissemination Factors
Level 1: Services to All Elementary Providing Alternative THinking Strategies (PATHS) Curriculum	**What:** The goal of the program is to facilitate the development of self-control, emotional awareness, and interpersonal problem-solving skills. The primary focus of the program is to prevent violence through the promotion of social competence, social understanding, and educational success. **How:** This curriculum is intended for delivery by teachers or counselors in regular education classrooms K–6. **Evidence:** Randomized trials with children in regular education classrooms, children receiving special education services including those with emotional impairments, and deaf/hearing-impaired children demonstrate positive effects.	Manualized lessons Set up as a multiyear, universal prevention model Materials available to involve parents Training and technical assistance are available Effective across multiple participant samples and across urban/rural settings Translated into Dutch, French, and Hebrew and implemented across the world
Middle School Second Step: Social Skills From Early Childhood to Grade 8	**What:** The goal of the program is to reduce impulsive and aggressive behaviors and increase protective factors and social-emotional competence. The primary focus of the program is to prevent violence through teaching empathy, problem solving, and anger management. **How:** This curriculum is intended for delivery by teachers or counselors in schools (PreK–8) and/or mental health agency settings. **Evidence:** Limited to a pre-post evaluation of a treatment and comparison at the middle school level. Much stronger support at the elementary level.	Manualized lessons Set up as a multiyear, universal prevention model Training and technical assistance are available Effective across multiple participant samples and across urban/rural settings. Spanish language supplements are available.

(Continued)

Table 6.2 (Continued)

Examples of Evidence-Based Programs by Level	Nature of the Program and Research Support	Transportability and Dissemination Factors
High School Too Good for Drugs & Violence	**What:** The goal of the program is to teach five essential life skills: (1) goal setting, (2) decision making, (3) bonding with prosocial others, (4) identifying and managing emotions, and (5) communicating effectively. The primary focus is to reduce risk factors and enhance protective factors related to alcohol, tobacco, and other drug use. **How:** This school-based curriculum is intended for delivery by teachers or counselors in schools K–12. **Evidence:** Pre-post randomized controlled trial demonstrating increased protective factors and reduction of risk factors.	Manualized lessons, workbooks Contains strong parental involvement component Training and technical assistance are available Effective across multiple participant samples and across urban/rural settings. Spanish version available
Level 2: Services to Some Elementary Incredible Years Dina Dinosaur Child Training Program (Small-Group Treatment Version)	**What:** The goal of this targeted treatment program is to promote social-emotional competence in elementary students who are at risk for later conduct problems. The primary focus of the program is to improve peer relationships, reduce aggression, and improve disruptive and noncompliant interactions with adults. **How:** The Small-Group Treatment Program can be implemented by trained counselors or therapists with small groups of children at school (PreK–Grade 6) or in the community. It is ideally offered in combination with the Parent Training Program. There is a Dina Classroom Curriculum that can also be used universally with all children as a Level 1 service.	Manualized lessons The program is a part of a multifaceted treatment program for parents and teachers Attending a formal training sessions over multiple days is highly recommended for those implementing the program. These costs and the skills necessary to implement this program may serve as barriers to school-based implementation. Technical assistance is available Effective across multiple participant samples and across urban/rural settings

Examples of Evidence-Based Programs by Level	Nature of the Program and Research Support	Transportability and Dissemination Factors
	Evidence: Multiple randomized controlled trials have demonstrated strong evidence for the Incredible Years Training series including the small group Dina program.	Translated into multiple languages and implemented across the world
<u>Middle School</u> Aggression Replacement Therapy	**What:** The goal of this targeted treatment program is to help adolescents better manage their anger and reduce aggressive behavior. The program can also be used as a Level 1 intervention with the primary focus on improving social skill competence and moral reasoning. The original focus of the program was to reduce aggressive behaviors in those involved in the juvenile justice system. **How:** Aggression replacement training is a cognitive-behavioral intervention can be offered by well-trained school professionals and/or mental health clinicians in schools Grade 6 to Grade 12 or within juvenile justice programs within the community. **Evidence:** The primary evidence to date is from residential treatment facilities and residential schools. Effectiveness of the program in those setting has been well established.	Structured lessons Training and technical assistance are available Cost of training and skills needed to implement this program may present challenges to school-based implementation Effective across multiple participant samples and across urban/rural settings
<u>High School</u> Functional Family Therapy	**What:** The goal of this targeted intervention program is to examine adolescents' behavioral problems within family relationship systems. This time-limited intervention has three specific phases: engagement and motivation, behavior change, and generalization. The program can be used as a Level 3 intervention for those experiencing serious dysfunction at school or in the community.	Multiple components related to both assessment and treatment Training and technical assistance are available Comprehensive approach to community-based implementation

(Continued)

Table 6.2 (Continued)

Examples of Evidence-Based Programs by Level	Nature of the Program and Research Support	Transportability and Dissemination Factors
	How: This family therapy approach can used by school counselors or mental health professionals working with children and adolescents (ages 10–18) at-risk for conduct problems and/or substance use. **Evidence:** The primary evidence to date revolves around recidivism rates. Both randomized trials and nonrandomized comparison group studies show that FFT significantly improves juvenile offense patterns.	Costs and training necessary may be particularly challenging for school-based implementation
Level 3a/3b: Services to Few Elementary Coping Cat	**What:** The purpose of this workbook-based intervention program is to help children (1) recognize anxious feelings and physical reactions to anxiety; (2) clarify feelings in anxiety-provoking situations; (3) develop a coping plan; and (4) evaluate performance and administer self-reinforcement. **How:** This individual therapy approach can be used by school counselors or mental health professionals working with children and adolescents (ages 8–13) presenting with severe anxiety. An intervention workbook adapted for use with older students up to age 17 is available. The program may be implemented via a Level 2/3 group approach. **Evidence:** There is strong evidence for the effectiveness of this program for the intended population from randomized controlled trials.	Manualized approach involving a structured workbook that is implemented by the treating clinician Training and technical assistance are available Parent involvement is a part of the treatment program Computer-assisted training is currently available to clinicians The program is available in Chinese, Hungarian, Japanese, Norwegian, Spanish

Examples of Evidence-Based Programs by Level	Nature of the Program and Research Support	Transportability and Dissemination Factors
Middle School Cognitive-Behavioral Therapy for Trauma in Schools (CBITS)	**What:** This intervention program is targeted to those who have experienced traumatic life events such as community and school violence, accidents and injuries, physical abuse and domestic violence, and natural and man-made disasters. The program is designed to reduce symptoms of post-traumatic stress disorder (PTSD), depression, and behavioral problems. It targets improved functioning, such as better grades and more consistent school attendance. In addition, peer and parent support and overall coping skills are taught. **How:** The program is typically delivered as a group intervention for children in Grades 6–9 but has been implemented with groups of high school students. **Evidence:** Research during the past decade has consistently supported the program's effectiveness.	Involves both teacher and parents within the intervention Includes some individual intervention sessions It has been modified for delivery by nonclinicians and in a variety of settings (urban, rural, suburban, and tribal)
High School Multisystemic Therapy	**What:** This intensive treatment program involves a family- and community-based approach. High risk juvenile offenders and their families are targeted. Adolescents functioning across home, school, and community settings are improved by increasing positive social behaviors and decreasing antisocial behavior. **How:** The intervention is typically administered by community-based therapists, though school counselors often play an important adjunctive role in the adolescents' treatment program. **Evidence:** Research during the past decade has consistently supported the program's effectiveness for serious juvenile offenders.	Time intensive treatment that requires the considerable availability of staff (on-call, 24/7) and limits use within schools Extensive training required to meet the complexity and severity of problems being addressed in therapy MST has been implemented and disseminated across the world and has been translated into multiple languages

among the resources presented in Resource D, and we encourage readers to become familiar with all of these evidence-based programs that have been documented within the profession.

SPECIAL TOPICS IN SCHOOL COUNSELING

Group Counseling

Group counseling can be a cost-effective approach to mental health interventions. Limited services, resources, and staff may be used effectively when multiple students are identified with the same need. Serving these students within a group approach can also enhance the effectiveness of the services being provided. Appropriate role models and social learning can be powerful techniques to improve behavior. The development of positive peer relationships, the feedback loop that is inherent within group settings, and the need for acceptance and approval from others can synergistically work together to create a support network for the challenges being faced by group members. Validation of problems and knowing that one is not alone in experiencing distressing thoughts, feelings, or actions too is an important process inherent when working in groups. In order for group counseling to work effectively, administrators, staff, and teachers need to be supportive of the time that may be taken from the child's regular classroom instructional periods. Minimizing this impact is essential. Accountability data pertaining to effectiveness of the group processes must be collected. This summary data report must be made available to multiple parties who have a vested interest in these outcomes. These include parents, teachers, administrators, and the students involved. Some type of report or progress note should be kept for each participating member. Progress toward both group and individual goals should be included within these notes and appropriately disseminated to those working with the student in future years.

Play Therapy

Many techniques requiring strong verbal skills and the ability to examine one's thoughts, feelings, and actions are not appropriate for young children. Play techniques allow for the use of manipulatives, toys, and other interactive material to guide the counseling relationship. Puppets, dolls, and other objects that can represent people, objects, or places in a child's life should be available within play therapy sessions. Typically, an open-ended play period typified by a nondirective, child-directed play will precede the therapy session. Increased directives and/or modeling of specific scenarios may then be implemented in the later part of the session. Books, sand, or story-telling techniques are other examples of play therapy sessions. The overall goal of these sessions is to provide an opportunity for children to present or play out their concerns or internal struggles within a nonthreatening and supportive environment.

Counseling Young Children

Counseling young children requires a special appreciation for routine, structure, consistency, involvement of adults in the child's environment, and a predominant focus on developing strengths or adaptive behaviors during the early years. The basic needs of young children must be assessed as a part of the counseling process. Biological routine (i.e., eating, sleeping), physical routine (i.e., exercise, play), and family routines (i.e., sharing in mealtime, child-directed play) are all essential to establish when working with young children and their families. These routines create certainty, predictability, and security for infants, toddlers, and preschool-aged children. Working with parents and teachers to assess for the presence of these routines, to watch for signs of the quality of these routines, and to ensure consistency with these routines are all important goals to implement and evaluate when counseling young children.

Counseling Diverse Populations

Diversity in culture, values, and beliefs is exponentially growing across the United States. An extensive knowledge of diverse counseling techniques is essential to match approaches to the unique needs of students receiving mental health services. It is likely that few if any interventions within the literature have been isolated as being effective for a minority group. The implication of such a paucity of knowledge for a given population is a need to treat every case or small group as its own experiment. Data pertaining to how one responds to an intervention are an essential part of the counseling process. Making sure that we work to know what treatment works, for whom, and under what conditions allows for continual improvement in service delivery. As a part of these efforts, counselors should have an awareness of normative behavior and beliefs of those populations with whom they work. Self-awareness of one's own cultural values too is a prerequisite for leading a student through mental health counseling techniques. Recognizing how traditional values and beliefs about the importance of education may be different from those within the counseling relationship or from the families of those students is essential. Understanding the culture and system that a student grows and develops within is important in formulating working hypotheses pertaining to areas of functioning that may need to be targeted within the counseling relationship.

CONCLUSION

Evidence-based counseling has multiple meanings. The first relates to need-ing to understand that there are literally hundreds of theory-based techniques that may be effective for a given child, presenting with a given challenge. Recognizing that relationships (i.e., trust, support, care) can serve as a cata-lyst for growth and change with many of these approaches makes it impera-tive that counselors collect progress monitoring data to support or refute the effectiveness of their selected techniques. Additionally, counselors have an ethical responsibility to be adept and aware of intervention programs that have empirical evidence for their use in school-aged populations. This sec-ond definition of evidence-based counseling requires professionals to under-stand the nuances of how those programs work, for whom they work, and under what conditions. Such factors and considerations are important to understand prior to intervention selection and should help to drive the data collection process that is undertaken at the onset of treatment. Such selection decisions and the importance of these decision processes take on an even greater value when working with special populations such as young children or with children from nonmajority backgrounds and cultures. Awareness of best practice approaches and model programs that may be used within a tiered approach to mental health service delivery can help to ensure a greater likelihood for a positive response to counseling interventions.

DISCUSSION QUESTIONS

1. What important considerations are necessary when considering what counseling interventions are deemed evidence based?

2. What limitations exist pertaining to evidence-based counseling pro-grams widely hailed within the literature?

3. How do you determine what counseling intervention is developmen-tally appropriate for the student for whom you will be providing services?

4. What evidence-based counseling intervention best links to a tiered approach to special education services? Why?

5. What challenges exist to the counseling relationship when a student is also prescribed a psychotropic medication intended to target school-related behaviors?

7 Developing and Assessing Counseling Interventions

The previous chapters have demonstrated the importance of school counseling interventions and how they fit within integrative, multi-level frameworks to provide supports at the secondary and tertiary prevention levels. Specific evidence-based counseling approaches and methodologies have been discussed, as well as the importance of utilizing the universal sources of change within counseling. The current chapter focuses on the role of assessment within data-based decision making, particularly with regard to assessing students' needs, measuring levels of performance, developing relevant and measurable goals for counseling, and measuring progress toward those goals. It is hoped that those reading this chapter will gain an understanding of how these practices fit within the framework of the problem-solving model introduced in Chapter 3.

THE ROLE OF ASSESSMENT WITHIN DATA-BASED DECISION MAKING

The growing push across the nation's schools for the implementation of RTI and PBIS systems has brought about a use of a common nomenclature that, until recently, was seldom used by most school personnel. Buzz words and phrases such as *evidence-based practice, functional assessment, fidelity of implementation, progress monitoring, gap analysis,* and *measurable outcomes* are just a few of the many terms that are used within these "problem-solving" systems. This use of terminology is fundamentally linked with the paradigm shift that is occurring in the field of education involving the emphasis on using valid and reliable data sources and empirical evidence to inform decision making (Reschly, 2008).

Both NASP and ASCA have established expectations for relying on empirical evidence in the provision of school-based services. NASP lists data-based decision making and accountability as the first functional competency within its *Blueprint for Training and Practice III* (Ysseldyke et al., 2006). Regarding the importance for school psychologists to be well versed within this competency, the *Blueprint* states that "Irrespective of the assessment method, the purpose of assessment remains clear: to define problems and student needs and assets, to estimate current status, to link results to the development of effective interventions, and to evaluate outcomes and inform future intervention decisions. Simply put, all assessment activities should relate to prevention and intervention" (p. 48). ASCA (2005), in its *National Model for School Counseling Programs,* maintains that the "monitoring of individual progress reveals interventions may be needed to support the student in achieving academic success. Data are necessary to determine: Where are we now? Where should we be? Where are we going?" (p. 116).

Chapter 3 highlighted the utility of the problem-solving model for use in RTI team decision making. A key feature of the problem-solving process is its reliance on assessment that uses valid and reliable data sources to guide decision making at each of the five phases *(problem identification, problem definition, plan development, plan implementation, plan evaluation)*. Without a system in place to assess student progress, school personnel cannot quantify current levels of need and, consequently, cannot measure whether newly implemented interventions are effective. The following sections highlight the critical opportunities for assessment to develop student counseling goals and objectives and to measure progress toward those goals while counseling intervention is provided.

DEFINING THE TARGET BEHAVIOR

Once a problem behavior is identified, the next step is to define it so that the RTI team can have an accurate and complete assessment of the student's current functioning. Typically, the information necessary to define a target behavior comes from indirect assessment data from teachers and other school staff who interact regularly with the student. A good definition allows for reliable recording from multiple observers (i.e., it should not be ambiguous). The use of an accurate and explicit definition of a target behavior is essential in carrying out the FBA. The evaluator (e.g., teacher, school psychologist, or counselor) must know exactly what behavior they are assessing so that all assessment and other FBA data pertain to the same behavior. A common approach when developing an operationalized definition is to ask if the definition passes the "stranger test," whereby any stranger could walk into the classroom and be able to pinpoint the target behavior based on the definition alone. The following are critical considerations in defining target behaviors, which include examples (and non-examples) for their use:

Consideration 1: When defining a target behavior, it is important to *describe the actual behavior,* rather than an outcome of the behavior:

Non-example: *Alyssa frequently makes her classmates upset.*

Example: *Alyssa makes derogatory comments directed toward her classmates, which include personal insults, taunting, and name calling.*

Consideration 2: When defining a target behavior, it is important to *state exactly what the student says or does,* rather than what can be implied:

Non-example: *Malik is not motivated.*

Example: *Malik begins work only after three reminders and is habitually late to class.*

Consideration 3: When defining a target behavior, it is important to *provide a list of specific examples* to accompany a general descriptor of the behavior:

Non-example: *Layne antagonizes peers.*

Example: *Layne antagonizes peers, which includes behaviors such as pushing peers in line while waiting for lunch, taking the personal belongings of peers, and touching peers inappropriately.*

Consideration 4: When defining a target behavior, it is important to *indicate a condition* in which the behavior occurs (e.g., setting, location, time):

Non-example: *Ricky is aggressive.*

Example: *Ricky hits other students during recess when he does not get his way.*

The development of a target behavior definition is a critical step within the process of collecting further assessment data needed to quantify the extent of a behavioral problem. Commonly, data should indicate that a student exhibits several challenging behaviors. Because the RTI team cannot effectively focus on all of these at one time, it is important to select only one, maybe two, behavior(s) (i.e., the most challenging and severe) to address. Assessing the severity of a problem behavior allows the RTI team to determine if it is of a nature and scope to warrant intervention (see *problem definition phase* of the problem-solving process discussed in Chapter 3). Typical criteria needed for target behaviors to be selected for intervention include behavior that is severe enough to put the child or someone else at risk for physical harm (e.g., physical aggression, self-injurious behaviors); behavior that disrupts the learning environment for the student and/or peers (e.g., classroom instruction distractions); and behavior that puts the student at risk (e.g., emotional issues, interpersonal conflict) for future academic, social, emotional, and/or behavioral problems.

FUNCTIONAL BEHAVIORAL ASSESSMENT

Once a problem behavior has been identified and defined, the RTI team moves to the next stage of the information gathering process by conducting an FBA to determine how best to address the problem behavior. A key principle in understanding why problem behaviors occur is that all behavior serves a function. Student behavior within the school or other environments is adaptive in that it either provides the student with something they want or removes something they do not want. Typically, students' behavior varies depending on the environment they are in and the specific conditions that are present. In other words, behaviors rarely happen within a vacuum, but instead are a direct result of environmental stimuli that trigger and/or maintain a response. Rather than working directly to alter the problem behavior itself, it is often advantageous first to attempt to alter the events that trigger and/or maintain that behavior. Members of the RTI team with expertise in behavior management (e.g., behavior interventionists, school psychologists) are trained to assess carefully these environmental stimuli through functional behavioral assessment.

Types of FBA

Functional behavioral assessment is a systematic process of gathering information about the events that trigger (i.e., *antecedents*) and maintain (i.e., *consequences*) problem behaviors (Crone & Horner, 2003). The complexity of the FBA can vary depending upon the level of the RTI framework that one is using and the severity of the specific problem behavior. For example, at the universal level of prevention, the FBA may be very brief (brief-FBA). Its predominant focus is on the classroom or school environment, with specific attention given to factors such as how the environment is arranged or how the schoolwide social-emotional/behavioral curriculum is implemented. Often, this assessment involves observing the student within one environment or setting. Typically, it is done when teachers refer the student and may benefit from consultative training and support to adapt their instruction, classroom management, or even the physical space or layout of the classroom. Ideally, with this consultative support, teachers can gain awareness of the antecedent or reinforcing variables that are in their power to alter or adapt (e.g., removing a distracting classroom stimulus, rearranging desk space, separating student from a distracting peer).

Other times, the FBA may be more involved, complex, and individualized (full-FBA). This requires assessment techniques that provide specific and detailed information about a student's behavior that may include parent and teacher interviews, extended classroom observations, and behavior rating scales or checklists. Typically, these are behaviors that have evolved over a longer period of time and have served some adaptive function for the student. These problematic behaviors may involve not only changes needed to the physical environment, but also specific skills training due to the presence of a skills deficit. In these cases, intervention is warranted at the secondary or tertiary level.

Conducting the FBA

A common approach to conducting the FBA is the A-B-C (antecedent-behavior-consequence) recording procedure (O'Neill et al., 1997). The ABC approach is an anecdotal method that uses a three-term contingency to note the events or situations that trigger a problematic behavior and the consequences that reinforce that behavior. This behavior observation technique first notes the *setting event* by describing the immediate environment in which the behavior occurs (e.g., day, time, classroom, classroom teacher, classroom subject, type of activity). The *A* (*Antecedent*) notes the specific events within the environment that "trigger" the behavior (e.g., peers or adults involved, requests made, activity being performed, emotional states). The *B* (*Behavior*) describes exactly what behavior occurred in concrete terms. The *C* (*Consequence*) records what happened as a result of the behavior (e.g., Did the student get attention? Get out of doing something? Gain something? What activities change or stop? What are the consequences for the student?). Take the following scenario, for example:

> *In math class, Andy's teacher assigns a worksheet and tells the class to take the next 10 minutes to complete it individually. Andy sits with his head down for the first 5 minutes before his teacher prompts him to complete the assignment. Andy immediately becomes disruptive and makes a derogatory statement about the class and indicates his refusal to complete the assignment. The teacher immediately sends Andy to the office with a discipline referral.*

A classroom observer who is evaluating Andy's behavior in this situation may use a specifically designed ABC recording form (see Resource E for a blank form; see Figure 7.1 for a completed incident example) to document the setting, triggering events, and maintaining consequence that might have contributed to the problem behavior (see Table 7.1 for a list of examples of common antecedents and consequences).

While an ABC recording of this incident provides an evaluator with useful information to begin to formulate a hypothesis regarding the function of Andy's behavior, it is only one data source. More assessment data are needed to develop accurately a *behavior-function hypothesis*. Because behavior is often the result of a complex interaction between many variables, it is important to use a multimethod, multisetting, and multisource assessment model (Steege & Watson, 2008).

A *multimethod* assessment approach should include a combination of *indirect* (e.g., interviews, rating scales, screening forms) and *direct* (e.g., observation and recording of behavior) data collection procedures (Steege & Watson, 2008). Structured interviews, rating scales (see Resource F for a sample form), and screening form data obtained from classroom teachers, school personnel, and families offer a relatively quick and easy way to make an initial assessment regarding the severity of a problem behavior. While these indirect forms of assessment typically do not provide the level of detail needed to identify the function of a behavior, they do provide the evaluator with useful data to guide more time-intensive direct assessment methods. These direct assessment methods are typically more reliable than indirect methods. Relying on an assessment of a problem behavior's severity based upon a teacher's memory or perception can be problematic as accurate data collection can be compromised. Instead, observing the problem behavior in the context of the natural environment and using data to quantify its severity can more closely approximate the actual presence of the student's behaviors. These direct assessment procedures rely upon the following objective recording methods, which are

Figure 7.1 ABC Recording Example

Setting Event	Antecedent	Behavior	Consequence
What was happening when behavior occurred?	*What happened right before behavior?*	*What did student do?*	*What was result of behavior?*
In math class, teacher assigns math worksheet for students to complete individually	In response to Andy laying his head down, teacher prompts him to work	Andy becomes disruptive, refuses work, makes derogatory statement	Andy leaves class, sent to office, gets out of doing work

Table 7.1 Examples of Common Antecedents and Consequences

Antecedents	Consequences
● **Distant (Removed in Time)**	Teacher attention (acknowledgment, calling on student)
Learning history (past success/failure)	Teacher praise
Home structures/procedures related to school/learning (e.g., homework monitoring)	Teacher reprimand
	Teacher ignoring
	Teacher redirection (to another behavior)
Home bedtime	Teacher error correction
Home responsibilities	Peer laughter
Home meal schedule/ practices	Peer attention (acknowledgment, interaction)
Medical conditions affecting behavior (e.g., medication, asthma)	Peer ignoring
	Peer disapproval/rejection
	Obtain desired objects
Home events prior to school day	Obtain/prolong desired activity
	Object taken away
Events en route to school	Activity terminated
Daily schedule	Negative feeling relieved (anxiety, anger, frustration)
	Positive sensation created (stimulation)
	Negative sensation relieved

Source: Hunley & McNamara (2010).

some of the more commonly used methods for collecting data on the target behavior: *frequency recording, duration recording, latency recording, interval recording,* and *momentary time sampling.* An overview of each of these recording methods is presented in Table 7.2.

A *multisetting* assessment approach should be used, because environmental factors have the power to initiate, sustain, or hinder problematic behaviors. Therefore, it is important to observe the student in the setting where the behavior is most likely to occur, as well as where it is least likely to occur. The selection of the observation period can be determined by the data from a scatter plot consisting of frequency counts of the challenging behavior, behavior incidence reports, and office discipline referrals. Conducting an analysis of these scatter plots can show trends as to when problematic behaviors tend to occur (e.g., times of day, days of week,

Table 7.2   Direct Observation Recording Methods

Recording Method	Question Addressed	When to Use	Type of Behaviors	Example
Frequency/ event recording	How often does behavior occur over a specified time?	Behavior is discrete and low frequency	Cursing, throwing objects, noncompliance, tardiness, absences, self-stimulatory behavior, negative self statements	Number of times student gets out of seat during one 50-minute class period
Duration recording	How long does behavior last?	Behavior is lengthy and low frequency	Arguing, out-of-seat behavior, noncompliance, crying, sleeping	Amount of time elapsed during tantrum behaviors
Latency recording	How much time elapses from prompt to behavior?	Elapsed time from prompt to behavior is of interest	Tardiness, task initiation, noncompliance	Amount of time for student to begin task after teacher gives direction
Whole-interval time recording	Does behavior occur during an entire interval?	Behavior is continuous and high frequency	On/off-task behaviors, out-of-seat behaviors, self-stimulatory behaviors, social isolation or withdrawal	Whether student is off task during entire 30-second interval
Partial-interval time recording	Does behavior occur at any time during an interval?	Behavior is lengthy and low frequency	On/off-task behaviors, out-of-seat behaviors, self-stimulatory behaviors, social isolation or withdrawal	Whether student is off task during any of the 30-second interval
Momentary time sampling	Does behavior occur at end of an interval?	Behavior is difficult to monitor continuously and multiple behaviors are observed simultaneously	On/off-task behaviors, out-of-seat behaviors, self-stimulatory behaviors, social isolation or withdrawal	Whether student is off task during the last second of the 30-second interval

classroom subjects). Using ABC recording during the peak times for problematic behaviors as well as the dormant times provides insight into those environmental conditions that are most likely to contribute to problems (Wheeler & Richey, 2010). Also, when it is suspected that a particular environmental condition may likely be the cause of a specific problem behavior, it is important to assess many students within that environment. If other students display a similar challenging behavior, it may confirm the precarious nature of the environment (e.g., physical space/classroom structure or classroom expectations).

A *multisource* assessment approach is useful, because data from multiple stakeholders who have direct contact with the student (e.g., teachers, school personnel, family) may provide insight into those specific practices that elicit the problem behavior and those that do not. Talking directly with the target student is often an overlooked step, but one that may elicit useful data. It is all too common within RTI team meetings to have the majority of teachers agree that a student is not able to do something, while one or two teachers report that the student performs well in their class and does not display a particular skill deficit. Typically, FBAs at this stage are more in-depth and require substantial data to tease apart whether or not a problematic behavior is the result of a *skill deficit* (i.e., a lack of previous learning experience pertaining to that skill or an actual disability) or a *performance deficit* (i.e., a lack of motivation or lack of reinforcement for engaging in the skill). VanDerHeyden and Witt (2008) refer to this as "can't do/won't do" assessment. Since the functions of these problem behaviors are different, depending upon the type of deficit they involve, the type of intervention would be different for each as well.

Identifying the Function of Behavior

After careful analysis of data obtained from multiple collection methods, the evaluator can see behavioral patterns emerge as a result of differing environmental conditions. By detecting a repeated pattern of challenging behavior under similar circumstances, a hypothesis regarding the function it serves the student can then be made.

As displayed in Figure 7.2, challenging behaviors typically serve the function of gaining access to something (i.e., positive reinforcement) or allowing escape from something (i.e., negative reinforcement). Students often act on the motivation to *gain* something they desire. This could be preferred tangibles, preferred activities, or social attention. For example, a student who is involved in a large-group activity in the classroom talks out, makes off-subject remarks, and gets his/her peers to laugh to obtain social attention, despite getting reprimanded by his/her teacher. Other times, a student's problem behaviors may serve the function of allowing *escape*

Figure 7.2 Functions of Behavior

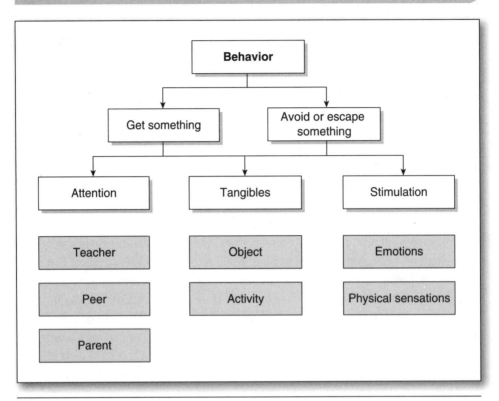

Source: Hunley & McNamara (2010).

from an aversive situation. This could be escape from a nonpreferred activity, difficult task, or nonpreferred social interaction. For example, Max is an eight-year-old student diagnosed with autism spectrum disorder. He is nonverbal but uses sign language and a DynaVox for communication. When his special needs resource room teacher gives him tasks to complete, he exhibits whining behavior, especially when the demand is particularly challenging or he does not want to complete the activity. As a result of this increased whining behavior, the teacher replaces the task with something less challenging to get him to stop this annoying behavior. Max has likely learned that whining can serve as an escape from a difficult or aversive task.

The function of a problematic behavior is not always initially apparent. Frequently, the *gain* misbehaviors appear indistinguishable from the *escape* misbehaviors (Crone, Horner, & Hawken, 2004). It is only after repeated observations at multiple times and settings and in conjunction with other data that a hypothesis regarding the function of the behavior can be made. This hypothesis is a data-based "guess" as to why the behavior occurs based upon a pattern of behaviors. By hypothesizing the function of a problem behavior, the RTI team can then select an appropriate replacement behavior to serve the same function as a part of the intervention plan.

Selecting a Replacement Behavior

By defining a target behavior, the RTI team has identified a behavior that has proved to be maladaptive within the student's learning environment. Also, through the FBA process, data have demonstrated that this behavior serves some function for the student in response to social or environmental stimuli that are present. Therefore, completely eliminating the behavior from occurring will be difficult unless the function of the behavior is understood in the selection of an appropriate intervention. In developing a function-based intervention, the goal is to provide the student with an alternative (i.e., replacement) behavior that serves the same purpose as the previous behavior, but is school appropriate. It should be reasonable that the student can not only learn the new skill, but also maintain the skill, either intrinsically or with the use of moderate extrinsic reinforcement. Specifically, natural rein-forcement is preferred in these situations.

Take the following scenario as an example: Amber is a third-grader who hits other students as a means of gaining social attention and interacting with peers. The RTI team determined that Amber would benefit from skills training that would teach her appropriate ways (e.g., using verbal or nonaggressive physical prompts to initiate conversation) of gaining social attention and interacting with peers. In this example, the replacement behavior fits logically with the function of the problem behavior and is likely to be reinforced by the natural environment. However, this example demonstrates a rather simplistic portrayal of how a replacement behavior is chosen; selecting a replacement behavior is rarely this easy in the real world. There are many factors to con-sider when identifying a replacement behavior with the greatest likelihood of leading to behavioral change. These considerations include the following:

- Is the replacement behavior functionally equivalent?
- What is the feasibility of providing the skills training to develop the replacement behavior?
- How well does the replacement behavior fit within the existing environment and classroom practices?
- What environment changes or modifications should be made to alter the student's behavior?
- How will the replacement behavior be reinforced (what antecedent triggers and maintaining consequences will be used)?
- What is the role of adults/teachers in developing the replacement behavior?
- What will the adults/teachers do differently to alter what the student does?

The RTI team, as part of a collaborative effort, answers these questions during the *intervention development phase* of the problem-solving process discussed in Chapter 3.

DEVELOPING INDIVIDUALIZED STUDENT GOALS AND OBJECTIVES

Once the RTI team has defined the target behavior (i.e., the behavior to be changed) and developed an intervention, it is necessary to delineate clear goals and objectives for the student to reach. Essentially, the development of goals is aimed at increasing positive behaviors (e.g., the ability to express anger in socially acceptable and healthy ways) while decreasing inappropriate behaviors (e.g., self-injurious behaviors). A goal for a student who exhibits excessive tantrumming would be to decrease tantrumming behaviors to an acceptable level. A goal for a student who displays poor social skills would be to increase their total amount of prosocial interactions. Well-written goals and objectives ensure that anyone reading the student's IEP knows exactly what the student is working to accomplish.

Present Level of Performance (PLP)

The development of individualized student goals and objectives is directly tied to a student's *present level of performance* (PLP) statement. The PLP should state what the student is currently able to do in the current setting and how a problem behavior impedes her or his ability to access the general education curriculum or function within the environment. An accurate present level of performance assessment provides a baseline from which to establish goals and objectives and to compare future progress. For this reason, it is vital that the problem behavior definition is easily measurable. Vague or ambiguous behavior definitions are likely to lead to measurement error.

The PLP should state a student's competency in positive terms (i.e., what they are able to do). By noting the presence of some behavior (i.e., rather than the absence), the RTI team is able to see and quantify that the student is capable of performing the behavior. A complete PLP statement should also provide information such as:

- The target student
- The target behavior
- Why the behavior is of concern

Additionally, a PLP statement should include specific *dimensions* of the behavior such as:

- Frequency (how often/at what rate it occurs)
- Duration (how long it lasts)
- Latency (how long until it begins)
- Topography (what it looks like)
- Location (where it occurs)
- Intensity (to what extent it occurs)

The following is an example of a PLP:

Mario is described as "very social" by his parents and teachers, at least in terms of his desire to engage with his peers. However, when faced with conflict situations, he struggles to regulate and express his emotions appropriately, often becoming angry and aggressive toward peers and teachers and violating school rules. Classroom observations indicate that Mario expresses his emotions appropriately (e.g., time-out, deep breathing, verbalize, write or draw his feelings) when in conflict situations 3 out of 10 times. School records indicate five disciplinary removals in the past three weeks (1.7 per week) due to aggressive, externalizing behaviors including yelling, cursing, and pushing at peers, as well as throwing objects. These disciplinary removals cause him to fall behind in his schoolwork and disrupt the safety of the learning environment for himself and others in the classroom. Mario's current levels of behavioral performance are significantly discrepant from the expected level of performance, which would be one or fewer discipline referrals per grading period and the appropriate emotional expression when in conflict situations of 9 out of 10 times as determined by the schoolwide code of conduct and PBIS-aligned disciplinary structure. A realistic goal would be for Mario to receive one or less discipline referrals per week and to use appropriate emotional response to conflict situations at least 8 out of 10 times.

This PLP statement not only quantifies the extent of the gap between Mario's *current* and *expected* levels of performance but also provides a baseline from which to develop and compare goals and objectives. It notes how his skills deficit adversely affects his involvement and progress in the general education curriculum. The target behaviors are performance based and measurable. Because "expresses his emotions appropriately" is a vague statement, specific examples that typify that behavior are also included. Once the PLP statement is written, the RTI team can then develop behavioral goals and objectives.

Developing Behavioral Goals and Objectives

Behavioral *goals* are broad statements that describe what the student can reasonably be expected to accomplish within an IEP year. Behavioral *objectives* are based upon the long-term goal, but consist of concrete skills needed in order to eventually reach the long-term goal. Objectives can be reached in a relatively short time span (three weeks to three months). For example, take the case of Zainab, a fifth grader who struggles to assert her needs in social situations. A long-term goal may be for Zainab to increase her use of assertive behavior at school. Specific short-term objectives for Zainab to master might include: (1) First, writing her needs in a notebook that she shows to her teacher at the end of each school day; (2) then, she will learn to state her needs directly to the teacher when in a situation that she does not feel comfortable or feels that she is treated unfairly; and (3) finally, she will learn to state her feelings and needs directly to her peers when in situations in which she feels that she is treated unfairly.

Essentially, each of the three short-term objectives consists of skills that Zainab would need to acquire in incremental steps (as each would build upon another) until the annual goal is met. Zainab's PLP should be used to develop goals and objectives as well as serve as a point of data comparison. Therefore, the goals and objectives should link directly to the PLP. Like the PLP statement, goals and objectives should be stated in a positive manner (i.e., what the student is to do). It should include the presence of the behavior you want to see, not the absence of the behavior you do not want (it is difficult to measure something that you cannot see). Take a look at the following example (and non-example) of a target behavior stated in positive terms:

Non-example: *Ruben will not hit or kick his classmates.*

Example: *Ruben will keep his hands and feet to himself.*

Goals and objectives should be selected with input from the student, as well as parents and teachers. Because goals and objectives are actually written statements that are included within a student's IEP, there should be complete agreement about them. They should be ambitious, yet reachable, given the appropriate skills training.

While goals are broadly worded in comparison to the specific nature of objectives, both goals and objectives are held to the same measurability standards as the PLP. Therefore, each goal and objective should note:

- Behavioral goal statement (observable and measureable)
- Service provider
- Criteria for goal attainment

- Time frame for goal attainment
- Conditions (or setting events)
- Evaluation method
- Evaluation frequency

The more clarity that is provided in the writing of intervention goals and objectives, the better the chances are of the intervention being implemented with integrity (Fuchs & Fuchs, 1989). The written goals and objectives should avoid the use of "hedge" words (e.g., *will better understand, feel more comfortable, will improve their*), which are ambiguous in nature (Twachtman-Cullen & Twachtman-Bassett, 2011). An observer can easily see and count a specific behavior such as "Ashton will raise his hand in class to be called on by the teacher." However, it is difficult to determine when "Ashton will distinguish between appropriate and inappropriate means of gaining the teacher's attention."

Let us now look at the following example of a long-term goal and its short-term objectives that are intended for a student involved in a group-based anger management counseling intervention. These goals and objectives link directly with the PLP statement we previously used with Mario.

Objective: *In a group setting, given direct instruction/examples of what is meant by appropriate anger expression and 10 story scenarios in which a character is presented with anger-provoking situations, Mario will list appropriate ways to express anger and the positive consequences of them, at an 80% level of accuracy, given indirect verbal cues and explanation regarding incorrect responses.*

Objective: *In a group setting, given direct instruction on recognizing body signs (e.g., clenched teeth, tense body, sweaty palms) and triggers to anger expression (e.g., desire to have something, someone not understanding you), and 10 videotaped scenarios involving exaggerated emotional cues of a character provoked into an anger outburst, Mario will correctly recognize the body signs and trigger for the anger outburst with 80% accuracy (8/10 scenarios), given indirect verbal cues.*

Objective: *In a group setting, given 10 open-ended role-play scenarios involving a conflict situation, Mario will demonstrate the use of appropriate strategies for handling anger from a self-generated list (e.g., time-out, deep breathing, verbalize, write or draw his feelings), across at least three turns, at least 80% of the time, given expectant waiting or gestural cues, as needed, and later will explain the reasons for his choice.*

Goal: *In a classroom setting, when presented with anger-provoking situations, Mario will demonstrate emotional control (e.g., recognize his body signs and triggers to anger) so as to express anger appropriately (e.g., time-out, deep breathing, verbalize, write or draw his feelings) 80% of the time by 6/15/12 as measured by the teacher-completed Anger Coping Evaluation Form and classroom observation.*

The goals and objectives listed are linked directly to the initial PLP statement. They state what Mario is expected to be able to accomplish, within what setting, under what circumstances, at what level of criterion, as measured by what. It is expected that if Mario masters each of the behavioral objectives, he likely would be able to meet the long-term goal within the specified period of time.

MEASURING RESPONSE TO INTERVENTION THROUGH SINGLE-CASE DESIGN

The last phase of the problem-solving process used by the RTI team is *plan evaluation.* Given the considerable time and resources used to screen and assess for problematic behavior, identify the function of the behavior, select a functionally equivalent replacement behavior, and implement an intervention that teaches that replacement, it is important to obtain empirical verification that these practices are effective.

One of the most common methodological approaches for use within applied settings (e.g., schools) in which treatment focuses on the individual student is single-case design (Kazdin, 1982). Single-case design relies upon the repeated observations of behavior over time in order for the evaluator to determine whether the behavior changes and if those changes are the result of an intervention. Rather than comparing the effects of intervention between two groups (treatment group vs. nontreatment group), single-case design compares the effects of intervention within one person (treatment phase vs. nontreatment phase). Therefore, each student serves as his or her own control. Because single-case designs deal with only one subject or a small group of subjects (as opposed to between-group designs), it is easier to conduct frequent assessment (often multiple data points per day or week). The use of frequent assessment allows the single-case design to be sensitive to detecting even small behavioral changes as they occur. Careful monitoring of these changes is needed to dictate whether the intervention should be continued, discontinued, or modified.

The basic steps involved in single-case designs include:

Step 1: Identify the target behavior (observable and measurable)

Step 2: Select the design (e.g., withdrawal, reversal, multiple-baseline, etc.)

Step 3: Select a measurement procedure (e.g., office discipline referrals, systematic direct observation, rating scales and/or checklists)

Step 4: Establish a baseline (include multiple data points)

Step 5: Introduce the intervention (e.g., individual therapy, social skills training, group counseling)

Step 6: Assess the results (treatment can be withdrawn and reintroduced to produce repeated measurement, if needed)

A-B Design

There are a number of single-case designs that may be useful for assessing a student's response to a counseling intervention within the school setting. Typically, these involve the comparison of two phases: (1) *baseline* (and *withdrawal*) *phase,* denoted by the letter *A;* and (2) *treatment phase,* denoted by the letter *B* (shown in Figure 7.3). Data collected in the baseline phase (stated within the PLP) are compared to data collected within the treatment phase in order to determine if a behavior change occurred. This approach is referred to as an A-B (baseline-treatment) design and is commonly used within school settings.

A-B-A Design

After the provision of a counseling intervention, eventually it will be withdrawn. This withdrawal design is represented by A-B-A. As depicted in Figure 7.4, data are collected after the treatment is removed to assess whether the changes are lasting.

Figure 7.3   A-B Design

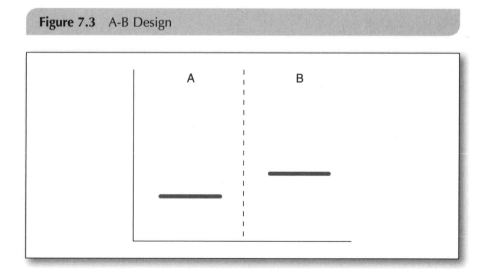

Figure 7.4 A-B-A Design

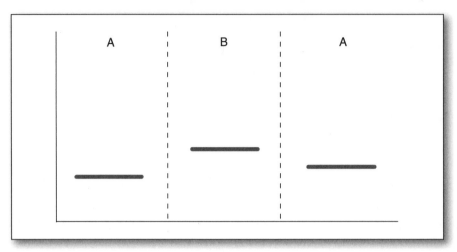

An inherent weakness in the previous two designs (A-B and A-B-A) is their inability to establish a functional relationship due to their omission of a treatment phase replication. However, in the case of school-based counseling interventions, the use of A-B and A-B-A designs will likely be the most commonly used. Because the goal of providing counseling services is to equip the student with skills training that produces a long-term and lasting change, it is likely that if quality, evidence-based counseling interventions are implemented with integrity there will not be a significant regression in the withdrawal phase (i.e., a student cannot "unlearn" perspective taking strategies) (Hunley & McNamara, 2010). There are a number of other single-case designs that school psychologists and school counselors may find useful.

A-B-A-B Design

While A-B designs can demonstrate whether a behavior change occurred, they cannot, however, demonstrate that the behavior change was a direct result from the treatment (Miltenberger, 2008). Typically, when it is important to determine if the treatment *caused* the behavior change, an A-B-A-B design is used. In this design the treatment is reintroduced (as shown in Figure 7.5). If performance dips during the withdrawal phase, but improves again when the treatment is reintroduced, it can reasonably be assumed that the intervention, indeed, was responsible for the performance increase (and not other variables).

Figure 7.5 A-B-A-B Design

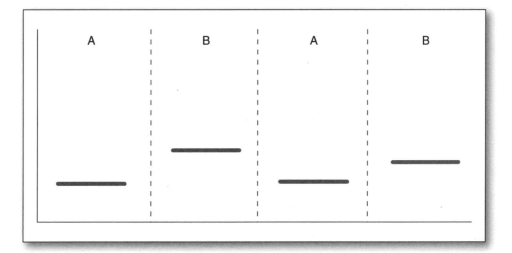

Multiple Baseline Design

The *multiple baseline design* shows whether behaviors across more than one baseline change as a result of a treatment. After performance data are collected across three or more behaviors demonstrated by a student, this design implements a treatment phase within each of the behaviors, but at separate times. This technique may prove useful in targeting multiple related behavioral problems within one student, especially when addressing potentially harmful or dangerous behaviors (e.g., physical aggression and self-harming behaviors) where it may be difficult or unsafe to withdraw treatment (Schloss & Smith, 1994). The multiple baseline design does not include a reversal stage, but it allows for replication by demonstrating a treatment's effect on multiple behaviors simultaneously (shown in Figure 7.6).

Alternating Treatments Design

The *alternating treatments design* is used to compare the effects of two or more treatments on a single behavior. Similar to the A-B-A-B design where the treatment is withdrawn and then reintroduced, the alternating treatments design withdraws the initial treatment, but introduces a second and *different* treatment while student performance is continually monitored (Zirpoli & Melloy, 1993). As these treatments are implemented alternately or in rotation (shown in Figure 7.7), the RTI team can discern what treatment approach is likely to be most effective with a particular student.

Figure 7.6 Multiple Baseline Design

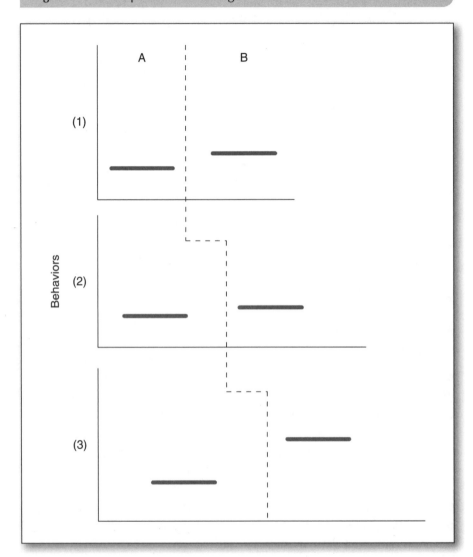

Changing Criterion Design

The *changing criterion design* is used to evaluate the incremental effects of a treatment on a behavior by continually increasing the criterion for reinforcement (see Figure 7.8). Essentially, the treatment phase is divided into "subphases," where each treatment condition that is met actually serves as the control for the next subphase, which uses an increased criterion for reinforcement (Zirpoli & Melloy, 1993).

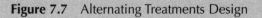

Figure 7.7 Alternating Treatments Design

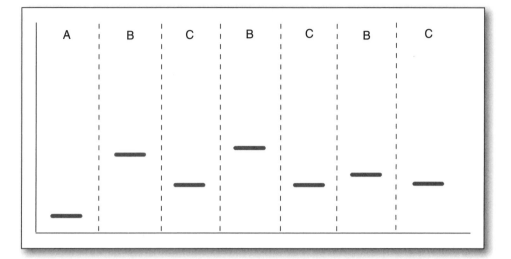

Figure 7.8 Changing Criterion Design

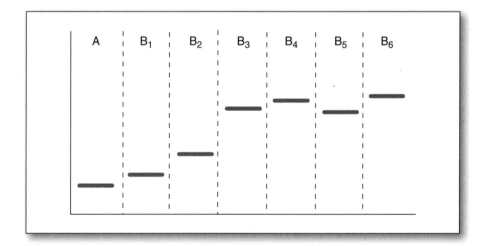

EVALUATING OUTCOMES

These single-case designs provide data for RTI teams to use in determining a student's response to a counseling intervention. Comparing intervention outcomes with baseline performance (as stated in the PLP) allows the team to determine intervention effectiveness. Single-case research relies on the demonstration of clinically significant (i.e., observable, measurable improvement in functioning) results within the individual rather than statistical significance (Alberto & Troutman, 1999). These improvement targets are delineated within the student's IEP goals and objectives as a quantitative indicator of intervention success. The type of outcome data that are selected by the RTI team will depend upon the specific problem behavior and the type of intervention used. Common measures include office discipline records, student-completed self-monitoring forms, goal attainment scaling (GAS) forms, direct observation, and behavior rating checklists. Typically, this outcome data are assessed by examining the change in means, levels of performance, and/or trends in performance.

Generally, an effective means of organizing and presenting intervention outcomes is through the use of a graph or chart. The use of a visual representation of data typically allows evaluators to notice slight changes in behavior that might not have been noticed otherwise (Casey, Skiba, & Algozzine, 1988). Also, graphs and charts provide a user-friendly method of presenting intervention outcomes to students, parents, teachers, and school staff. Visual representations can easily be developed using data management software such as Microsoft Excel or ChartDog Graphmaker (available at www .interventioncentral.org/tools/chart_dog_graph_maker).

If a student is responsive to the counseling intervention and has met established goals and objectives, the RTI team can then elect to develop a plan to phase out or exit the student from services. It is important to phase out supports while ensuring that the behavior is maintained. If the student is responsive to the intervention, but making slower than expected progress, the RTI team may elect to change the intensity of supports or provide ancillary supports. If the student is unresponsive to the intervention, the team may elect to reexamine their target behavior definition and its function hypothesis. Typically, more data would be collected and intervention integrity would be re-assessed to determine why the intervention was ineffective. Remember, the steps involved in the problem-solving framework are permutable and represent a continual process of assessment and evaluation. Further, regarding the dynamic process involved in the problem analysis procedure, Christ (2008) stated, "It is the collection, summary, and use of information to systematically test, reject, or verify relevant hypotheses to establish problem solutions" (p. 159).

CONCLUSION

While it may appear that the RTI team's progression through the phases of the problem-solving process occurs in a linear and static sequence, this is rarely the case. However, an emphasis on the use of data to guide decision making at each of the five phases of the problem-solving model will undoubtedly make the process as efficient and effective as possible. Hopefully, this chapter provides the reader with an overview of the importance of using data to identify behaviors of concern, quantify the severity of those behaviors, develop measurable goals and objectives for behavioral change, and evaluate the effects of counseling interventions on behavior. For further discussion of these pertinent topics, the reader is directed to a number of guidebooks on the market that provide a more detailed and step-by-step approach to conducting functional behavior assessments (e.g., Cipani & Schock, 2010; Steege & Watson, 2009), writing measurable IEP goals and objectives (e.g., Bateman & Herr, 2006; Twachtman-Cullen & Twachtman-Bassett, 2011), and evaluating the response to counseling intervention through single-case design (e.g., Riley-Tillman & Burns, 2009).

DISCUSSION QUESTIONS

1. What is FBA? Why is FBA important when developing interventions for students who demonstrate problematic behavior?

2. How do objectives relate to goal statements? How do objectives and goal statements relate to the present levels of performance (PLP) statement?

3. Discuss the importance of stating target behaviors in observable and measurable terms. Provide examples of target behaviors stated in both measurable and nonmeasurable ways.

4. Discuss the purpose of single-case designs.

5. Discuss how the effectiveness of an intervention is demonstrated or not demonstrated in the A-B, A-B-A, A-B-A-B, multiple baseline, alternating treatment, and changing criterion designs.

8 Case Studies

Many of the ideas and concepts presented in the previous chapters are illustrated through case studies in this chapter. The first two cases focus on the RTI problem-solving process (Problem Identification, Problem Definition and Analysis, Intervention Development, Treatment Implementation, and Treatment Evaluation) within an immediate time frame. The final two cases look at the provision of responsive counseling across time for individual students to demonstrate the influence of interventions and environmental factors throughout developmental periods or phases.

CASE 1: THE PROBLEM-SOLVING PROCESS WITHIN THE CASE OF A FIFTH GRADER WITH ANGRY, AGGRESSIVE, EXTERNALIZING BEHAVIORS

Background Information

Mario is an 11-year-old Hispanic male in the fifth grade at Spartan Elementary School. He has repeatedly demonstrated angry, aggressive, externalizing behaviors both in and outside of the classroom. Mario is described as "very social" by his parents and teachers, at least in terms of his desire to engage with his peers. However, when faced with conflict situations, he struggles to regulate and express his emotions appropriately, often becoming angry and aggressive toward peers and teachers and violating school rules. School records indicate five disciplinary removals in the past three weeks due to angry, aggressive, externalizing behaviors including yelling, cursing, and pushing at peers, as well as throwing objects. These disciplinary removals have caused him to fall behind in his schoolwork and disrupt the safety of the classroom environment for himself and others.

Mario has been unresponsive to the Level 1 research-supported socio-emotional classroom curricula, established code of conduct, and PBIS-aligned disciplinary structure, as well as Level 2 classroom-based selected supports (behavioral contract with mystery motivator program). The following sections provide an overview of the problem-solving process that an RTI team might follow in using relevant behavioral data sources to guide treatment decision making in the case of Mario.

Problem Identification

Mario was identified by the fifth-grade-level team through its universal screening process to identify students demonstrating (a) trouble with interpersonal problem solving and anger management, (b) disruptive classroom behaviors, and/or (c) academic underachievement. Members of the RTI team provided teacher training and consultative support to ensure that the schoolwide research-supported socio-emotional classroom curricula and classroom management strategies were implemented with integrity. The team ensured that the use of minimally intrusive classroom-based behavioral interventions targeted directly at Mario's FBA-demonstrated needs were tried. By implementing and evaluating the fidelity and outcome efficacy of these primary supports, the RTI team determined that Mario was truly unresponsive to these evidence-based practices. The RTI team identified several challenging behaviors that Mario exhibited. However, they decided to select only one problem behavior (the most severe), as trying to address three or four behaviors at once would be too much to effectively focus on at one time.

Problem Definition

At this point, the RTI team has ascertained that a problem truly exists that adversely affects the classroom learning for Mario and his peers. The next step was to assess whether the nature and severity of the problem was enough to require additional supports in order for him to be successful in the school environment. The school psychologist conducted another FBA to understand the functional antecedent and consequent events linked with Mario's problem behaviors. Results from the FBA, as well as behavioral and emotional assessments, teacher screening scales, parent and teacher interviews, discipline and attendance records, and academic performance data were used to quantify Mario's present level of performance (PLP) and define his behavioral functioning in operational terms. By obtaining a valid and reliable assessment of his present performance, the RTI team was able to compare this to Mario's expected levels of performance, based on his classroom peers and local norms (schoolwide code of conduct). Understanding the extent of this behavioral achievement gap allowed the RTI team to dictate the type and intensity of supports needed and provided a baseline in which to compare later progress.

Intervention Development

The RTI team worked with Mario's teachers to develop a common set of goals and objectives for Mario to work toward. These goals and objectives were targeted directly at his skill deficits as indicated by FBA data (inability to self-regulate anger/negative emotions) that had academic, functional, behavioral, and social relevance. A list of potential empirically supported interventions was generated. Each of these interventions was evaluated for its empirical support, target skill development, and feasibility of implementation. The RTI team, as well as Mario and his family, reached a consensus regarding his participation in a Level 2 "pull-out" treatment intervention called the *Anger Coping Program* (Larson & Lochman, 2004). The Anger Coping Program is a cognitive-behavioral anger counseling group that incorporates weekly sessions over the course of a semester to provide anger management skills training aimed at improving perspective taking, problem solving, recognition of emotions associated with anger arousal, and reducing impulsive and aggressive responses to anger. The goal of programs at the selected prevention level is to equip students with the skills to replace their maladaptive behaviors with more educationally and socially responsible ones.

Plan Implementation

Once an appropriate intervention plan had been selected, the RTI team devised how it would be carried out and how implementation integrity would be evaluated. Team member communication at this stage was important as the effectiveness of the plan would be dependent on numerous stakeholders who contribute to its implementation. The intervention implementers held weekly meetings with Mario's classroom teachers to obtain useful information to guide in goal setting and discuss his progress within the classroom. These teachers were also relied on to look for and reinforce any incidences of Mario using newly developed skills, such as appropriate anger control in the classroom setting. The RTI team obtained informed parental consent from Mario's parents and told them that they would receive monthly updates regarding Mario's progress at school. Mario's parents were also informed that they would be relied on to provide the RTI team with updates regarding his behavior progress at home.

Treatment Evaluation

A multimodal progress-monitoring and evaluation plan was developed whereby a system of weekly teacher-completed behavior evaluations (Anger Coping Evaluation Form), school records (office discipline reports and grades), and classroom observations were used to assess Mario's progress throughout the semester. These periodic progress updates were used to compare Mario's performance to baseline levels collected at the start of the intervention. Outcome data collected at the end of the 18-week Anger Coping Program indicated that Mario's behavioral goals and objectives had been reached and that his academic progress had returned to expected levels. His weekly score on the Anger Coping Evaluation Form had increased from 12 out of 30 at baseline to 23 out of 30 after treatment. His weekly average for office discipline referrals decreased from 1.7 at baseline to 0.5 after treatment. His appropriate response to conflict situations of 30% of the time at baseline increased to 80% after treatment, as indicated by classroom observations. The intervention demonstrated success, and the RTI team worked to establish a follow-up plan (exit from services plan) where Mario's newly developed skills would be maintained, while slowly phasing out the supports he required. The team arranged for booster sessions to be conducted with Mario on an individual or group basis at the outset of his sixth-grade school year. These sessions would occur biweekly and slowly phase out based on his progress-monitoring data and weekly classroom teacher feedback.

Case Discussion

This case study was organized within the framework of the RTI problem-solving model introduced in Chapter 3. This case discussion and the accompanying intervention planning form (see Figure 8.1) are intended to provide an overview of the treatment decision-making process (also, see Resource B for a blank intervention planning form). Specifically, it is intended to demonstrate how the use of data drives decision making at each of the five phases of the problem-solving process. The RTI team's role in obtaining meaningful data is vital in ensuring that only the most minimally intrusive interventions (but that are targeted directly to students' specified needs) are used. The *Anger Coping Program* was provided as an example of a group counseling intervention that was specifically targeted to students at high risk for academic failure, poor peer relationships, and school drop-out. While its implementation at Level 2 within an RTI or a PBIS framework was geared to addressing specific skill deficits that Mario demonstrated, its focus was still preventative in nature. By addressing the core difficulties that Mario showed with emotional self-regulation within a once-a-week group session, it was hoped that more intrusive supports at the tertiary level were not needed.

Figure 8.1 Intervention Planning Form: Case Study 1 (Mario)

Student Information

| Target Student: | Mario P. | Date of Birth: | 2/13/2001 | Age: | 11 |

Gender: Male   School: Spartan Elementary   Grade: 5th

Phase 1: Problem Identification

How was student identified (e.g., grade-level team referral, etc.)? Universal screening, Grade-level team referral

Description of presenting problem: Mario frequently exhibits angry, aggressive, externalizing behaviors within the classroom that disrupt the safety of the learning environment. He is unresponsiveto the Level 1 schoolwide disciplinary structure, as well as Level 2 classroom-level behavioral supports.

Identify the assessment procedures used by the RTI team (e.g., archival data, behavior screening tools, discipline logs, FBA data, interviews, observations, etc.):

Assessment Procedure	Date	Results/Comments
Classroom observation	10/20/11, 10/21/11	Appropriate emotional response to conflict situations 3/10 times
Teacher and parent interviews/ checklist instrument	10/24/11, 10/25/11	Indicates deficits in ability to self-regulate negative emotions
School records: office discipline referrals & academic performance	10/24/11	16 discipline referrals this semester; failing 2 courses due to absences
Anger Screening Scale (teacher report) Children's Inventory of Anger; Behavior Assessment of System for Children–2 (student, parent, & teacher report)	10/24/11, 10/27/11	Elevated scores on all anger/ emotional control domains
Functional Behavioral Assessment (FBA)	11/7/11	Angry, aggressive behaviors in response to conflict situations. Skill deficit in anger control/regulation.

If a problem does exist, is it significant enough to warrant further investigation?

X Yes (Continue to Phase 2)

☐ No (Continue to monitor behavior; collect more data)

Phase 2: Problem Definition

Present Level of Performance (baseline): Mario is described as "very social" by his parents and teachers, at least in terms of his desire to engage with his peers. However, when faced with conflictsituations, he struggles to regulate and express his emotions appropriately, often becoming angry and aggressivetoward peers and teachers, and violating school rules. School records indicate 5 disciplinary removals in the past 3 weeks due to aggressive,

(Continued)

Figure 8.1 (Continued)

externalizing behaviors including yelling, cursing, and pushing at peers, as well as throwing objects. These disciplinary removals cause him to fall behind in his schoolwork and disrupt the safety of theenvironment for himself and others in the classroom.

Expected Level of Performance (goal; based on classroom or school wide expectations and/or local or national norms): Goals established by Mario's teachers in conjunction with the RTI team include limiting discipline referrals to no more than one per week and expressing his emotions appropriately when in conflict situations 8 out of 10 times.

How severe is the gap between present and expected levels of performance? Mario currently receives 1.7 discipline referrals per week and expresses his emotions appropriately when in conflict situations 3 out of 10 times. These are significantly discrepant from the expected level of performance, which would be 1 or fewer discipline refereeak per grading period and the appropriate emotional when in conflict situations of 9 out of 10 times. A realistic short term goal would be for Mario to receive 1 or fewer discipline referrals per week and to use appropriate emotional response to conflict situations at least 8 out of 10 times.

Operational definition of target behavior (must be measureable and observable): In a classroom setting, when presented with conflict situations (e.g., not getting hisway, being told to do something), Mario responds with a demonstration of anger (e.g., yelling, cursing, pushing, throwing an object) 80% of the time, as measured by classroom observation.

What is the function of the target behavior (based upon FBA results)? Anger release

Specific Skill Deficit(s): Self-regulation of anger

What, if any, additional supports is student currently receiving? Level 1 research-supported classroom curricula in social & emotional learning; Level 2 classroom based selectedsupports (behavioral contract with mystery motivator program)

Is the nature and severity of the problem enough to require additional supports?

[X] Yes (Continue to Phase 2)

[ ] No (Continue to monitor behavior; collect more data)

Phase 3: Intervention Development

Write a meaningful, measureable, and observable behavioral goal (with short-term objectives):

Objective: In a group setting, given direct instruction/examples of what is meant by appropriate anger expression & 10 story scenarios in which a character is presented with anger-provoking situations, Mario will list appropriate ways to express anger & the postive consequences of them, at an 80% level of accuracy, give indirect verbal cues & explanation regarding incorrect responses.

Objective: In a group setting, given direct instruction on recognizing body signs (e.g., clenched teeth, tense body, sweaty palms) & triggers to anger expression (e.g., desire to have something, someone not understanding you),& 10 videotaped scenarios involving exaggerated emotional cues of a character provoked into an anger outburst, Mario will correctly recognize the body signs and trigger for the anger outburst with 80% accuracy (8/10 scenarios), given indirect verbal cues.

Objective: In a group setting, given 10 open-ended role-play scenarios involving a conflict situation, Mario will demonstrate the use appropriate strategies for handling anger from a self-generated list (e.g., time-out, deep verbalize, write or draw feelings), across at least 3 turns, at least 80% of the time, give expectant waiting or gestural cues, as needed, and later explain the reasons for his choice.

Goal: In a classroom setting, when presented with anger-provoking situations, Mario will demonstrate emotional control (e.g., recognize his body signs and triggers to anger) so as to express anger appropriately (e.g., time-out, deep breathing, verbalize, write or draw feelings) 80% of the time by 6/15/12 as measured by the teacher-completed Anger Coping Evaluation Form and classroom observation.

Identify Potential Empirically Supported Interventions:

Intervention	Empirical Support (circle one)	Specific Skill Development	Ease of Implementation	Comments
Anger Coping Program (ACP)	⟨Strong⟩ / Mixed / Weak	Anger management & problem-solving skills	18 sessions; relatively easy	Our co-leaders have been trained on program
Student-Created Aggression Replacement Education (SCARE) program	Strong / ⟨Mixed⟩ / Weak	Anger management & coping skills	15 session; relatively easy	Limited effectiveness studies; considered USDE "promising program"
Too Good for Violence	Strong / Mixed / ⟨Weak⟩	Prosocial & behavior skills	9 sessions; relatively easy	Limited effectiveness studies

Selected Intervention: Anger Coping Program (ACP)

Intervention description: Cognitive-behavioral anger counseling group. Weekly sessions are designed to promote anger management skills by improving perspective taking, problem-solving skills, recognition of emotions associated with anger arousal, and reducing impulsive and aggressive responsed to anger.

Is the intervention developmentally appropriate?　　　　　Yes ☒　No ☐

Is the intervention directly linked to the results of the FBA?　Yes ☒　No ☐

Figure 8.1 (Continued)

Is the intervention directly linked to the goal statement? Yes ☒ No ☐

Is the intervention directly linked to socially valid outcomes? Yes ☒ No ☐

Is the entire RTI team (and student) in agreement on the appropriateness of the intervention? Yes ☒ No ☐

If yes to all previous 5 questions, proceed to Phase 4.

Phase 4: Intervention Implementation

Person(s) responsible for carrying out intervention: School psychologist and school counselor (co-leaders)

Intervention setting: Conference room Beginning Date: 01/08/12 Ending Date: 06/05/12

Frequency of Intervention: 45 minutes/day 1 days/week 18 weeks

Materials needed: Video-camera, TV, VCR, items used as tokens within a point-based system, reinforcers, deck of playing cards, and dominoes.

Briefly describe the extent of collaboration/coordination needed across other settings (e.g., home, community): Need to obtain informed parental consent; will provide monthly progress updates to parents.

Intervention Integrity

Has a treatment integrity evaluation plan been developed? Yes ☒ No ☐

Description of treatment integrity evaluation plan (include what measures will be used): A treatment integrity checklist has been developed with 10 interventionsession components.

Who will conduct integrity checks? School counselor

How often will integrity checks be conducted? Weekly

Do data indicate that plan was implemented with integrity?

☒ Yes (Continue to Phase 5)

☐ No (Analyze why; provide additional training to implementers; revise intervention; change intervention)

Phase 5: Intervention Evaluation

Standard(s) used to determine level of performance: Problem behaviors identified by his teachers and the RTI team as being incompatible with the schoolwide code of conduct and classroom expectations were included in a behavior rating scale (the Anger Copying Evaluation Form).

What progress-monitoring tools will be used? Anger Coping Evaluation Form, classroom observation, discipline reports

Briefly describe the progress-monitoring process: Mario's teachers will complete the Anger Coping Evaluation Form on a weekly basis; Mario will be observed within the classroom; office discipline reports will be monitored. Weekly meetings will take place withMario's teachers to ensure intervention goals stay consistent; parents will receive monthly progress reports.

Person(s) responsible for progress monitoring: School psychologist, school counselor, Mario's teachers, RTI team

How often/when will progress-monitoring data be collected? Weekly from the Anger Coping Evaluation Form, counseling session and classroom observations, and teacher interview results.

Progress-monitoring/outcome efficacy summary:

Progress-Monitoring Date	Progress Made (Compare baseline data to current performance)
11/18/11 (baseline)	1. 3 wks baseline data using teacher-completed Anger Coping Evaluation Form; Score = 12/30 2. Office discipline referrals = 1.7 per week average (5 discipline referrals in 3 weeks) 3. Classroom observation of appropriate response to anger-provoking situations = 30% of time
2/1/12	1. Anger Coping Evaluation Form (averages from all teachers) = 18/30 2. Office discipline referrals = 0.7 per week average (2 discipline referrals in 3 weeks) 3. Classroom observation of appropriate response to anger-provoking situations = 50% of time
3/15/12	1. Anger Coping Evaluation Form = 20/30 2. Office discipline referrals = 0.7 per week average (4 discipline referrals in 6 weeks) 3. Classroom observation of appropriate response to anger-provoking situations = 60% of time
5/1/12	1. Anger Coping Evaluation Form = 22/30 2. Office discipline referrals = 0.5 per week average (3 discipline referrals in 6 weeks) 3. Classroom observation of appropriate response to anger-provoking situations = 70% of time
6/15/12 (final)	1. Anger Coping Evaluation Form = 23/30 2. Office discipline referrals = 0.5 per week average (3 discipline referrals in 6 weeks) 3. Classroom observation of appropriate response to anger-provoking situations = 80% of time

Intervention Status/ Recommendations
Check the most appropriate box(es)

[X] Performance goals have been met

    [X] Maintain behavior;phase out supports

    [ ] Employ ongoing FBA to evaluate possible shift(s) in function of behavior

    [ ] Develop new goals

(Continued)

Figure 8.1 (Continued)

☐ Performance goals have not been met, but progress has been made

☐ Continue intervention, but with increased intensity
☐ Revise intervention
☐ Select new intervention

☐ Performance goals have not been met, no progress has been made

☐ Introduce additional tiers of support
☐ Progress to next level of support
☐ Referral to Special Education

Notes regarding future plan: Arrange and conduct booster sessions with Mario on individual or group basis at outset of 6th grade progress–monitoring data. school year. Begin with biweekly sessions and phase out supports based upon

Discussion Questions

1. Why would it be important to select one, maybe two, behavior(s) to work with at a time, even if data suggest a student exhibits multiple challenging behaviors? How would you determine which behaviors are most severe and, thus, should be targeted for intervention?

2. In the case of Mario, what might the RTI team do if the periodic progress-monitoring data indicate that he is not on pace to meet his established goals?

CASE 2: INTENSIVE TERTIARY SCHOOL-BASED SERVICES FOR A NINTH GRADER WITH ACUTE SCHOOL REFUSAL ASSOCIATED WITH SOCIAL ANXIETY

Background Information

Kelly is a 14-year-old Caucasian female in the ninth grade at Woodside High School. She is currently experiencing an acute episode of school refusal behavior. She has missed nine of the last 10 school days. After attempting to return to school a week ago, Kelly did not tell anyone but reportedly experienced a panic attack and has not been to school the past five days. Her parents report extreme distress associated with school, including resistance to their attempts to get her to attend. In the past week, Kelly and her parents report that she is experiencing frequent/severe headaches and an upset stomach, including vomiting. Kelly is reported by her parents as being shy and somewhat anxious in social and performance situations, though the severity of her current symptoms and resulting dysfunction has not been observed in the past. A specific trigger or antecedent to this acute episode was identified as a recent decline in her relationship with her best friend, Cally, and an emerging discomfort in being around her peers. Kelly feels as if her classmates are isolating her and talking negatively behind her back. Kelly has no history of receiving Level 1 or 2 RTI services within the high school, but she did attend a three-month social skills training group run by the middle school counselor as a result of teacher nomination. Group notes indicated Kelly effectively participated in this Level 2 intervention approach. According to parent report, Kelly has no history of psychological or psychiatric treatment within the community pertaining to her current symptoms.

Problem Identification

Kelly was identified for services by the school principal who was notified of her frequent absences by the school attendance office. This behavior is in marked contrast with a history of strong school attendance and exceptional academic performance (GPA 3.87) within a rigorous college preparation course load. Kelly has missed nine of the last 10 school days. After hearing of the school's concerns, Kelly's parents got her in to see her physician to rule out any medical causes of her current problems. Following the determination that Kelly's difficulties were primarily psychological in nature, the RTI team and her parents decided on the need and importance of developing a school reentry plan. The purpose of that plan was to appropriately treat Kelly's social anxiety in a way that would restore a gradual resumption of school attendance over a two-week period of time. By the end of those two weeks, the goal was to have Kelly back in school as expected (five out of five days). Kelly's self-report of social anxiety symptoms at baseline fell within the clinically significant range as measured by the *Multidimensional Anxiety Scale for Children* (MASC). Symptom reduction, including close monitoring and assessment of panic-like symptoms, was warranted. Kelly's physician prescribed a short-acting anti-anxiety medication (i.e., alprazolam) to be taken as needed (i.e., when panic-like symptoms emerge, such as difficulties breathing, feeling as if she was going to die).

Parent consultation was deemed necessary as interview data suggested they may be negatively reinforcing Kelly's symptoms and behaviors by giving significant attention to her physiological symptoms (headaches/stomach aches) and by trying to make her as comfortable as possible (i.e., renting her movies, getting her favorite foods for lunch) once their attempts to force her to attend school each morning have been unsuccessful.

Problem Definition

The RTI team determined that intensive assessment, consultative, and intervention services were necessary to allow Kelly to benefit from her educational programming. Following an office visit and blood work, Kelly's physician reported no medical or biological reason for her current school refusal and socially anxious behaviors. The school psychologist conducted an FBA that clearly demonstrated Kelly's school refusal was the result of her avoidance of an anxiety-provoking situation. In sum, her school refusal behavior and feelings of anxiety were further reinforced by her absence from school, presenting a complex set of circumstances in need of intensive, individualized counseling services.

Intervention Development

The RTI team worked to develop a comprehensive action plan involving Kelly, her parents, and her teachers. The school psychologist developed a school reentry plan with Kelly that helped to break down the barriers (i.e., social anxiety) getting in the way of her attendance. This plan was shared with all RTI team members and Kelly's parents. The goals and objectives of the reentry plan were targeted directly at her skill deficits as indicated by FBA data (not attending school was negatively reinforcing her socially anxious behaviors). A list of potential empirically supported interventions as described by the Association for Cognitive and Behavior Therapies website (www.effectivechildtherapy.com) was developed. Each of these interventions was evaluated for its empirical support, target skill development, and feasibility of implementation. The RTI team, given the severity of Kelly's symptoms and resulting dysfunction, decided that all three interventions recommended for this condition be targeted for implementation. The goal of programs at this tertiary level of service delivery is to equip students with the skills to replace their maladaptive behaviors so that they can benefit from their educational programming. Specific treatment components used within the reentry plan included the following: relaxation training, graduated exposure to her hierarchy of anxiety-provoking situations, cognitive restructuring, setting up contingencies for school attendance, and goal setting/

monitoring via teacher consultation. Parent training via consultation was implemented to ensure a smooth morning and evening routine that focused attention on positive behaviors while ignoring negative behaviors associated with Kelly's school refusal.

Plan Implementation

The primary treatment goal was to ensure Kelly's reentry back into school. Team member communication at this stage was extremely important as the effectiveness of the plan was dependent upon numerous stakeholders who contributed to its implementation. The RTI team obtained informed parental consent from Kelly's parents as well as a two-way release of information for effective communication with Kelly's primary care physician and community-based psychologist who would take over the psychological care of Kelly following successful completion of short-term cognitive behavioral treatment and parent/teacher consultation.

Treatment Evaluation

A multimodal progress-monitoring and evaluation plan was developed that clearly linked progress to Kelly's success with her reentry plan (i.e., a set of steps with increasingly more anxiety-provoking steps). School records (office discipline reports and grades) and teacher/parent feedback via daily behavior report cards (social anxiety) were used to provide periodic progress updates and to compare Kelly's performance to baseline levels collected at the start of the intervention. Outcome data collected indicated short-term goals were met, and Kelly resumed her school attendance. Her MASC scores revealed gradual improvement across time with all subscale scores falling well below clinically significant levels two months following the onset of this treatment plan. The intervention demonstrated success, and the RTI team worked to establish a follow-up plan (exit from services plan) where Kelly received psychological services from a community-based psychologist.

Case Discussion

This case study was organized within the framework of the RTI problem-solving model introduced in Chapter 3. This case discussion and the accompanying intervention planning form (see Figure 8.2) are intended to provide an overview of the treatment decision-making process. Cognitive-Behavioral Therapy was provided as an example of an individual "best practice" intervention that meets the acute nature and

Figure 8.2 Intervention Planning Form: Case Study 2 (Kelly)

Student Information

Target Student:	Kelly.H.	Date of Birth: 10/26/1998	Age: 14

Gender: Female   School: wood High School   Grade: 9th

Phase 1: Problem Identification

How was student identified (e.g., grade-level team referral, etc.)? Principal; Child Study Team

Description of presenting problem: Kelly has been absent from school 9 out of the last 10 days. The principal was informed of her absences from the attendance office. A phone call to percents revealed significant symptoms of social anxiety and social refusal. Level 3 services will be provided given the severity of symptoms and resulting dsyfunctiond of Kelly.s behaviors on school funtioning.

Identify the assessment procedures used by the RTI team (e.g., archival data, behavior screeing tools, discipline logs, FBA data, interviews, observations, etc.):

Assessment Procedure	Data	Results/Comments
Parent Interview (School Psychologist)	2/5/12	Social anxiety is reported leading to avoidance of school. Kelly is experiencing significant distress and associated physiological symptoms (vomiting, headaches).
Child Interview (School Psychologist)	2/5/12	Deficits in ability to control her anxiety pertaining to attending school and facing situations in the hall and classroom that are causing her significant distress. Kelly is particularly worried about facing her former best friend and attending classes where she feels that other girls are talking negatively about her.
School records: Grades and Attendance	2/6/12	Academic performance has been strong (GPA 3.87); no problem attending school have been noted prior to her current difficulties.
Multidimensional Anxiety Scale for Children (March 2012; self–report)	2/5/12	Elevated scores on all social anxiety subscales (physical symptoms, social anxiety, harm/avoidance, separation and panic) are noted.
Functional Behavioral Assessment (FBA)	2/6/12	Negative reinforcement; avoidance of fear/anxiety-provoking situations is reinforcing school refusal behaviors. Acute set of circumstance in need of immediate intervention.

If a problem does exist, is it significant enough to warrant further investigation?

X	Yes (Continue to Phase 2)
	No (Continue to monitor behavior; collect more data)

Phase 2: Problem Definition

Present Level of Performance (baseline): Kelly sis described by her parents as achievement-oriented, shy, and socially anxious. This is the first time that these issues have led to absence from school. In the past two weeks, Kelly has been absent 9 out of 10 school days and has missed the entire last week. An antecedent to these events was relationship difficulties with her best friend, Cally who since the holiday beaks has associated with a different peer group, leaving Kelly feeling isolated and disconnected from others within the high school Kelly reports that no one likes her, that others are talking negatively about her in the hails and in her classes, and that she is not as smart as the students in her advanced courses. The most recent day of attendance she experienced a panic attack.

Expected level of Performance (goal; based in classroom or schoolwide expectations and/or national norms): Goals established by the RTI tam include regular school attendance (daily) and appropriate coping for discomfort associated with social interactions with peers, specifically positively adapting to her current perceived and actual relationship challenges.

How severe is the gap between present and expected levels of performance? A significant gap appears in kelly's current attendance behavior and expected levels of this behavior. Kelly is currently experiencing clinically significant levels of behaviors associated with social anxiety. Examples include physiological (headaches, stomachaches), cognitive (fear of being judged/performing poorly), and behavioral (school refusal) symptoms are leading to high levels of resistance to go school. Avoiding school and these anxiety-provoking situations are negatively reinforcing her irrational fears and beliefs.

Operational definition of target behavior (must be measureable and observable): School attendance (currently 0 out of 5 days): social anxiety symptoms (including vomiting, headaches) in the clinically significant range on the MASC.

What is the function of the target behavior (based upon FBA results)? Escape from anxiety-provoking situation

Specific Skill Deficits(s): The ability to manage her anxiety and resume attendance at school.

What, if any, additional supports is student currently receiving? No current supports in place. Consultation with primary care doctor to rule out medical or physiological reasons for her increase in anxiety symptoms and school absences was recommended to her parents.

Is the nature and severity of the problem enough to require additional supports?

| X | Yes (Continue to Phase 3) |
| | No (Continue to monitor behavior; collect data) in response to current supports) |

(Continued)

Figure 8.2 (Continued)

Phase 3: Intervention Development

Write a meaningful, measureable, and observable behavioral goal (with short-time objectives):

Objective: To work with kelly to develop a school reentry plan. Initial goals pertain to relaxation training and exposure to anxiety–provoking situations via a set of gradual introduction of feared stimuli including leaving home, arriving at school, interactions in the hallway, and class attendance. Kelly well successfully master one reentry plan goal per day so that within a period of one week she is back in school as expected.

Objective: To work with Kelly's parents and teachers to focus on reinforcement of school and class attendance. Specific attention will be given to reducing any unintended "negatively" reinforcement of avoidance behaviors.

Goal: With appropriate supports at home via parent and at school via short–term therapy and consultation with teachers, Kelly will resume her regular attendance at school (five out of five days) and reduce her symptoms of social anxiety to below clinically (<84th percentile) as measured on the MASC Consultation with her primary care physician for possible treatment of panic symptoms and referral to outside psychological services for additional assessment of depression symptoms.

Identify Potential Empirically Supported Interventions (Source: www. Effectivechildtherapy.com):

Intervention	Empirical Support (circle one)	Specific Skill Development	Ease of Implementation	Comments
Cognitive-Behavioral Therapy for school refusal behavior	Strong / (Mixed) / Weak	Reduction of anxiety via relaxation training and targeting of maladaptive cognitions via cognitive restricting. School attendance is keystone target behavior.	Challenging, given the need to meet student's needs initially in the home setting and the intensity of services needed to achieve school reentry	School psychologist will undertake direct therapy efforts and consult with family/physician regarding treatment plan. Following short-term CBT, a referral to outside psychological services will be made.
Parent training pertaining to increasing reinforcement of school attendance and decreasing reinforcement of maladaptive behaviors	Strong / (Mixed) / Weak	Positive reinforcement of coping behaviors and school attendance	2 sessions; relatively easy via consultation	Targeted skills development as well as open communication about progress and outcomes associated with primary care psychological services

Teacher training pertaining to support attendance	Strong	Reduction of behaviors that may contribute to school refusal behavior	2 sessions; relatively easy via consultation	School psychologist will visit with teachers from the first two periods on Kelly's schedule.
	(Mixed)			
	Weak			

Selected Intervention: Cognitive–Behavioral Therapy with Kelly initially at home to address acute dysfunction (i.e., school refusal).

Intervention Description: Cognitive–Behavioral Therapy with Kelly. Initially, within the home setting to develop skills necessary to leave home in the morning to attend school. Once school attendance occurs, continued therapy sessions until short-term goals of therapy have been met. Brief consultation sessions with parents' and teachers to eliminate the function of Kelly s school refusal behavior are needed.

Is the intervention developmentally appropriate? Yes [X] No [ ]

Is the intervention directly linked to the results of the FBA? Yes [X] No [ ]

Is the intervention directly linked to the goal statement? Yes [X] No [ ]

Is the intervention directly linked to socially valid outcomes? Yes [X] No [ ]

Is the entire RTI team (and student) in agreement on the appropriateness of the intervention? Yes [X] No [ ]

If yes to all 5 previous questions, proceed to Phase 4.

Phase 4: Intervention Implementation

Person(s) responsible for carrying out intervention: School psychologist and classroom teachers (first two periods)

Intervention setting: Home/School Beginning Date: 2/7/12 Ending Date: As needed

Frequency of Intervention: As needed minutes/day 5, initially days/week 4–6 weeks

Materials needed: MASC self-report forms, brief consultation report to share with primary care physician, daily report card pertaining to social anxiety to be completed by parents and teachers (first 2 class periods).

Briefly describe the extent of collaboration/coordination needed across other settings (e.g., home, community): Need to obtain informed parental consent; need to consult with family physician and outside psychological service provider.

Intervention Integrity Yes [X] No [ ]

Has a treatment integrity evaluation plan been developed?

(Continued)

Figure 8.2 (Continued)

Description of treatment integrity evaluation plan (include what measures will be used):
A treatment integrity checklist has been developed with 5 intervention session components (home–based therapy, school–based therapy, parent/teacher/physician consultation.

Who will conduct integrity checks? School psychologist

How often will integrity checks be conducted? Weekly

Do data indicate that plan was implemented with integrity?

| X | Yes (Continue to Phase 5) |
| | No (Analyze why; provide additional training to implementers; revise intervention; change intervention) |

Phase 5: Intervention Evaluation

Standard(s) used to determine level of performance: Kelly's progress on her reentry plan. Anxiety reduction and her coping with her negative and intrusive concerns pertaining to others' judgments and perceptions.

What progress-monitoring tools will be used? Attendance records; Multidimensional Social Anxiety Rating Scale; reentry plan

Briefly describe the progress-monitoring process: The school psychologist will gather attendance data and compare it to the reentry plan developed to ensure that Kelly is making improvements in reducing her anxiety associated with school attendance. Parents and teachers will also provide feedback to the school psychologist via daily report cards for social anxiety–related behaviors.

Person(s) responsible for progress monitoring: School psychologist, parents, teachers

How often/when will progress-monitoring data be collected? Attendance–daily; MASC–weekly within therapy sessions; teacher and parents feedback via daily behavior report (appropriately coping with social anxiety)

Progress–monitoring/outcome efficacy summary:

Progress–Monitoring Date	Progress Made (Compare baseline data to current performance)
2/6/12 (baseline)	1. School Attendance= 0 out of 5 days in past week 2. MASC Scores= clinically significant on all subscales
2/13/12	1. Partial school attendance as expected within her reentry plan (3 out of 5 days, first 2 partial days) 2. MASC Scores= clinically significant on only harm/avoidance and social anxiety subscales

2/20/12	1. School attendance as expected within her reentry plan (5 out of 5 days, first 2 partial days) 2. MASC scores= clinically significant only on social anxiety subscale
3/20/12	1. School attendance= 5 out of 5 days (Goal met after 2 weeks of treatment plan, consistent with expectations) 2. MASC scores= clinically significant only on social anxiety subscale
4/20/12 (final)	1. School attendance= 5 out of 5 days 2. MASC scores= No subscales within clinically significant range

Intervention Status/Recommendations
Check the most appropriate box(es)

[X] Performance goals have been met

    [X] Maintain behavior; phase out supports
    [ ] Employ ongoing FBA to evaluate possible shift(s) in function of behavior
    [ ] Develop new goals

[ ] Performance goals have not been met, but progress has been made

    [ ] Continue intervention, but with increased intensity
    [ ] Revise intervention
    [ ] Select new intervention

[ ] Performance goals have not been met, no progress has been made

    [ ] Introduce additional tiers of support
    [ ] Progress to next level of support
    [ ] Referral to Special Education

Notes regarding future plan: Arrange for community-based follow-up with Kelly pertaining to the development of coping mechanisms for her social anxiety and to assist with processing peer relationship challenges that may arise.

significant impairment associated with Kelly's school refusal behavior. While its implementation at Level 3 within an RTI or a PBIS framework was geared to addressing the primary need to get Kelly back in school, its focus was on short-term functioning and transitioning her to additional supportive treatment at school and within the community as needed. By addressing the core dysfunction that Kelly was demonstrating, this case provides an example of short-term treatments that may be closely aligned to the function associated with maladaptive and dysfunctional behaviors.

Discussion Questions

1. Given a case such as school refusal due to severe social anxiety, what are the challenges and issues that arise from an RTI's team engagement in assessment and intervention services within the home setting?

2. What might the RTI team do to prevent Kelly's future school refusal behavior?

SCHOOL-BASED COUNSELING ACROSS DEVELOPMENTAL PHASES

The long-term outcomes for children and adolescents are not always foreseeable. Predictions, or prognoses, can be made based on children's risk factors, protective mechanisms, and response to intervention, but much can change over time for children and adolescents due to their maturation/development, experiences, learning, and changes in their environment. In order to bring attention to the developmental perspective, Cases 3 and 4 illustrate the provision of counseling services across time, from elementary school through high school.

CASE 3: SOCIAL SKILLS TRAINING AND COUNSELING ACROSS DEVELOPMENTAL PHASES FOR A STUDENT WITH HIGH-FUNCTIONING AUTISM

Background Information

Kevin, an African American male, lived with his mother and step-father in a suburban area. His mother was a criminal defense attorney, and his step-father was a sales manager for a pharmaceutical company. His step-father's son, who was a couple of years older than Kevin, occasionally visited on weekends. Kevin had minimal contact with his biological father and half-sister who lived in another state. Kevin grew up in a warm, stable home environment.

Kevin's early development was mildly delayed in the areas of social communication and motor coordination due to hypertonia. He also exhibited some mild sensory sensitivities and restricted patterns of interest. His delays became more apparent when he entered kindergarten, particularly in the area of social communication, and he was referred for a multidisciplinary autism evaluation. Kevin qualified for special education services as a student with autism, specifically Pervasive Developmental Disorder–Not Otherwise Specified (PDD–NOS) and he began to receive speech therapy services, occupational therapy, and social skills training. The following sections provide an overview of the social skills and counseling interventions Kevin received throughout his elementary, middle, and high school years. His deficit in social communication was the most significant area of concern targeted for intervention.

Elementary School

It was apparent early on that Kevin was intelligent and had no trouble learning academic concepts. He was ahead of most of his peers academically and was quite knowledgeable in areas of particular interest to him as well. The specific areas of concern included that Kevin talked excessively about areas of interest to him (e.g., Pokémon), he had difficulty taking turns during peer group activities, he was socially withdrawn, he had poor eye contact, he used limited gestures and facial expressions when communicating with others, he spoke in a monotone voice, he had difficulty picking up social cues, he was poorly organized and inattentive (e.g., he lost or misplaced materials and papers, he had trouble shifting his attention, etc.), and he had difficulty managing transitions and unexpected changes in his normal routine.

Kevin began to receive pull-out speech therapy services as well as social skills instruction from the school psychologist when he was in kindergarten; both services primarily targeted social communication and social skills. The school psychologist collaborated with his general education classroom teacher to select two "typical" peers to participate in a "friendship group" with Kevin. The group sessions involved fun, interactive games and social skills lessons targeting specific skills, such as joining in interactive play, recognizing and expressing emotions, sharing, taking turns, and making and keeping friends. The sessions typically involved various strategies, including teaching and modeling specific skills, use of social stories designed specifically for Kevin, and role playing. The school psychologist and speech therapist also collaborated with one another and with Kevin's classroom teacher to track his progress and develop strategies to increase generalization of skills into the classroom setting. One of the primary strategies they used to promote generalization was through the use of peer mentors. The school counselor already provided schoolwide Level 1 classroom guidance lessons (tailored for each grade level) promoting peer cooperation that laid the groundwork for the use of peer mentors or "buddies." This enabled the teacher to reinforce and build upon the schoolwide theme of peer cooperation to facilitate

Kevin's participation with his classmates as well as teach, model, and prompt prosocial interactions. These services and strategies (with adaptations) continued throughout elementary school.

The combination of peer support from his "typical" peers and direct social skills instruction was beneficial for Kevin. He was accepted by his classmates, and he increased his prosocial interactions. He continued to demonstrate qualitative differences in his social interactions compared to his classmates, but he made efforts to generalize the specific social skills he was learning because he felt safe and accepted. Over time many of his classmates increasingly recognized his positive attributes, particularly his intelligence and his dry and quirky sense of humor. Before he entered middle school, Kevin was dismissed from speech therapy, but he continued to receive social skills training from the school psychologist.

Middle School

The transition from elementary school to middle school can be stressful for any student, but especially for students with disabilities such as autism. The school psychologist at the middle school attended Kevin's transition IEP meeting at the end of his fifth-grade year so plans could be developed for a smooth transition for Kevin. His sixth-grade teachers and school staff at the middle school were provided information and guidance concerning Kevin's needs so that appropriate plans were in place. The first couple of weeks were indeed stressful for Kevin, but the transition plans were successful and he soon settled into a routine.

The school psychologist initially met with Kevin individually before seeing him in a social skills group with two other boys who also were previously identified with autism. By the conclusion of the second group session, the school psychologist was convinced that Kevin recognized that he was more intelligent and exhibited fewer atypical behaviors compared to the other boys in his group. The school psychologist was concerned that Kevin's self-esteem might suffer from remaining in the group and that he might react negatively as a result. Because of this, the school psychologist (without bringing much attention, if any, for the reason behind the proposed change) offered to meet with Kevin individually instead. Kevin, too, liked the idea of individualized sessions instead of the group sessions. The individualized sessions targeted social communication, increasing assertiveness in social interactions, and organizing his assignments. Kevin had a couple of friends who he sat with at lunch who held similar interests as him, mainly video games and video and print comic characters. He began playing the violin in the sixth-grade orchestra and participated sporadically in after-school clubs, including the chess club and stop-motion animation club. Throughout middle school Kevin performed well academically, maintained a small group of friends, and enjoyed playing in the orchestra.

High School

Kevin was both excited and nervous as he began high school. Once again, the transition was stressful for him, but he handled the change with relatively little support. He continued to receive social skills counseling as a related service by the school psychologist at the high school. Kevin enjoyed having a supportive adult whom he could touch base with. He continued his involvement in the orchestra, and he maintained connections with a few close friends from middle school and became acquainted with some new students as well.

In the spring of his freshman year, Kevin was re-evaluated for special education services. While he continued to exhibit mild symptoms character-istic of autism he no longer demonstrated an educational need for special education services. At that time he was dismissed from special education services, but he continued to receive support through a 504 Accommodation Plan due to his diagnosis of autism/PDD–NOS. Throughout high school, he met regularly with one of the school counselors who provided guidance and support. Kevin sought advice from the counselor on how he could become more popular with his peers, especially girls. They also discussed transition planning for post–high school. Kevin had become increasingly interested in computers as well as video technology and production. He took a theater production class and found a niche in providing technical support. Throughout high school he assisted in behind the scenes technical support for the school's theatrical performances. Kevin performed well academically throughout high school. In the spring of his senior year, his post-graduation plans were to enroll in a nearby university where he planned to major in film and digital media. After college, he thought that he would either pursue a career in film and media production or possibly attend law school like his mother, but spe-cialize in copyright law.

Case Discussion

The positive schoolwide climate of Kevin's elementary school was a key factor in setting the stage for his positive adjustment and growth throughout his school-age years. The combination of peer support and acceptance he received along with the commitment his teachers, service providers, and school staff made in facilitating Kevin's social development propelled him toward success. Indeed, Kevin had several other protective factors in his favor, including grow-ing up in a positive family environment with available resources, his innate intelligence, and his desire to excel. Furthermore, his autistic symptoms were relatively mild. One could assume that his transition to college would still be challenging, especially if he lived away from his parents. He would likely not have the benefit of previously established relationships in his new environment and would have to make new friends and acquaintances. With his qualitative social impairments and tendency toward social withdrawal he might be at risk for social isolation. At the same time, Kevin could build upon the positive experiences he had from high school. He would also continue to have support available to him at his university due to his being identified as an individual with autism under his 504 Accommodation Plan.

Discussion Questions

1. What are some examples of integrative mental health services in this case?

2. What was Kevin's response to social skills training and counseling? What factors may have influenced his interest in counseling?

3. What were some considerations in group formation in social skills/ counseling as well as general education setting interventions in Kevin's case?

4. At any point in Kevin's case, what additional interventions could have been considered or tried? Are there other approaches or interventions you might have tried?

CASE 4: SUPPORTIVE INTERVENTIONS FOR A STUDENT WITH BOTH LEARNING AND EMOTIONAL-BEHAVIORAL PROBLEMS

Background Information

Amanda was the second-born of four children who lived with her biological parents in a metropolitan area. Her parents both worked hard to support the family, and her maternal grandmother assisted with child care when needed. Both of her parents completed their education through high school, but neither had attended college. Her father received some technical training after high school. Amanda, herself Caucasian, lived in an ethnically diverse community. Her family was involved in church that was a meaningful source of spiritual and social support for them. This case focuses primarily on the educational supports that Amanda received for her learning problems and subsequent emotional-behavioral problems.

Elementary School

In her early elementary school years, Amanda struggled to keep pace with her classmates academically. When she was in second grade she began to receive Level 2 academic support. Her teachers and parents hoped that she would begin to catch up with her classmates as she was shy and immature compared to her peers. In third grade she continued to struggle despite Level 2 interventions, so she received additional intensive supports targeted directly at her academic skill deficits identified through the systematic problem-solving case study process at Level 3A. After still showing inadequate progress to these interventions, she was referred for a special education evaluation at Level 3B. Amanda qualified for special education services as a student with a Specific Learning Disability in the area of Reading Comprehension. She was also suspected of having ADHD, Primarily Inattentive Type, but her parents were hesitant about this potential diagnosis and did not want to pursue an additional evaluation at that time. Amanda benefited from the specially designed instruction that targeted her reading skill deficits. She attended a special reading class where she received individualized attention in a small-group setting. She made slow, steady progress academically throughout elementary school.

During third and fourth grades, in addition to her academic support, Amanda participated in a girls' self-esteem group led by the school counselor. It appeared that she benefited from the group as she established friendships with a couple of the girls in the group and her confidence was improving too. In fifth grade she continued to progress academically with support. Her self-confidence also continued to improve, so it was determined that she no longer needed counseling support.

Middle School

During the summer before sixth grade, Amanda was coerced by her 15-year-old male cousin into sexual contact. She did not initially tell anyone about the event because her cousin told her not to tell, and she also felt partly responsible for allowing it to happen. In sixth grade Amanda's grades began to drop, she engaged in inappropriate attention-seeking behaviors of a sexual nature, and she became increasingly withdrawn and moody. She received several detentions and discipline referrals, but her inappropriate behaviors persisted. The school counselor began meeting with Amanda regularly to assess the potential causes of her problems (or the functions of her behavior) and to provide her support. Amanda's parents also sought assistance and counsel from the youth leader at church to encourage her. In November and December she became verbally abusive at home toward her parents and siblings. The week before her extended holiday break from school, Amanda told her mother that she wanted to kill herself. Her parents also discovered cut marks on her arms and wrists. Concerned for her safety, her parents took her to the hospital. She was referred to an inpatient psychiatric treatment facility where she stayed for 10 days. During her hospitalization she revealed to one of the therapists that she had had a sexual encounter with her older cousin, but that no one was to know about this. The therapist, though, explained to her that due to the nature of the incident that this would need to be reported. During her stay she was also prescribed medications for her depression and mood instability and was referred to a therapist for ongoing outpatient therapy.

When Amanda returned to school after the holidays, her mother updated the school counselor regarding recent events and Amanda's current functioning. Within a couple of weeks after returning to school, Amanda's inappropriate behaviors resurfaced. Her IEP Committee recommended that Amanda's three-year evaluation (due in the spring) be pulled forward and that a psychological evaluation be completed as well. Amanda qualified for special education services as a student with an emotional disturbance in addition to continuing to requalify with a specific learning disability. Her schedule was adjusted so that she received support in the self-contained social-emotional classroom one period each day, and she received the support of a classroom aide in her regular classes. Also, a behavior management plan IEP was developed and she was provided special education counseling as a related service. The goal of these changes was to provide Amanda the amount of social-emotional support she needed so she could focus on her schoolwork and learn to apply positive coping strategies. With the increased structure and supports in place, Amanda's work completion increased and her behavior generally improved. She did, though, continue to engage in some inappropriate attention-seeking behaviors (especially seeking attention from boys), she got into arguments with many of her female classmates, and she continued to cut and scrape on her arms and wrists.

Throughout middle school Amanda met with her private therapist about every other week, she received weekly counseling as a related service at school from the school psychologist, and she continued to meet regularly with the school counselor. With consent, communication between the private therapist and school service providers facilitated ongoing assessments and interventions. Amanda's behavior management plan provided strategies for teachers to support her in gaining attention in appropriate ways and to use positive coping strategies when experiencing challenging emotions. Teachers and staff were encouraged to monitor any attempts or signs of self-injury and report this to the school nurse, school counselor, and/or school psychologist. At the same time, teachers and staff were encouraged not to bring attention to her self-injury so as not to inadvertently reinforce the behavior. Both the school psychologist and school counselor worked with Amanda, her teachers, and parents to identify positive activities that she could become involved in at school. She did not want to become involved in any school activities, though, and she felt that most of her peers rejected her.

In counseling sessions, both the school counselor and school psychologist provided Amanda support and acceptance, listened to her, and encouraged her to express her emotions appropriately. She would become defensive and start to "shut down" if the topic of her self-injuring was ever brought up. Both school service providers did not press her on this topic, but instead they expressed interest in her, honored her experiences, and expressed empathy. They worked with her on areas that she brought to them, such as arguments and "drama" she was having with other girls in school and being rejected by her peers. Both the school psychologist and school counselor also attempted to instill hope and expectancy of change during sessions with Amanda as well as evoke within her motivation for change. They attempted to build on her strengths, such as her fashion sense and sense of humor. Amanda, though, held strong negative self-attributions as she viewed herself as "dumb," "ugly," and "no good." Both service providers worked with her in identifying and challenging her irrational and destructive thoughts. At times she seemed to be developing more positive views about herself, but then she would revert back to the negative self-thoughts. Amanda had at least one or two teachers, in addition to her teacher in the self-contained classroom, who reached out to her to support her and build her confidence each year. She was hospitalized one other time during middle school, but with the supports in place she moved on to high school relatively stable.

High School

Amanda continued to receive her special education supports in high school. During her freshman year she was quiet and withdrawn, but she applied herself academically. She continued to cut on herself superficially when she experienced stress. During the school year she found a boyfriend who was two years older than her, and they became sexually involved. Her grades began to drop. She failed two classes one grading period and failed another class the following grading period, but she was able to pass all of her classes for the year.

In the fall of her sophomore year, Amanda discovered that she was pregnant. Both she and her parents did not want to terminate the pregnancy, but they were undecided whether she would keep her baby or adopt her baby out. Amanda and her boyfriend broke up, but her boyfriend wanted to be involved in his baby's life and offer as much support as he was able. Amanda received proper medical attention and prenatal education. She wanted to take good care of herself so that she would have a healthy baby. Her self-injurious behaviors decreased in intensity and frequency during her pregnancy. Amanda also decided that she would not let her unexpected pregnancy keep her from graduating from high school. She and her mother sought guidance from the school counselor and school administrators regarding options and plans for Amanda continuing her education during and after her pregnancy. Amanda requested and was approved transfer to attend an alternative school in the district designed for pregnant and parenting students. Also, her grandmother offered for her to live with her during and after the pregnancy and she soon moved in.

Because of her low-income status, Amanda qualified for federal assistance from the Women, Infants, and Children (WIC) program. WIC provided her a counselor to assist her with the special challenges of being a teen mother. School was also a source of support for her. She was able to pursue her education in a small setting with other girls like herself. In addition to her academic courses and IEP, the school provided students pertinent information and guidance (e.g., prenatal care, breast feeding, and parenting), support from social workers, and an on-campus daycare. After careful consideration, Amanda and her family decided that she would raise her child. She gave birth to a healthy boy and continued her education.

Amanda experienced mild to moderate depression during and after her pregnancy. She also continued superficial cutting and scraping during times of stress, though the intensity and frequency continued to decrease over time. With the support of her family, church, school staff and students, and WIC, Amanda did not give up on her education. While in school she watched girls like herself graduate each year and go on to pursue higher educational and vocational pursuits. Upon her own graduation from high school, she planned to pursue training as a nursing aide and eventually become a registered nurse.

Case Discussion

Amanda appeared to benefit from the individualized educational supports she received at school. Without these supports it is likely she would have regressed further academically, emotionally, and behaviorally. Amanda experienced some challenging events and circumstances, but she dealt with her problems as best as she knew how, including coping with difficult circumstances and emotions through self-injury.

In counseling, Amanda did not want to talk about her self-injury, but she responded favorably to supportive counseling and CBT. Research has found that individuals who self-injure value having someone to talk *with* and someone who will listen to them as opposed to being told to stop what they are doing (Heslop & Macaulay, 2009). In their study, Heslop and Macaulay reported, "What participants found most helpful was help to change their ways of thinking, not their ways of behaving" (2009, p. 103). Kress and Hoffman (2008) discuss the use of *motivational interviewing* (MI) and the *transtheoretical model* (TTM), also referred to as the stages of change model, in enhancing clients' readiness for change in nonsuicidal self-injuring individuals. The purpose of MI is to increase clients' motivation for change and hopefulness so they will respond favorably to interventions that promote goal attainment. Kress and Hoffman (2008) pose that Miller and Rollnick's (2002) four basic principles for fostering client change in MI (expressing empathy, developing discrepancy, rolling with resistance, and supporting self-efficacy) may be useful in working with individuals who self-injure. They also emphasize that some clients may need more directive intervention to ensure safety and that MI should only be used as an adjunct to evidence-based interventions, such as Dialectical Behavioral Therapy (DBT) for nonsuicidal self-injury. Amanda's service providers used the basic principles for fostering client change in sessions in response to her resistance. At the same time, her service providers and school personnel took her *self-injuring behavior* very seriously to ensure her safety. Hoffman and Kress (2010) provide recommendations for minimizing counselor and client risk while enhancing client care with adolescents who present with nonsuicidal self-injury.

In Amanda's case, while her self-injuring continued, the intensity and frequency decreased over time. Her ability to cope with difficult emotions was improving. By the time of her graduation from high school, her prognosis appeared fairly good. Because she did not display characteristics of significant psychopathology or a personality disorder, such as borderline personality disorder, she had positive social supports in her life, and she demonstrated resiliency, it appeared that Amanda would have the necessary coping skills to pursue her future goals effectively.

Discussion Questions

1. What initial steps should school mental health service professionals take when they learn a student is self-injuring?

2. In Amanda's case, what are some possible functions for her self-injuring?

3. At any point in Amanda's case, what additional interventions could have been considered or tried? Are there other approaches or interventions you might have tried?

4. How much influence would you estimate each of the "common factors" (reference Chapter 9) might have had in Amanda's case? What aspects of counseling might have been most helpful?

5. What are the educational rights of pregnant and parenting teens? (reference state and federal laws)

Part II

Special Topics in School-Based Counseling

Part II examines special topics in school-based counseling, including advancing one's clinical skills in counseling, professional development as a counselor, and emerging models for difficult service delivery areas in school mental health. Chapter 9 focuses on the development of clinical skills for counselors, emphasizing both professional and personal development. We provide a self-evaluation survey for counselors (Resource G) to facilitate self-awareness as a first step to goal setting for a personal and professional growth plan (Resource H). Finally, Chapter 10 addresses difficult service delivery areas (i.e., family support services, medication management, substance-abuse counseling) as well as other important topics—social skills programs, vocational counseling, counseling vulnerable populations, and program development and funding.

9 Developing Clinical Skills

W ith the strong emphasis on evidence-based interventions in research, laws, and professional guidelines, the topic of "common factors" in counseling or psychotherapy is easily neglected. Common factors are the basic processes that all therapies share, such as showing empathy and acceptance to the client, providing support, and developing goals and activities with the expectation of progress. It is recommended that counselors design and implement evidence-based interventions based on quality functional assessments of students' needs. Practitioners should also remember the counselor's ability to establish therapeutic relationships with clients is central to providing effective therapeutic services.

This chapter examines ways school-based mental health professionals can access or utilize common factors and, more broadly, the *sources of change* in therapy. In short, practitioners can accomplish this through developing and advancing their clinical skills. Whether one is a new therapist or experienced, examining and developing one's knowledge base, skills, and use of judgment can promote professional growth and revitalization. One of the main goals of this chapter is to spark self-reflection so counselors can develop their own personal and professional growth plan.

USING EVIDENCE-BASED METHODS AND COMMON FACTORS IN COUNSELING

As we reviewed in Chapter 6, psychological therapy is often effective for many children and adolescents. The "great psychotherapy debate" (see Wampold, 2001) in psychological therapy outcome research poses two different explanations for client change. One side of the debate argues that client change is due primarily to specific methods and techniques (e.g., evidence-based interventions) while the other side attributes client change to common factors that all therapies share. Lambert (2003) proposed four common factors that account for client change and estimated their relative contribution to therapy outcomes: (1) *factors outside of therapy* (e.g., client characteristics and other extratherapeutic factors)—40%, (2) *common factors in therapy* (e.g., common processes and structure shared by most treatments, person-centered facilitative conditions and the therapeutic alliance)—30%, (3) *placebo effect (or hope and expectancy)*—15%, and (4) *specific treatment methods*—15%. Lambert and Barley (2002) offer that the best way to improve psychotherapy is for therapists to learn to improve in their ability to relate to clients.

Rosenfeld (2009), in *Beyond Evidence-Based Psychotherapy: Fostering the Eight Sources of Change in Child and Adolescent Treatment,* proposes eight elements that account for change in psychotherapy based on his review of the research: (1) evidence-based techniques, (2) client characteristics, (3) the therapeutic alliance, (4) therapist characteristics, (5) common processes present in most techniques, (6) extratherapeutic forces (e.g., family, school and community factors), (7) problem-related factors (e.g., severity and intensity of the client's problems), and (8) placebo effects. Rosenfeld states "the therapist's mission is to contribute to fostering change by maximizing the impact of these forces" (p. 13). He further emphasizes that treatment is influenced by the therapist's ability to integrate specific therapy techniques and common factors into the therapist. Regarding this integration, he states "when they are fully incorporated into the therapist, the techniques become effective because they are seen as a spontaneous exposure of the therapist's genuine reaction to the client" (p. 14).

Realistically, the relative contribution of the various factors or sources responsible for client change varies by individual case. Also, there is often an interactive effect between the factors. For example, research indicates that specific methods/techniques can enhance the structure of therapy as well as assist in the development of the client-therapist relationship (Carr, 2009; Hubble, Duncan, & Miller, 1999; Langer, McLeod, & Weisz, 2011; Sprenkle & Blow, 2006; Wampold, 2001). Another example of the interactive effect is when multisystemic treatment approaches (e.g., involving families and schools) help to alleviate a source of problems in one or more settings that enables the client to apply strategies learned in counseling sessions. Or, when a student with ADHD is better able to learn new skills in counseling and apply them in the classroom as a result of psychopharmacological intervention. Overall, the interrelationship between common factors and specific techniques/evidence-based interventions (as well as all the sources of change) can result in increased therapeutic effectiveness (see Figure 9.1).

Throughout this book we have emphasized that school-based counselors who use a collaborative, multisystemic approach can foster change by

Figure 9.1 Specific Methods and Common Factors Work Together

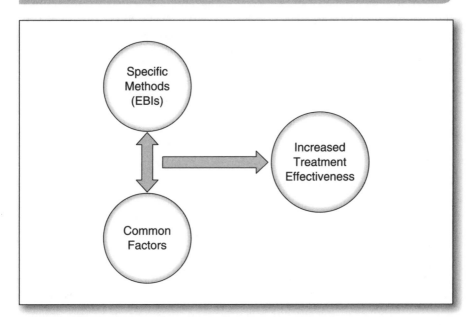

maximizing the positive impact of extratherapeutic forces. This may be accomplished through active participation in RTI, parent and teacher consultation, community partnerships, and providing information to families about programs and resources. The other sources of change, including specific techniques, common factors, the child's characteristics, and the placebo effect, can be maximized by school-based counselors as well. Counselors can maximize the sources of change in therapy when they understand the interactional nature of these forces and can utilize specific therapy techniques and common factors within the individualized context of the child or adolescent. The ability to maximize the sources of change in therapy comes through acquiring knowledge and training, developing one's clinical skills, the natural abilities and background of the therapist, and ongoing personal and professional development and growth.

THE THERAPEUTIC RELATIONSHIP

The therapeutic relationship, also referred to as therapeutic alliance, working alliance, and client-therapist bond, has shown to have moderate to large relationships with treatment outcomes (Gelso & Hayes, 1998; Karver, Handelsman, Fields, & Bickman, 2005; Shirk & Karver, 2003). Other than extratherapeutic factors/client characteristics, the therapeutic relationship is the most predictive force in therapy outcomes. In his classic book, *On Becoming a Person,* Carl Rogers (1961) presented the simple philosophical position that humans require acceptance that leads to growth and *self-actualization.* Rogers presented his Therapeutic Triad, consisting of empathy, warmth (or unconditional positive regard), and genuineness (or congruence), as foundational processes in forming therapeutic relationships with clients. These were not described as techniques counselors apply tactically but rather as processes embodied in the person of the counselor.

Empathy is defined in the *Merriam-Webster Online Dictionary* (2012) as "the action of understanding, being aware of, being sensitive to, and vicariously experiencing the feelings, thoughts, and experience of another of either the past or present without having the feelings, thoughts, and experience fully communicated in an objectively explicit manner." Erskine, Moursund, and Trautmann (1999), in *Beyond Empathy: A Therapy of Contact-in-Relationship,* discuss three aspects of empathy: inquiry, attunement, and involvement. Once again, therapists should be careful not to apply these aspects of empathy in a technical manner, but rather in a natural, authentic way. Inquiry involves asking questions and listening. Effective inquiry necessitates asking questions with a purpose, such as to express interest, draw out, learn about the client's experiences, and facilitate contact enhancement. Erskine and colleagues (1999) explain that effective inquiry brings attention to contact, including internal contact (e.g., what the client is feeling or experiencing), external contact (e.g., what the client is noticing), and client-therapist contact (e.g., what the client is thinking or feeling about the therapist's comments). Inquiry is enhanced by attunement, described by Erskine (1998) as

> *More than just understanding or vicarious introspection, attunement is a kinesthetic and emotional sensing of the other—knowing their rhythm, affect and experience by metaphorically being in their skin, and going beyond empathy to create a two-person experience of unbroken feeling connectedness by providing an reciprocal affect and/or resonating response.* (p. 236)

Then, *involvement* is how the therapist demonstrates emotion and authenticity. Erskine and colleagues (1999) describe four therapeutic activities to demonstrate the aspect of empathetic involvement: acknowledgment (of the client's thoughts, feelings, behaviors, fantasies, and sensations as well as the client-therapist relationship), validation (or giving meaning to the client's experience), normalization (e.g., providing clients reassurance that their thoughts, behaviors, or feelings are not atypical under a set of circumstances), and presence (e.g., the therapist is present in the relationship and is "willing to be known as well as to know, in contact both with the client and with her [the therapist's] own experience") (Erskine, n.d.). *Warmth* (or *unconditional positive regard*) and *genuineness* (or *congruence*) may be viewed as facets or extensions of empathy. For example, both unconditional positive regard and congruence are reflected in Erskine and colleagues' (1999) description of empathetic involvement (see above). Unconditional positive regard is fully accepting clients for who they are despite poor choices they may have made. This acceptance helps build respect and trust with clients. Then, genuineness involves therapists sharing their thoughts and feelings with clients about the therapy process. This entails a sense of "give-and-take" in the therapeutic relationship—being "real," honest, and transparent. Therapists should be careful not to be impulsive or destructive in their attempt at being genuine. In counseling children and adolescents, therapists should work to establish developmentally appropriate therapeutic relationships and boundaries.

ROLE AND FUNCTION OF THERAPIST: THEORETICAL ORIENTATION

The working alliance provides the foundation for therapy. How and to what degree the therapeutic relationship is used as a vehicle for change, though, will vary depending on the goals of counseling, the therapeutic modality, the counselor's style and personality characteristics, and the client's characteristics. For example, both CBT and SFBT advise that a sound therapeutic relationship is necessary for therapy to be effective, though the therapeutic relationship is not the main focus of intervention. Both CBT and SFBT are structured and directive (yet collaborative) approaches based on an educational model. In contrast, in Psychodynamic Interpersonal Therapy (PIT), for example, the therapeutic relationship is the primary process or activity responsible for change. In PIT the therapist utilizes the "here-and-now" experiences within the therapeutic relationship to identify patterns, generate hypotheses, and facilitate reparative experiences.

As we presented in Part I of this book, CBT, SFBT, and psychoeducational approaches are ideal theoretical approaches for school counselors. Each counselor, though, has his or her own unique counseling style and may utilize other theoretical approaches that may be appropriate in school settings. In a survey of school counselors, Frye (2005) found that school counselors preferred activities from a variety of theoretical orientations using an eclectic approach to meet the personal and social needs of students with disabilities. A large portion of school counselors utilize an eclectic/integrative approach suggesting they adapt their role and function as a therapist based on the client's needs. In terms of specific or "pure" therapies, school-based mental health professionals use a variety of approaches with preferences influenced by their specialized training area, including CBT, SFBT, Psychoeducational/Social Skills Training, Supportive Therapy, Narrative Therapy, Adlerian/Play Therapy, and Reality or Choice-Based Therapy.

Teyber and McClure (2011) propose that therapists are more effective when they use a "case formulation" or "case conceptualization" approach that involves exploring various theoretical frameworks. They state, "while core conditions [e.g., empathy, warmth and friendliness] are necessary, they are insufficient—therapists also need to discern more clearly a focus for treatment that clarifies what's really wrong, how this came about, and what needs to be done to change it" (p. 7). Norcross and Beutler (2011) explain that integrative psychotherapies individualize both the therapeutic techniques and relationship stances for each unique client. They discuss five client characteristics integrative psychotherapists assess to guide treatment decisions: (1) diagnosis, (2) stages of change, (3) coping style, (4) reactance level, and (5) patient preferences (see Norcross & Beutler, 2011). Similarly, Lazarus (1976), in his Multimodal Therapy (MMT), developed a comprehensive therapy that assesses and intervenes at multiple dimensions of personality utilizing the acronym BASCID (Behavior, Affect, Sensation, Imagery, Cognition, Interpersonal, and Drugs/Biology). Whether a therapist is integrative or adheres strictly to a specific theoretical orientation, individualizing to the specific needs of the client will enhance the therapeutic alliance.

In this book we have specifically focused on the role of school-based counseling within the PBIS/RTI process. RTI is a collaborative process whereby each stakeholder has a relationship with the student. RTI, particularly in Level 3, also employs a case study approach that facilitates a highly individualized intervention plan implemented by a team holistically. The impact of relationship, then, extends beyond the confines of the "therapeutic relationship" with the professional counselor to include all members who develop a relationship with the student. For example, the student may form a particularly strong bond with a favorite teacher, inclusion teacher, classroom aide, or an administrator. Ideally, the student will develop positive, trusting relationships with all team members. In regard to formal therapy, the therapeutic relationship is foundational. We discuss ways counselors can build strong therapeutic relationships with clients throughout this chapter (see Figure 9.2).

Figure 9.2 Keys to Building Strong Therapeutic Relationships

- Use of Therapeutic Triad (empathy, warmth, and genuineness)
- Friendliness, humor, interpersonal skills
- Provide a therapeutic structure (e.g., clear direction)
- Facilitate positive expectancy
- Use a guiding theoretical model appropriate to context
- Individualize counseling approach based on the client's unique characteristics (e.g., developmental level, cultural background, personality, interests, learning style, preferences, and motivation for therapy)
- Utilize your own personal strengths as a counselor
- Develop improvisational abilities (e.g., apply knowledge flexibly and in the moment)
- Be self-aware and open to feedback
- Attend to your own emotional health as a therapist

USING STRATEGIES AND TECHNIQUES WITHIN THE THERAPEUTIC STRUCTURE AND PROCESS

While each counseling relationship is unique, psychological counseling follows a process that generally applies to all theoretical orientations. For example, Hackney and Cormier (2001) describe the following stages of counseling: (1) rapport and relationship building, (2) assessment/problem definition, (3) goal setting, (4) initiating interventions, and (5) termination. The process and structure of therapy is built on professionalism and ethics. As a part of this, counselors should help clients understand the characteristics, conditions, procedures, and parameters of counseling. Karver, Handelsman, Fields, and Bickman (2006), in a meta-analysis of therapeutic relationship variables, found a weighted mean effect size in the moderate range (.40) for therapist's *direct influence skills* (e.g., active structuring of a session, providing a rationale for a treatment approach, giving specific instructions) on child and adolescent outcomes. By developing a therapeutic structure, the therapist sets the counseling process in motion, establishes appropriate boundaries within the therapist-client relationship, and communicates professional competence to the client. Therapeutic strategies and techniques are used within the therapeutic structure and process. The counselor's case conceptualization, theoretical orientation, and personal approach guides the counselor in selecting appropriate strategies and techniques.

Strategies and Techniques in Therapy

Strategies and techniques are the tools counselors use to influence change. Using a case study approach helps counselors select the right tools for specific clients. Some strategies and techniques are very specialized and applicable to specific child or adolescent concerns (e.g., systematic desensitization, parent-child interaction therapy, eye movement desensitization and reprocessing) and may require specialized training to use them. Other strategies and techniques are general approaches that can be applied across many contexts (e.g., normalizing the client's experience, cognitive reframing, role-playing). Table 9.1 lists common strategies and techniques used in counseling. Specialized treatments often incorporate multiple counseling strategies and techniques into the specialized treatment approach. For example, *Dialectical Behavioral Therapy* (DBT) involves multiple techniques, including self-monitoring, behavioral-chain analysis, developing adaptive methods for coping with negative emotions, guiding clients to experience and tolerate primary emotions without experiencing secondary emotions, and interpersonal skills training. The foundational or basic counseling skills (See Corey, 2009; Egan, 2009), such as active listening, use of body language, use and types of questions, paraphrasing, focusing, reflecting meaning and feeling, structuring, summarizing, recognizing patterns, self-disclosure, immediacy, challenging, goal setting, problem solving, teaching skills, and evaluation, are used throughout all interactions with the client, including in the use of specific strategies and techniques. Effective use of basic counseling skills enhances the potential effectiveness of strategies and techniques implemented by the counselor.

Creativity and Improvisation in Therapy

The creative and improvisational abilities that experienced and skillful therapists display, often referred to as the "art of therapy," is akin to the expertise demonstrated by individuals in other fields, such as a master or professional musician, pilot, chef, or athlete. There is always a combination of experience and natural ability involved when progressing from novice, to experienced, to masterful.

Over time and through practice, therapists can apply their knowledge base with skill and flexibility in the moment. Binder (1993) and others (Bennett-Levy, 2006; Plionis, 2007) discuss types of knowledge (declarative, procedural, and tacit) therapists use in the therapy process. These types of knowledge demonstrate progression of skill and coordination. Ultimately, real-life practice requires applications, adjustments, and readjustments that become "instinctive." First, *declarative knowledge,* or factual information counselors learn (e.g., conceptual understandings and

Table 9.1 Common Counseling Techniques

Counseling Technique	Description of Technique	Theoretical Orientation
Anticipatory Guidance/ Flagging the Minefield	Assist client in identifying potential barriers to goal attainment and developing proactive solutions	Supportive Therapy; SFBT
Bibliotherapy	Use of reading materials (fiction or nonfiction) as an adjunct to or as a part of therapy sessions	Adaptable to theory
Choice-based, reality approach	Deal with current issues; focus on personal responsibility 5 basic needs: power, love, freedom, fun, and survival 3 questions counselors ask to see if clients are meeting their needs: (1) What do you want? (2) What are you doing to get what you want? (3) Is it working?	Reality Therapy
Cognitive Restructuring	Assist client in identifying and correcting negative automatic thoughts; ABCD Model (**A**ctivating Event—**B**elief or Thoughts—**C**onsequences of Feelings and Behaviors—**D**ispute the Irrational Thought); challenge distorted thinking by asking for evidence; consider alternative perspectives	CBT; REBT
Exception to the problem	Have client identify times when the problem behavior is not occurring; encourage client to continue what is working at those times	SFBT; Narrative Therapy
Exposure	Often used with relaxation and guided imagery; gradually exposing clients to something they fear	CBT
Externalizing the problem	Help clients understand they are not the problem, but rather the problem is the problem; put distance between (or separate) the client and the problem	Narrative Therapy
Here-and-now	Focus on the present moment instead of past or future; therapist observes client's body language, verbal and nonverbal behaviors, inconsistencies, therapist's own internal reactions to client-therapist interactions	Gestalt Therapy; Existential and Phenomenological theoretical orientations

(Continued)

Table 9.1 (Continued)

Counseling Technique	Description of Technique	Theoretical Orientation
	Therapist uses "I" messages; therapist shares his/her experiences with client in the here-and-now; client interprets, not therapist; promotion of clients' self-awareness so clients can recognize the choices they can make and how their choices can influence their environment	
Journaling and Logs	Journaling can assist clients in expressing and processing emotions, monitoring emotions, clarifying thoughts and feelings, and problem solving; use of a log to keep track of behaviors, thoughts, or feelings	Adaptable to theory
Mapping the Influences of the Problem	Assist the client in identifying the influence of the problem on the client; assist client in identifying how the client affects the problem; used within the "externalizing the problem" frame	Narrative Therapy
Miracle Question	"Suppose tonight, while you slept, a miracle occurred. When you awake tomorrow, what would be some of the things you would notice that would tell you life had suddenly gotten better?" The question promotes a goal focus and helps the therapist see what the client wants; it helps promote a solution-focused context instead of a problem-focused one	SFBT; Narrative Therapy
Problem Solving	Use of problem-solving methods with client such as the Six-Step Problem Solving Process (Identify the problem, Analyze the problem, Generate possible solutions, Select and plan the solution, Implement the solution, and Evaluate the solution); write down the pros and cons of each potential option	CBT
Reframing	Assisting the client in considering alternative perspectives, explanations, or interpretations of a situation	CBT; Narrative Therapy

Counseling Technique	Description of Technique	Theoretical Orientation
Relaxation	Various relaxation strategies, including deep breathing, visualization, guided imagery, progressive muscle relaxation, distraction (e.g., music, play, games)	Adaptable to theory; holistic health/mind-body
Replacement Behaviors (identifying coping mechanisms)	Replacing maladaptive thoughts or behaviors with positive thoughts or behaviors; brainstorm with client potential replacement behaviors; develop a plan to implement the replacement behaviors	CBT; Psychoeducation
Role Play and Modeling	Enacting a scenario with a client can be useful for practicing social interaction and communication skills, perspective taking, gaining insight, and problem solving; counselors can model new skills through role play	Adaptable to theory
Scaling	Client rates his real or perceived experience, typically on a 0 to 10 scale; used to move past "black and white" thinking, for self-monitoring and awareness, and for communicating degrees of intensity to the therapist	SFBT; CBT
Self-Talk	Assisting the client in identifying negative thought patterns and replacing negative or irrational self-talk with positive self-talk	CBT; REBT
Supportive Approach	Use of sympathetic listening, praise, reassurance, encouragement, education, limit setting, advice, reassurance, and validation	Supportive Therapy

Abbreviations: Cognitive-Behavioral Therapy (CBT), Rational-Emotive Behavioral Therapy (REBT), Solution-Focused Brief Therapy (SFBT)

schemas about human behavior and counseling), is required before the therapy process can be enacted. Then, *procedural knowledge* involves *application* of skills. Regarding the developmental growth and progress of therapists (from novice to experienced), Bennett-Levy (2006) explains "Their knowledge 'chunks' and problem solving strategies become progressively elaborated and refined, and they build a formidable repertoire of representative when-then rules, plans, procedures and skills" (p. 59). Finally, Plionis (2007) describes *tacit knowing* as "automatic and identifies the master clinician" (p. 203). Tacit knowing capabilities allow for improvisation by the therapist. Plionis (2007) states, "Improvisation relies on highly disciplined and automatic procedural knowledge and on a highly self-regulated ability to allow for reflection and adjustment of performance in the therapeutic moment: reflection in action" (p. 203).

Characteristics of Master Therapists

As mentioned above, master therapists are able to apply their vast clinical knowledge automatically and with keen self-regulation in the context of a dynamic therapeutic relationship. Jennings and Skovholt (1999) provide additional insight regarding qualities of master therapists through a qualitative study of 10 peer-nominated therapists who were highly regarded in their practice communities. Each master therapist was nominated by at least four peers in a metropolitan area. All of the peer-nominated therapists worked in full-time private practice and had 21 to 41 years of psychotherapy experience. The theoretical orientations of the therapists varied: psychodynamic ($n = 4$), family systems ($n = 2$), integrative ($n = 2$), and existential-humanistic ($n = 2$). Through a systematic qualitative analysis of recorded interviews nine themes emerged within three major domains: cognitive, emotional, and relational. Within the cognitive domain, results indicate that master therapists are voracious learners, draw extensively from accumulated experience, and value cognitive complexity. Within the emotional domain, master therapists are emotionally receptive and nondefensive, are mentally healthy and mature individuals who attend to their own emotional well-being, and are aware of how their emotional health affects work quality. Finally, within the relational domain, the study shows that master therapists possess strong relationship skills, are experts at using those skills in therapy, and believe that the foundation for therapeutic change is a strong working alliance. It is worth emphasizing that this study identifies *personal qualities* of master therapists more than their technical skills or treatment methods. It reasons that cultivating these kinds of personal qualities can promote growth as a therapist.

COUNSELOR DEVELOPMENT AND GROWTH

Professional development and growth is an ongoing process whether one is new to the field or a seasoned professional. There are countless areas of counselor competency, some of which are general and foundational to all counselors (e.g., basic counseling skills, application of ethical guidelines and principles) and other areas that may be specialized (e.g., working with specific populations, working in special settings, treating specific types of problems, utilizing specific forms of intervention). Demonstration of practice competencies as a counselor involves the integration of knowledge, skill,

Figure 9.3 Integrating the Core Areas of Counselor Competence

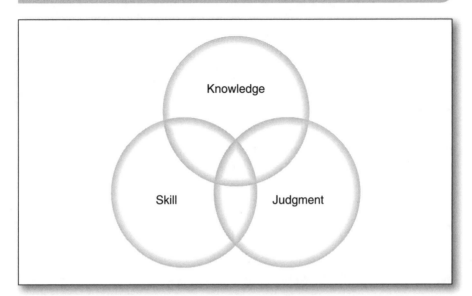

and judgment (see Figure 9.3)—similar to the types of knowledge discussed earlier in this chapter (declarative, procedural, and tacit).

While there may be identifiable characteristics or traits of highly effective therapists, each therapist is a unique individual who brings his or her own mix of strengths and weaknesses. Therapists should build on their natural strengths and resources. They should also seek awareness of any personal weaknesses that may interfere with or impede the therapy process and seek growth in these areas. This requires self-reflection, openness to feedback, courage, and commitment. Pursuit of professional excellence is admirable and will lead to growth. At the same time, therapists should be careful not to judge themselves too harshly as this will only lead to burnout. Professional vitality and growth can be fostered through having a sense of humor, not taking oneself too seriously, having a support network, and actively pursuing interests and activities separate from work.

Self-Awareness as a Counselor

There are various methods counselors may use to increase self-awareness regarding their clinical skills and levels of proficiency, including self-reflection methods (e.g., self-rating instruments, journaling, tracking trends with clients) and receiving feedback from others (e.g., supervisors, professional peers). According to research by Kruger and Dunning (1999), during self-analysis the least skilled counselors tended to greatly overestimate their performance while the most highly skilled counselors slightly underestimated their performance.

As already discussed, master therapists were viewed as being emotionally receptive, open to feedback, nondefensive, and aware of their own emotional health. Self-awareness can empower counselors to build on their strengths as well as identify areas in which they can make improvements.

We have provided a counselor self-evaluation survey (Resource G) to facilitate self-awareness as a first step to goal setting for a personal and professional growth plan. There are numerous roles that school mental health providers fulfill. The self-evaluation survey focuses on the role of therapy or closely related aspects (e.g., consultation in conjunction with therapy to support generalization). Once again, it is important for counselors to recognize and embrace their strengths as these are the areas that they can build on to potentially make the greatest impact.

Developing a Personal and Professional Growth Plan

Professional organizations (e.g., ACA, APA, ASCA, NASP, SSWAA) support professional development and continuing education in order to ensure the most appropriate services are provided to students/clients. Employment settings (e.g., schools) often include individual growth plans for semi-annual/ annual review. We have included a personal and professional growth plan form (Resource H) for school-based mental health professionals (the growth plan form is to be used in conjunction with, and following completion of, the self-evaluation survey). Once again, this growth plan focuses primarily on therapy and related aspects. Also, we emphasize both professional and personal areas of growth because the therapeutic relationship (which is greatly influenced by the *person* of the therapist) is such a crucial source of change in therapy. Many training programs too often focus on teaching professional objectives and neglect the personal formation of counselors. Having said this, it is important to recognize that the training and development of counselors is a developmental process. The needs of beginning therapists who have little experience are not exactly the same as early or mid-career counselors.

Caring for and supporting others can be an emotional drain for mental health professionals, especially when counselors are burdened with limited resources and support. Professional effectiveness and longevity requires ongoing sustenance and self-care.

CONCLUSION

The therapeutic relationship provides the foundation for effective counseling. A well-established therapeutic alliance positions counselors to maximize each of the sources of change in therapy. The development of clinical skills is a process by which therapists become increasingly skillful in applying their clinical knowledge in the moment with clients. Individual therapists have unique qualities and strengths that they can integrate into their clinical practice. By doing so, clients may experience their therapist as genuine and authentic.

Professional growth is an ongoing process. Counseling experience alone does not result in increased expertise and effectiveness. When therapists do not engage in ongoing professional growth opportunities or they neglect their own personal needs, then burn-out, stagnation, and deterioration of service delivery may follow. Pursuing professional growth opportunities and attending to one's own personal needs can result in increased competence, vitality, and effectiveness.

DISCUSSION QUESTIONS

1. How do "common factors" and evidence-based methods work together in counseling?

2. Which sources of change have the greatest impact on therapy outcomes? What are the implications for counselors?

3. Explain therapeutic structure and process.

4. What is your primary theoretical orientation to counseling? Why? Explain your theoretical orientation.

5. What are some characteristics of a "master therapist"?

6. What methods (e.g., learning style, formats) for professional growth and development are most beneficial for you?

10 Special Topics in School-Based Counseling

We have described how responsive school-based counseling fits within an integrative mental health framework to promote students' optimal school functioning. Research is bearing out the benefits of responsive counseling in schools, especially within a collaborative, integrative framework. PBIS and RTI are guiding models for providing comprehensive and integrative mental health services in schools. A school's culture and climate, which includes responsiveness to the varied needs of students, families, and the school, is the engine that drives effective service delivery.

Within the realm of mental health in schools, there is a wide range of mental health concerns that impact students' educational progress, including internalizing and externalizing problems related to neurobiological and/or environmental factors, concomitant learning and social-emotional problems, ADHD, developmental disabilities, social problems, family problems, substance abuse, eating disorders, concerns about gender or sexuality, physical or sexual abuse, delinquency and gang-related behaviors, homicidal or suicidal behaviors, and major psychiatric conditions. As pointed out in Chapter 1, Foster et al. (2005) found that the greatest mental health concern as ranked by schools was social, interpersonal, or family problems. The study also found that family support services, medication management, and substance abuse counseling were ranked as the most difficult services to deliver in schools. In this concluding chapter we discuss best practices and emerging models for addressing these difficult service delivery areas (e.g., family support services, medication management, substance abuse counseling) as well as other important topics—social skills programs, vocational counseling, counseling vulnerable populations, and program development and funding.

Research is showing us that schools can improve mental health service delivery by implementing comprehensive, multifaceted approaches. The specific pieces and processes used to successfully develop integrated school mental health services will vary based upon the unique contexts of schools and communities.

BEST PRACTICES AND EMERGING MODELS FOR DIFFICULT SERVICE DELIVERY AREAS

Family Support Services

Family support is a crucial component in addressing children's mental health, but it has shown to be a difficult service to deliver in schools. Multiple barriers contribute to the difficulty of delivering family support services effectively, including families' financial constraints and lack of insurance, transportation barriers, lack of time, language barriers, insufficient school and community-based resources, stigma surrounding mental health issues, poor school-family relationships, lack of trained school staff, lack of communication and organizational structure, minimal administrative support, and disagreement about goals and responsibilities (Christenson, Whitehouse, & VanGetson, 2008; Foster et al., 2005). While these barriers can be formidable, there is a movement toward increased school-family partnerships. Innovative models of family support services in schools are showing promise in helping to overcome the barriers to effective service delivery.

Christenson and colleagues (2008) recommend that schools organize mental health services for the child/family system at the universal, selected, and indicated levels (Levels 1–3). As an example of this, the Oregon Research Institute is currently conducting an effectiveness trial of EcoFIT (an evidence-based model that emphasizes service delivery to parents of high-risk students, a primarily Level 3 intervention) integrated with PBIS (systems for positive behavioral management at Levels 1–3) (Child and Family Center, n.d.; Institute of Educational Sciences, n.d.; Positive Family Support, n.d.). In the EcoFIT/PBIS study, Level 1 involves schools creating a family resource center and providing parents information about the school's expectations as well as specific information about their child's social, emotional, and academic adjustment to the school context. In Level 2 interventions, parents receive daily and/or weekly data on their child's attendance, completion of academic tasks, and behavior. The Oregon Research Institute identified *Check-In/Check-Out* (a behavior education program) as an example of a Level 2 intervention that can be utilized in the EcoFIT/PBIS model. Horner and colleagues (2012) provide a PowerPoint presentation of *Check-In/Check-Out* at the following URL: http://www

.pbis.org/common/pbisresources/presentations/BEP_CICO_Anne.ppt. For students who require additional support at Level 3, *Family Check-Up* (FCU; the primary component of EcoFIT) is used to assess support needs. According to the Child and Family Center (n.d.), in the EcoFIT/PBIS study, FCU "has been revised to focus more exclusively on parental monitoring of their student's adjustment at school and of their peer group, and specific parenting practices relevant to those outcomes" (para. 1). Schools then identify available support services to complement the FCU intervention to support families. Research updates and training opportunities in using EcoFIT can be found at the University of Oregon's Child and Family Center web site (http://cfc.uoregon.edu/index.htm).

Another family support model, the School-Based Child & Family Support Teams (CFST) program, has been implemented in participating North Carolina schools through a state initiative (Center for Child and Family Policy, n.d.; North Carolina Department of Health and Human Services, n.d.). In CFST, the school nurse and social worker take the lead in working with parents, school staff, and local agencies in identifying students who need assistance. Any student who is having trouble passing school or living in his or her home is eligible to participate. The nurse and social worker work with the parent to identify others who may help the child and family access helpful resources (e.g., extended family members, friends, neighbors, mental health professionals, and/or individuals from community agencies). These individuals comprise the Child and Family Team that meets regularly to develop and update plans for the student and family. CFST is currently being evaluated by Duke University's Center for Child and Family Policy (see the center's website [http://www.childandfamilypolicy.duke.edu/] for further information about CFST and research findings). Early study results show that the CFST program is working for high-risk families.

EcoFIT/PBIS and CFST are both collaborative, integrative models for delivering family support services in schools. While programs such as these will not completely alleviate all the barriers to family support services, they show potential in making significant improvements. For example, systematic programs can help clarify roles and streamline effective communication, schools can receive training in implementing well-developed, evidence-based programs, and schools and communities can identify strategies to overcome significant barriers to effective service delivery for families (e.g., the CFST program utilizes home visits that helps reduce transportation and financial barriers for some families).

There are a variety of niche programs and services that schools can implement to support the child/family system across Levels 1–3 within the overall PBIS framework. Examples include programs for parents (e.g., parenting and health workshops, literacy training, resource assistance), home notes, newsletters, websites for parents, support for PTA/PTO, volunteer programs for parents, home-school prevention programs, after-school and summer programs, parent training, and family counseling. For further information about schools partnering with families visit the U.S. Department of Education's Family Involvement Partnership for Learning website (http://www2.ed.gov/parents/academic/help/partnership.html). To be most efficient and effective, schools will offer interventions and programs, such as family support services, within an integrated system of care.

Adelman and Taylor (2010) address the school's role in transitions and transformations in the delivery of mental health services. They advocate for a broadened perspective that "embeds mental health into a continuum of systematically interconnected school and community interventions" (p. 75), and they provide strategies for embedding mental health in school improvement that are beyond the scope of this book. They further emphasize the importance of mapping, resource analysis, gap analyses, and setting priorities as "basic processes in transforming systems" (p. 79). There are several examples of school districts and communities that are taking the lead in integrating schools and broader community mental health systems. For example, the *Berkeley Integrated Resources Initiative* (BIRI), involving a partnership between the Berkeley Unified School District, the City of Berkeley, the University of California at Berkeley, and the broader community, adopted the *Comprehensive Systemic Intervention Framework* developed by Drs. Adelman and Taylor of the UCLA Center for Mental Health in Schools (Schear & Warhuus, January 2007). Another example is the *Integrated Mental Health Services in the Schools* project, a collaborative effort between Alegent Health and Omaha Public Schools (Innovative Programs, n.d.).

Medication Management in Schools

There is a demand currently for greater involvement of schools in addressing the needs of students who are prescribed with psychotropic medications (i.e., medications that affect the central nervous system). Recognizing the safety risks in prescribing to children, Kubiszyn (1994) was the first to identify appropriately trained school psychologists as ideal candidates to undertake leadership roles in working with students, families, school staff, and prescribing physicians in matters regarding medication management in the school setting. However, there is limited literature that clearly delineates the medication-related roles in which school psychologists are needed to undertake, and even less that examines the involvement of school counselors.

The need for clearly defined medication-related roles for school-based practitioners is apparent as nearly all school psychologists have *at least* one student prescribed with psychotropic medication on their caseload (Carlson, Demaray, & Hunter-Oehmke, 2006). Moreover, practicing school psychologists report that roughly one-fourth (23%) of students on their caseloads are prescribed with a psychotropic medication (Shahidullah & Carlson, 2013). Given the adverse effects that these drugs can have on school performance (Kubiszyn, 2011), school psychologists are needed to work effectively with these students to achieve positive school outcomes. Also, school counselors who have at least a basic knowledge of the uses of psychotropic medication will likely "be better equipped to handle diverse client problems and more able to make appropriate medication referrals when necessary (Ponterotto, 1985; p. 114).

The scope of school practitioners' roles related to working with students prescribed with medication depends on the standards of practice for the jurisdictions in which they work (McGrath et al., 2011). Legislation prohibiting the discussion of medication by school personnel has been passed in several states, resulting in the need for practitioners to be particularly cautious within their consultation with families and their physicians (McGrath et al., 2011). Though school practitioners will not likely undertake active roles in treatment decision making, they are needed to undertake critical support roles by ensuring that students' cognitive, emotional, and behavioral concerns are met in a safe and effective manner. The data-based problem-solving model introduced in Chapter 3 serves as a framework, whereby decisions regarding the school-based management of medications can be made.

A role that counselors and school psychologists, as members of an IEP or RTI team, may be in a position to undertake is that of coordinating with agencies outside the school setting to establish a system of collaborative care. Specifically, school psychologists can identify behaviors that may be appropriate for intervention and share data with the school-based intervention and/or RTI team that may assist a parent or caretaker in referring their child to a medical professional. By contributing relevant cognitive, emotional, and behavioral functioning assessment data from within and outside the classroom, these practitioners can provide necessary information a parent may need in making the appropriate referral. School psychologists and counselors may be needed to identify key community resources that offer psychological, psychiatric, or medical support to children and adolescents. These are important roles as it is often difficult, particularly within poor urban and rural settings, to gain access to quality mental health service (Goldman, 2009). With the "severe maldistribution" of child and adolescent psychiatrists in low-income areas, where access is significantly reduced (Kim, 2003), and the overall shortage of pediatric psychiatrists in general (Thomas & Holzer, 2006), students in need of pharmacotherapy may find it difficult to locate a provider. Students from low-income families, especially, are likely to become reliant on the school to locate quality health care service providers, such as school-based health clinics. School-based health clinic services may be more accessible to students and their families than traditional community-based health clinics as their services typically provide comprehensive and collaborative support that link with the services a student already receives at school (Rappaport, 2001).

Roberts, Floress, and Ellis (2009) recognize that once a student is seeing a physician, whether in a school- or community-based health clinic, school psychologists can work within a consultative capacity to ensure the appropriateness, safety, and transportability of a medication treatment into the school setting. These authors specifically demonstrated how the behavioral consultation model (Kratochwill & Bergan, 1990) can be used to evaluate the effect of psychotropic medication within a problem-solving approach. Further, medication monitoring protocols (e.g., School-Based Medication Evaluation Program [SBME]; Gadow, 1993; Methylphenidate Placebo Protocol; Hyman et al., 1998; The Agile Consultative Model for Medication Evaluation [ACMME]; Volpe, Heick, & Gureasko-Moore, 2005) may be utilized within the framework of Kratochwill and Bergan's (1990) problem-solving model. Using this model of evaluation, school psychologists can offer empirical support to prescribing physicians to inform treatment decision making. School psychologists' training in data-based decision making, intervention, and program evaluation make this an ideal role for them to undertake (Roberts et al., 2009).

In an article recognizing the impact that psychotropic medication can have on children and their school performance, DuPaul and Carlson (2005) identified school psychologists as key facilitators of enhanced communication and collaboration between families, school staff, and physicians. These authors showed that appropriately trained school psychologists can help families and physicians make informed decisions regarding medication as a treatment option by being an information resource regarding the child's social-emotional, behavioral, and academic functioning across an array of settings. Due to the difficulty in observing students within the school setting, physicians acknowledge the usefulness of receiving a short summary (one to three paragraphs) of relevant diagnostic information followed by a more detailed psychoeducational report from school personnel when consulting with students diagnosed with attention deficit/hyperactivity disorder (ADHD) (HaileMariam, Bradley-Johnson, & Johnson, 2002). This information provided by school psychologists is helpful in developing the least restrictive treatment plan.

Once a medication regimen has begun, DuPaul and Carlson (2005) recognized the roles that school psychologists can undertake in monitoring and evaluating treatment effects through record reviews, clinical interviews, direct observation, behavior rating scales, and school-based medication-evaluation protocols. Using these monitoring and evaluation procedures, periodic progress updates can be provided to physicians for potential medication titration, change, or discontinuation. School psychologists and counselors can also help ensure that long-term progress is sustained by providing school-based psychosocial interventions as adjuncts to pharmacotherapy (DuPaul & Carlson, 2005). This emphasis on the use of psychosocial and combined interventions as evidence-based child treatments is also supported by the American Psychological Association (2006). School psychologists and counselors appear to be in the best position to provide these therapeutic supports in the form of Cognitive-Behavioral Therapy, motivational interviewing, behavioral management instruction, social skills training, and family support groups. Shahidullah and Carlson (2012) recognized that these sessions provide ideal avenues to identify and address any psychosocial issues affecting medication treatment adherence and compliance, and to monitor for adverse effects and/or contraindications.

Substance Abuse Counseling

The abuse of illicit substances such as alcohol, tobacco, marijuana, and amphetamines by adolescents is a major concern. Because these practices directly affect a student's learning and education, it is important that not only prevention but also intervention efforts occur within the school setting, where they can be intertwined within the PBIS framework. A major goal of PBIS is to provide early evidence-based supports to prevent later negative outcomes, such as substance abuse. These PBIS supports provide knowledge and information, affective education, and behavioral skills training to offer youth an awareness of the obstacles they may face and equip them with the inter- and intra-personal skills needed to overcome those obstacles. However, given the myriad risk (biological, psychological, and environmental) and causal factors for substance abuse, it is unlikely for all students to respond to these supports. Therefore, many school counselors and school psychologists will encounter youth who struggle with dependence and risky and/or destructive behaviors that stem from substance abuse.

Though a school psychologist, school counselor, or school drug counselor may be trained to work with students with problems related to drug use, a multidisciplinary team approach is recommended. A common approach that has been traditionally used within schools is the use of *Chemical Assessment Referral and Education* (CARE) teams (Gonet, 1994). These teams play pivotal roles in identifying students at risk by evaluating assessment and screener results and communicating frequently with school staff who work regularly with the students. CARE teams often implement school and districtwide prevention programs, and coordinate intervention and treatment services. Also, they organize and facilitate family and teacher training on recognizing the signs of potential substance abuse. A comprehensive assessment of the severity of risk for drug problems includes factors such as social, emotional, behavioral, interpersonal, and learning problems; medical concerns; family history; and home life. A CARE team approach provides a better chance of identifying problems early through the use of a comprehensive case-finding method. These assessment practices occur as part of the primary prevention focus of PBIS.

Primary Prevention

An effective PBIS system establishes a schoolwide drug and discipline policy as part of its expectations and rules. Comprehensive support is provided to help students meet these expectations and prevent problem behaviors, such as drug abuse. Examples of universal drug prevention programs include *Project Alert* (Ellickson, Bell, & Harrison, 1993) and *Project Star* (Pentz, Cormack, Flay, Hansen, & Johnson, 1986), which are designed to reduce the onset and regular use of drugs among youth and foster an awareness of the social influences on the temptation to use drugs. Other types of support include social skills training, such as "assertiveness training or the ability to say no in a variety of different ways, the ability to analyze pressure techniques from media and peers, and decision-making skills" (Gonet, 1994, p. 81). Methods for positive coping, such as stress reduction and anger management techniques, are also taught, modeled, and practiced. These support programs are typically incorporated within the school curriculum and offered in conjunction with health, physical education, science, or other relevant coursework.

Another component of an effective PBIS system is providing training and support to teachers and school staff on how to look for and recognize those students who may need additional and more intensive prevention support. Teachers may be the best personnel to identify students who may be at risk. They typically spend the most time with students and can recognize when students show deviations in their learning and behavioral performance. By identifying atypical student behavior and negative performance trends they can refer the student to the appropriate support personnel. As part of RTI or CARE teams, school counselors and school psychologists can intervene and provide support at the secondary level to prevent more serious drug use patterns or drug-related problems from developing.

Secondary Prevention

According to Gonet (1994), "secondary prevention is using an intervention to identify and work with individuals who are exhibiting high-risk behaviors for involvement with alcohol and other drugs, for using alcohol and other drugs, or for getting in trouble with their drug use" (p. 89). Once a student has been referred to an RTI or CARE team, further assessment is conducted to examine the magnitude and scope of the concerns. Along with other assessment protocols (e.g., behavioral checklists; substance abuse problem checklists; direct observation; student, family, and school staff interviews; academic, school discipline, and attendance records), an FBA is conducted to identify and address causal or antecedent factors that predict substance abuse. This evaluation data help determine if a student's altered or maladaptive behaviors are drug related and if so, the severity of those behaviors in order for the appropriate supports to be provided. Gonet (1994) identifies counseling (e.g., motivation counseling, group counseling, and/or crisis intervention) as a critical school-based early intervention method.

Secondary school-based drug abuse prevention programs (e.g., *Coping Power Program;* Lochman & Wells, 1996) provide students with the opportunity to look objectively at how their drug use is affecting themselves and others, understand the negative consequences of drug use, and identify alternatives to drug use. Students who are unresponsive to these supports are referred to the appropriate community agencies for more individualized and intensive support. Typically these services are provided within alternative school settings such as residential school programs or outside the school setting such as outpatient and day treatment facilities or inpatient treatment facilities.

Tertiary Prevention

Tertiary prevention involves reducing risks and providing support to students with a substance dependency in order for them to manage behaviors for a successful re-entry into school. Two support programs specifically designed for use at the tertiary level are *Project Towards No Drug Abuse* (Project TND; Sussman, Dent, & Stacy, 2002) and the *Reconnecting Youth Program* (RY; Eggert, Nicholas, & Owen, 2004). These programs focus on developmental issues that adolescents face and reducing drug use through better management of their emotions and moods. They aim to reduce current substance abuse, but typically do not utilize a direct treatment approach that other substance abuse counseling methods may use.

Substance abuse counseling often utilizes directive empowerment approaches that increase a client's intrinsic motivation for change. A common approach is *motivational interviewing* (MI), which is defined as "a goal-directed, client-centered counseling style for eliciting behavior change by helping clients to explore and resolve ambivalence" (SAMHSA's National Registry of Evidence-based Programs and Practices, 2007, para. 1). This approach is commonly used by school counselors due to its relatively brief and solution-focused nature that contributes to its cost and time effectiveness (Wood & Hinkelman, 2008). However, due to either a lack of trained school-based personnel, time restrictions, or the severity of a student's substance abuse behavior, this treatment often occurs outside the school setting.

In these cases, school counselors and school psychologists will not be involved within the direct treatment of the chemical dependency, but rather, will play vital roles in support. According to Gonet (1994), these support roles include: (1) making referrals for chemical dependency assessments, (2), educating students and their parents about the disease of addiction, (3) educating students and their parents about treatment and how to select a treatment program, (4) helping ease the transition from treatment back to the school environment, (5) supporting and reinforcing a student's recovery program, and (6) providing relapse prevention. Providing these support services often places school counselors and school psychologists as the liaison between the treatment agency, the school, and the student's family. Collaborating and coordinating efforts amongst these stakeholders highlights the importance in approaching a student's treatment from a broader systemic perspective.

For examples of research-based drug abuse prevention programs that can be implemented at the universal, secondary, and tertiary levels of a school's PBIS system, visit the National Institutes of Health, National Institute of Drug Abuse (NIDA) at www.drugabuse.gov/publications/preventing-drug-abuse-among-children-adolescents. Also, to view SAMHSA's searchable online registry of more than 160 interventions supporting mental health promotion, substance abuse prevention, and mental health and substance abuse treatment, visit the National Registry of Effective Programs and Practices at www.nrepp.samhsa.gov/.

OTHER IMPORTANT TOPICS IN SCHOOL-BASED COUNSELING

Social Skills Programs

Along with family problems, social and interpersonal problems were the greatest mental health problems ranked by schools in the 2005 SAMHSA study (Foster et al., 2005). The promotion and development of students' social skills is a major emphasis of school-based counseling within Levels 1–3 of PBIS. Social skills interventions and programs may target specific skills (e.g., taking turns in conversations), a specific area (e.g., conflict resolution skills), or the various dimensions of social skills (e.g., peer relational skills, self-management skills, academic skills, compliance skills, and assertion skills; see Gresham, Sugai, & Horner, 2001). Some students experience unique social challenges related to a disability such as ADHD or an autism spectrum disorder. For example, children with ADHD may have trouble with talking out or interrupting others, taking turns, and picking up social cues.

Children with an autism spectrum disorder may have trouble with joint attention, using and understanding nonverbal communication, initiating and maintaining conversations, understanding nonliteral language, expressing interest in others, and perspective taking. Social skills interventions and programs should be developed to meet the specific needs of a population, subgroups, and individuals. Across Levels 1–3 there are various types of interventions that can be used to teach and promote social skills, including schoolwide social and emotional learning programs, teaching and reinforcing cooperative learning skills in the classroom, leadership and social skills clubs, use of peer models (e.g., peer buddy programs, peer-mediated social skills training), applied behavioral analysis (ABA), social skills groups, role playing, social scripts, social stories, comic strip conversations, video modeling, movie making, and computer-based programs. There are many examples of innovative community and school-based programs designed to enhance students' social skills. It is important to emphasize the generalization of social skills by supporting the student in practicing these skills in his or her natural settings through re-teaching, modeling, practicing, and reinforcing the targeted social skills.

The first large-scale meta-analysis of universal (Level 1) school programs that enhance students' social and emotional development found that students in these programs showed significant improvement in their social and emotional skills, caring attitudes, and positive social behaviors and declines in disruptive behavior and emotional distress compared to students in control groups (Durlak et al., 2011). Meta-analytic research indicates that certain types of social skills training results in larger treatment effects for students in general education than for students who receive special education services (Kavale & Forness, 1999). More recently, a review of studies between 2001 and 2008 of different treatments for social deficits of individuals of autism found that social skills groups and video modeling met the criteria to be classified as established and promising EBPs, respectively (Reichow & Volkmar, 2010). Clinicians are increasingly relied upon to provide social skill support for students with high-functioning autism due to the increased recognition of this disability and the greater emphasis on inclusion (White, Keonig, & Scahill, 2007). In working with students with high-functioning autism, Winner (2010) suggests that practitioners prioritize teaching nuanced social skills because students with high-functioning autism who appear "neurotypical" or normal will be held to higher expectations for their social behaviors compared to those who are more obviously socially impaired. She also points out the greater risk of mental health challenges for students with social skills deficits who have higher levels of social awareness. Practitioners should be attuned to students' emotional reactions to their own social skill deficits as this can inform intervention planning.

Vocational Counseling

For many students, the transition from high school to post-school life is challenging. This task is even more difficult for those students who struggled to meet the day-to-day expectations of their high school environment, particularly those with disabilities. Fortunately, many schools will have a Transition Services program to assist students with disabilities (and those considered to be "at risk" of dropping out of school) and their families with the transition to their post-school life. These services include, but are not limited to, support in pursuing post-secondary education, vocational training, employment, integrated employment (including supported employment), independent living, and community participation. They typically begin toward the end of middle school and include the use of a *Transition IEP* to delineate which services will be provided by the school in order for the student to meet established goals and objectives for post-school outcomes.

Typically, the personnel that work within a transition services team include vocational specialists, vocational education instructors, transition specialists, rehabilitation counselors, general and special education teachers, educational diagnosticians, administrators, county case managers, and other community liaisons. The role that school counselors and school psychologists play in these transition services teams is dependent on the specific needs of the district and competencies of other personnel involved. However, given their expertise in learning and behavior theory and adolescent psychology and development, school counselors and school psychologists are, undoubtedly, excellent candidates to play collaborative roles in these vocational programs (Levinson, 1993). Levinson (2008) posits their roles as contributors to a transition services team as a best practice approach.

Similar to other support programs a school may offer, a student's post-school intentions may best be guided through the development of goals and objectives. By clearly delineating post-school plans, measurable transition goals and objectives serve as benchmarks to ensure that appropriate supports are provided. By linking goals and objectives with vocational aspirations, students are more likely to be invested in the process of skill development. As with any type of planning activity, outcome efficacy is best assured through the use of data to guide decision making and monitor progress. Like other skill development practices discussed throughout this book, the first and most critical step involved in planning a vocational counseling program is *assessment* (Levinson, 2004). Again, this is where school psychologists' expertise in measurement and program evaluation and school counselors' expertise in vocational assessment can be a valuable resource to the transition services team.

Assessment should be *multimodal,* directly linked with social outcomes, and, ideally, fit within a larger service delivery system (Levinson, 2008). The role of school psychologists and counselors is to identify the skills a student currently has and what skills they need in order to look for, obtain, and maintain a job. A number of assessment tools might be used, such as career interest inventories and occupational aptitude assessments. This assessment data can be paired with data already obtained from psychoeducational evaluations (e.g., intellectual ability, academic achievement, adaptive behavior functioning, personality and social skills assessments) to develop a comprehensive school-to-work transition plan (Levinson, 2004). School counselors and school psychologists may be relied upon to plan transition supports, carry them out, or provide consultative support to those that do.

As not all schools have a vocational planning program established, some school psychologists and counselors may be relied upon to incorporate components of vocational counseling within their preexisting counseling practices (Levinson, 2008). These personnel can implement either group or individualized training focused on employability (e.g., self-determination and self-advocacy) skills. They can provide vocational guidance by helping students develop timelines and tasks lists for the job search process. Also, they can facilitate social skills development through mock interviews and role play.

Typically, students who school psychologists, in particular, will work extensively with are those who present with more severe needs (e.g., intellectual disabilities, learning disabilities, and emotional impairments). The needs of these students typically require the school psychologist's involvement in planning for extended school services, transition to postsecondary training, or living supports. A student's needs may be addressed through a functional assessment where their work characteristics are identified so that the intensity of support services can be specified. School psychologists are trained to administer a number of adaptive behavior assessments (e.g., *AAMR Adaptive Behavior Scales* [ABS]; *Inventory for Client and Agency Planning* [ICAP]; *Scales of Independent Behavior–Revised* [SIB–R]; *Vineland Adaptive Behavior Scales*), which are important in post-school vocational planning for developmentally disabled youth or those with more severe needs. These adaptive behavior assessments can be used to identify obstacles to a student's ability to obtain and maintain employment. For students with more debilitating disabilities, the goal of vocational assessments is to delineate suitable job tasks within real work environments in the community. Goals and objectives can be developed with these students that focus on developing both socially and vocationally relevant skills.

For those school psychologists and counselors that find it difficult to take on direct vocational counseling responsibilities in addition to their current counseling caseload, they may be expected to serve in a consultative capacity to other personnel (e.g., transition services team, case managers, career center staff, guidance staff) (Levinson, 1993). They can interpret the results of comprehensive vocational assessments to guide in career planning and goal setting. They can work closely with teachers and the transition services team in developing academic and vocational IEPs and in identifying and establishing connections with local, state, and federal post-education transition agencies (e.g., Department of Assistive and Rehabilitation Services [DARS]; Department of Vocational Rehabilitation [DVR]; Office of Vocational and Adult Education [OVAE]). Also, they may be relied upon to communicate with the families of those students that they have existing working relationships with through previous correspondence within counseling, consultation, referral, and/or other IEP meetings. Also, an essential component in establishing the sustainability of any school-based program is evaluating outcomes to ensure that the practices were effective. School counselors and school psychologists may be needed to develop program assessment tools and methods to evaluate whether or not students successfully met their goals as delineated within their Transition IEP. Annual review meetings or other school staff/parent conferences are great places for results of these assessments to be shared and discussed.

Counseling Vulnerable Populations

The counseling relationship is built on a foundation of strong communication, trust, and commitment. A subset of the student population may be particularly vulnerable when it comes to receiving mental health services in the schools. These include students who are under great duress in terms of their living situation and financial circumstances (i.e., homeless), students who must be in counseling as a result of a decision handed down in the juvenile justice system, students who are English Language Learners (ELL) or struggling to adapt to the majority culture/language, or students with a history of being physically/sexually abused who may have a serious mistrust of adults in general.

Homeless Youth

Homelessness affects large numbers of children in the United States, as estimates put the number of youth age 18 and younger who live in emergency and transitional shelters at roughly 44,000 (Smith & Smith, 2001). A number of issues are important for counselors to keep in mind when providing services to youth who are from unstable homes or those experiencing serious financial strain. Counselors may need to be especially aware of a student's need to have her or his own space within the school setting or a strong affinity for boundaries to help cope with the uncertainty and lack of routine associated with homelessness. The importance of academic and peer functioning are especially challenged in youth who are working to get their basic needs met and have trouble finding the time to be engaged in their studies outside of school. Peer relationships are especially important to assess, as this typical level of social support may be truly missing within the life of a child who is living with uncertainty surrounding their neighborhood or community of residence. For information and resource support to assist homeless youth, refer to the National Coalition for the Homeless website (http://www.nationalhomeless.org/factsheets/youth.html).

Court-Appointed Counseling

No one likes to be forced into doing something. Free will and choice are essential to one's feelings of self-worth and competence. Such choice and decision making are also important to building a meaningful relationship with someone. Youth who are prescribed counseling as a part of the juvenile justice system present with a number of barriers to effective service delivery. Creating important connections with these youth, recognizing how you as their counselor will impact their status in the juvenile justice system, and working collaboratively with those adults and individuals that are key players within this referral source are key to building a solid relationship from which counseling interventions may be implemented effectively. Walters, Clark, Gingerich, and Meltzer (2007), through funding from the National Institutes of Correction, published a thorough guide entitled *A Guide for Probation and Parole: Motivating Offenders to Change,* that describes use of *motivational interviewing* as an intervention with this population (see http://static.nicic.gov/Library/022253.pdf).

Youth Who Are ELL

Communication is essential within the counseling relationship. Children and adolescents who have a lack of familiarity or who lack the skills to speak and understand English require considerable adaptations within the counseling process. Working to secure informed consent is especially important to consider when working with ELL students. Special consideration of how to elicit treatment preferences, how to accurately understand the student's particular concern, how to ensure that interventions are being carried out as intended, and how to get problems resolved is needed. An interpreter and translation of documents that are important to providing counseling services must be in place. Working with a family member or peer who can help to break down the communication barriers is essential. See the NEA website (http://www.nea.org/home/32346.htm) for further information about ELL.

Youth With a History of Abuse

Trust is essential for the counseling relationship. Students who have reasons to mistrust adults or those in authority may present with unique needs within the counseling relationship. Counselors must recognize the deeply personal and individual response that a student may demonstrate as a result of previous trauma. Identifying emotions, behaviors, and cognitions that may arise as a result of that history is important within the counseling relationship. Equally important is understanding the physiological and biological symptoms that may correspond with the psychological harm caused by such a history. In some cases, it may be too difficult for a child to be ready for counseling, and instead supportive services or building a relationship will need to be the primary focus of the counselor. Prevent Child Abuse America (http://member.preventchildabuse.org/site/PageServer?pagename=adv_ main) has further information about prevention and treating child abuse.

Program Development and Funding

The current state of research pertaining to child and adolescent mental health interventions has provided considerable guidance to practitioners. Yet, this knowledge base has only recently emerged in the past few decades, and issues of implementation and dissemination often serve as significant barriers to widespread use of interventions that have been determined to be effective through rigorous research methodologies. Those providing counseling services in schools can actively participate in the field's need for further knowledge generation through program development and through seeking funding to bring evidence-based treatments into their districts.

Program development can best be understood within the process of a logic model. The first step is to accurately understand the mental health needs within your district. This includes examining both the assets and weaknesses of existing services and the challenges or problems in need of change. Important stakeholders and necessary collaborations are also important to identify within this process. Specific inputs or resources necessary to address the need and missing services are essential to identifying reasonable outputs or goals to address within the district. This includes both short- and long-term goals associated with the program under development. When developing programs or adopting evidence-based interventions for use within your district, the field of implementation science has much to offer with respect to providing guidance for successfully carrying out these efforts (Fixsen, Naoom, Blase, Friedman, & Wallace, 2005). For example, program development efforts must be thought of within a deliberate two- to four-year window of time, if they are reasonably expected to be sustained across time. Moreover, six stages of implementation should receive attention within any data-based approach to program development, including (1) exploring the adoption or replication of an evidence-based intervention; (2) preparing for the implementation to begin within the district; (3) attending to the key variables within early implementation including training, ensuring organizational supports, and setting a structure that facilitates frequent problem solving around implementation barriers; (4) ensuring that implementation is happening in a manner that is expected and that processes become routine and integrated into existing practices; (5) sustaining the new intervention through additional training and seeking funding to support the program in future years; and (6) testing innovations and improvements once the new intervention is being carried out as intended.

Program development requires considerable time, attention, collaboration, and persistence. Making changes to school-based mental health services and adopting new practices or programs can pose significant barriers given the resources and training necessary for these efforts. Multiple system-level supports should be examined to obtain the funding that may be necessary to put good ideas into action. Local, state, and national initiatives can be targeted for start-up or full implementation grant support. Collaborating with other agencies or institutions such as universities may provide a successful route toward acquiring the resources necessary to support program development and/or implementation in your district. Numerous federal agencies support the implementation of evidence-based practices, including the Institute for Educational Sciences, the Office of Special Education Programs, the National Institute of Mental Health, and Office of Juvenile Justice and Delinquency Prevention, to name a few. State-level (e.g., the Early Childhood Investment Corporation in Michigan supported early mental health consultation practices in early childhood classrooms across the state) and local-level grant supports may also be sought (e.g., the Michigan State University Extension Program Development Fund Grant supported the county-level implementation of the Incredible Years).

CONCLUSION

School mental health professionals fill an important role in educating today's youth. These professionals may serve in a variety of capacities, including providing responsive counseling services for students who require additional support to overcome barriers to their academic and/or social progress in school. In this book we have focused specifically on the role of responsive school-based counseling within the framework of PBIS/RTI. There is a growing body of research demonstrating the benefits of school-based counseling within Levels 1–3. Furthermore, research supports the implementation of integrative, collaborative systems of care in schools and communities. For information regarding research and decision-making guidance in developing and supporting school mental health systems of care, learn about the School Mental Health Capacity Building Partnership (SMH-CBP) national initiative at www.nasbhc.org/, as well as visit the University of South Florida's Research & Training Center for Children's Mental Health website at http://rtckids.fmhi.usf.edu/sbmh/default.cfm.

There is a large and growing amount of information in different specialty areas in the counseling and mental health field. It is unrealistic for practitioners to become expert, let alone knowledgeable, in all these areas. This is another good reason for implementing integrative, collaborative models of care. Practitioners should develop competencies within their specified roles and take care of their own personal wellness needs. Through professional development and growth, practitioners can also develop specialty areas, broaden their areas of knowledge and expertise, and/or take on programmatic leadership roles.

DISCUSSION QUESTIONS

1. What are some national trends in the provision of school mental health services?

2. In counseling, what specific areas do you feel most competent to address? What areas do you feel least prepared and competent to address?

3. What are some specific ways practitioners can facilitate improvements in school mental health systems of care?

Resource A

Treatment Integrity Checklist

Intervention Implementer: _____   School: _____

Date: _____   Time: _____   Evaluator: _____

Intervention: _____

<u>Evaluator Directions</u>: Either the person implementing the intervention or an observer completes this form at the end of each day that the intervention is conducted.

Intervention Tasks	Completed		Comments
	Yes	No	

Total Number of Tasks Completed (Yes) = ___/___ (Out of Total Number of Tasks Required)

= _____% Total Effective Treatment Integrity

Resource B

Intervention Planning Form

Student Information

Target
Student: _____

Date of
Birth: _____

Age:
_____

Gender: _____

School: _____

Grade _____

Phase 1: Problem Identification

How was student identified (e.g., grade-level team
referral, etc.)? _____

Description of presenting
problem: _____
_____
_____

Identify the assessment procedures used by the RTI team (e.g., archival data, behavior screening tools, discipline
logs, FBA data, interviews, observations, etc.):

Assessment Procedure	Date	Results/Comments

If a problem does exist, is it significant enough to warrant further investigation?

☐ Yes (Continue to Phase 2)
☐ No (Continue to monitor behavior; collect more data)

Present Level of Performance
(baseline): _____
_____
_____
_____
_____

Expected Level of Performance (goal; based on classroom or schoolwide expectations and/or local
or national norms): _____
_____
_____
_____

(Continued)

(Continued)

How severe is the gap between present and expected levels of performance? _____

Operational definition of target behavior (must be measureable and observable): _____

What is the function of the target behavior (based upon FBA results)? _____

Specific Skill Deficit(s): _____

What, if any, additional support is student currently receiving? _____

Is the nature and severity of the problem enough to require additional supports?

☐ Yes (Continue to Phase 3)

☐ No (Continue to monitor behavior; collect data in response to current supports)

Phase 3: Intervention Development

Write a meaningful, measureable, and observable behavioral goal (with short-term objectives):

Objective:
_____
_____
_____
_____

Objective:
_____
_____
_____
_____

Objective:
_____
_____
_____
_____

Goal:
_____
_____
_____
_____

Identify Potential Empirically Supported Interventions:

Intervention	Empirical Support (circle one)	Specific Skill Development	Ease of Implementation	Comments
	Strong			
	Mixed			
	Weak			
	Strong			
	Mixed			
	Weak			
	Strong			
	Mixed			
	Weak			

Selected
Intervention: _____

Intervention
description: _____
_____

Is the intervention developmentally appropriate?   Yes ☐   No ☐

Is the intervention directly linked to the results of the FBA?   Yes ☐   No ☐

Is the intervention directly linked to the goal statement?   Yes ☐   No ☐

Is the intervention directly linked to socially valid outcomes?   Yes ☐   No ☐

Is the entire RTI team (and student) in agreement on the appropriateness of the intervention?   Yes ☐   No ☐

If yes to all previous 5 questions, proceed to Phase 4.

Phase 4: Intervention Development

Person(s) responsible for carrying out
intervention: _____

Intervention
Setting: _____   Beginning Date: _____   Ending Date: _____

Frequency of
Intervention: _____ minutes/day _____ days/week _____ weeks _____

Materials
needed: _____
_____

Briefly describe the extent of collaboration/coordination needed across other settings (e.g.,
home, community): _____
_____

(Continued)

(Continued)

Intervention Integrity

Has a treatment integrity evaluation plan been developed?　　　　　　Yes ☐　　No ☐

Description of treatment integrity evaluation plan (include what measures
will be used): _____
_____

Who will conduct integrity
checks? _____
_____

How often will integrity checks be
conducted? _____

　　　Do data indicate that plan was implemented with integrity?

　　　☐ Yes (Continue to Phase 5)
　　　☐ No (Analyze why; provide additional training to implementers; revise intervention; change intervention)

Phase 5: Intervention Evaluation

Standard(s) used to determine level of
performance: _____
_____
_____

What progress-monitoring tools will be
used? _____

Briefly describe the progress-monitoring
process: _____
_____
_____

Person(s) responsible for progress
monitoring: _____

How often/when will progress-monitoring data be
collected? _____
_____

Progress-monitoring/outcome efficacy summary:

Progress-Monitoring Date	Progress Made (Compare baseline data to current performance)

Intervention Status/Recommendations

Check the most appropriate box(es)

☐ Performance goals have been met

    ☐ Maintain behavior; phase out supports

    ☐ Employ ongoing FBA to evaluate possible shift(s) in function of behavior

    ☐ Develop new goals

☐ Performance goals have not been met, but progress has been made

    ☐ Continue intervention, but with increased intensity

    ☐ Revise intervention

    ☐ Select new intervention

☐ Performance goals have not been met, no progress has been made

    ☐ Introduce additional tiers of support

    ☐ Progress to next level of support

    ☐ Referral to Special Education

Notes regarding future
plan: _____
_____
_____
_____

This form can also be found and printed at
http://www.corwin.com/counselinglevels2and3

Resource C

Resources for Counselors, Students, and Parents

RESOURCES FOR COUNSELORS— PUBLISHING COMPANIES, MANUALS, CURRICULA, COUNSELING FORMS, BOOKS, DVDS/MULTIMEDIA, CHILD THERAPY TOYS AND GAMES

Boys Town Press (www.boystownpress.com)

The Bureau for At-Risk Youth (www.at-risk.com)

Center for School Mental Health Analysis and Action (www.schoolmentalhealth.org/Resources/Clin/QuickGuide.pdf)

Childswork Childsplay (www.childswork.com)

Child Therapy Toys (www.childtherapytoys.com)

Counseling Forms Online (www.CounselingFormsOnline.com)

Courage to Change (www.couragetochange.com)

Creative Therapy Store (www.creativetherapystore.com/)

James Stanfield (www.stanfield.com)

MindWare (www.mindware.com)

PBIS World.com (www.pbisworld.com/)

Psychology Tools (www.psychologytools.org/cbt.html)

The School Counselor Toolkit (www.School-Counselor.org)

Social Skills Central (www.socialskillscentralstore.com)

The Therapy Shoppe (www.therapyshoppe.com)

Whole Person Associates (www.wholeperson.com)

BOOKS FOR CHILDREN AND ADOLESCENTS WITH AUTISM

The Aspie Teen's Survival Guide: Candid Advice for Teens, Tweens, and Parents, From a Young Man With Asperger's Syndrome, by J. D. Kraus; Age Level: Teens and tweens

Can I Tell You About Asperger Syndrome?: A Guide for Friends and Family, by Jude Welton; Age Level: 7–15

Freaks, Geeks & Asperger Syndrome: A User Guide to Adolescence, by Luke Jackson; Age Level: Teens

Keisha's Doors/las Puertas De Keisha: An Autism Story/una Historia De Autismo Libro Uno (Spanish and English Edition), by Marvie Ellis (Author) and Jenny Loehr (Illustrator); Age Level: Young children

Look Me in the Eye: My Life With Asperger's, by John Elder Robison; Age Level: Teens and up

My Social Stories Book by Carol Gray; Age Level: 9 and up

The New Social Story Book, by Carol Gray; Age Level: Elementary school age

Preparing for Life: The Complete Guide for Transitioning to Adulthood for Those With Autism and Asperger's Syndrome, by Jed Baker; Age Level: 16 and up

Since We're Friends: An Autism Picture Book, by Celeste Shally and David Harrington; Age Level: Preschool through second grade

Social Skills Picture Book for High School and Beyond, by Jed Baker; Age Level: Teens and up

Tacos Anyone? An Autism Story (English and Spanish Text) (Spanish and English Edition), by Marvie Ellis (Author) and Jenny Loehr (Illustrator); Age Level: Young children

Take Control of Asperger's Syndrome: The Official Strategy Guide for Teens With Asperger's

Syndrome and Nonverbal Learning Disorders, by Janet Price and Jennifer Engel Fisher; Age Level: 10 and up

What It Is to Be Me!: An Asperger Kid Book, by Angela Wine; Age Level: 4 and up

BOOKS FOR CHILDREN AND ADOLESCENTS (ADHD, SOCIAL-EMOTIONAL CONCERNS, TRAUMA, MENTAL ILLNESS, SUBSTANCE ABUSE)

The ADHD Workbook for Teens: Activities to Help You Gain Motivation and Confidence, by Lara Honos-Webb; Age Level: 13 and up

Anger and Anger Management (Teen Mental Health), by Charlie Quill; Age Level: 12 and up

Antisocial Behavior (Teen Mental Health), by Frank Spalding; Age Level: 12 and up

Anxiety and Panic Attacks (Teen Mental Health), by Judith Levin; Age Level: 12 and up

Beyond the Blues: A Workbook to Help Teens Overcome Depression, by Lisa Schab, Age Level: 13 and up

Coping With Post-Traumatic Stress Disorder: Dealing With Tragedy, by Carolyn Simpson and Dwain Simpson; Age Level: 12 and up

Depression, Anger, Sadness: Teens Write About Facing Difficult Emotions, by Al Desetta, Keith Hefner, and Laura Longhine; Age Level: 14 and up

Depression and Mood Disorders (Teen Mental Health), by Judith Levin; Age Level: 12 and up

Drugs and Mental Illness (Drug Abuse Prevention Library), by Maia Miller; Age Level: 12 and up

Investigating Depression and Bipolar Disorder: Real Facts for Real Lives (Investigating Diseases), by Abigail Meisel; Age Level: 14 and up

Mind Race: A Firsthand Account of One Teenager's Experience With Bipolar Disorder, by Patrick E. Jamieson and Moira A. Rynn; Age Level: 12 and up

Monochrome Days: A First-Hand Account of One Teenager's Experience With Depression, by Cait Irwin, Dwight L. Evans M.D., and Linda Wasmer Andrews; Age Level: Teens

Obsessive-Compulsive Disorder (Teen Mental Health), by Sandra Giddens; Age Level: 12 and up

A Terrible Thing Happened—A story for children who have witnessed violence or trauma, by Margaret H. Holmes, Sasha J. Mudlaff, and Cary Pillo; Age Level: 4 and up

Up and Down the Worry Hill: A Children's Book About Obsessive-Compulsive Disorder and Its Treatment, by Aureen Pinto Wagner; Age Level: 4 and up

What to Do When Your Temper Flares: A Kid's Guide to Overcoming Problems With Anger, by Dawn Huebner and Bonnie Matthews; Age Level: 8 and up

What to Do When Your Brain Gets Stuck: A Kid's Guide to Overcoming OCD, by Dawn Huebner and Bonnie Matthews; Age Level: 8 and up

What to Do When You Worry Too Much: A Kid's Guide to Overcoming Anxiety, by Dawn Huebner and Bonnie Matthews; Age Level: 6 and up

THERAPEUTIC BOOKS FOR CHILDREN (PUBLISHING COMPANIES)

JayJo Books (www.jayjo.com)—books for children with chronic illness and other conditions

Magination Press (www.maginationpress.com)—storybooks, picture books, and workbooks to help children deal with a variety of psychological concerns and challenges

BOOKS FOR PARENTS ABOUT CHILDHOOD AND ADOLESCENT AUTISM

1001 Great Ideas for Teaching and Raising Children With Autism or Asperger's, Revised and Expanded 2nd Edition, by Ellen Notbohm and Veronica Zysk

Asperger's Syndrome: A Guide for Parents and Professionals, by Anthony Attwood

Facing Autism: Giving Parents Reasons for Hope and Guidance for Help, by Lynn M. Hamilton

Helping Your Child with Autism Spectrum Disorder: A Step-By-Step Workbook for Families, by Stephanie B. Lockshin, Jennifer M. Gillis, and Raymond G. Romanczyk

Parenting Your Asperger Child: Individualized Solutions for Teaching Your Child Practical Skills, by Alan Sohn and Cathy Grayson

A Parent's Guide to Asperger Syndrome and High-Functioning Autism, by Sally Ozonoff, Geraldine Dawson, and James McPartland

A Parent's Guide to Autism: Answers to the Most Common Questions, by Charles A. Hart

BOOKS FOR PARENTS ABOUT CHILDHOOD AND ADOLESCENT ANXIETY, OCD, DEPRESSION, MOOD INSTABILITY, SCHIZOPHRENIA, AND SUBSTANCE USE

The ADD & ADHD Answer Book: Professional Answers to 275 of the Top Questions Parents Ask, by Susan Ashley

Adolescent Depression: A Guide for Parents (A Johns Hopkins Press Health Book), by Espen J. Aarseth

Adolescent Drug & Alcohol Abuse: How to Spot it, Stop it, and Get Help for Your Family, by Nikki Babbit

Anxiety-Free Kids: An Interactive Guide for Parents and Children, by Bonnie Zucker

Freeing Your Child From Anxiety: Powerful, Practical Solutions to Overcome Your Child's Fears, Worries, and Phobias, by Tamar E. Chansky

If Your Adolescent Has Depression or Bipolar Disorder: An Essential Resource for Parents (Adolescent Mental Health Initiative), by Dwight L. Evans M.D. and Linda Wasmer Andrews

If Your Adolescent Has Schizophrenia: An Essential Resource for Parents, by Raquel Gur and Ann Braden Johnson

Parenting Children With ADHD: 10 Lessons That Medicine Cannot Teach, by Vincent J. Monastra

Rescuing Your Teenager From Depression, by Norman T. Berlinger

Survival Strategies for Parenting Children With Bipolar Disorder: Innovative Parenting and Counseling Techniques for Helping Children With Bipolar Disorder and the Conditions That May Occur With It, by George T. Lynn

Talking Back to OCD, by John S. March

What to Do When Your Child Has Obsessive-Compulsive Disorder, by Aureen Pinto Wagner

RESOURCES FOR PARENTS AND FAMILIES

Active Parenting Publishers (www.ActiveParenting.com)

Military Family Resources (www.militaryfamily.com)

Parenting.org from Boys Town (www.parenting.org)

The Stepfamily Foundation Inc. (www.stepfamily.org)

SUPPORT FOR PARENTS AND FAMILIES OF CHILDREN WITH DISABILITIES

Attention Deficit Disorder Association (www.add.org/)

AutismWeb: A Parent's Guide to Autism Spectrum Disorders (www.autismweb.com/)

Children and Adults With Attention Deficit/Hyperactivity Disorder (www.chadd.org)

Children's Disabilities Information (www.childrensdisabilities.info/)

ED.gov U.S. Department of Education (www2.ed.gov/parents/needs/speced/edpicks.jhtml)

LD Online (www.ldonline.org/)

National Alliance on Mental Illness (www.nami.org)

National Center for Learning Disabilities (www.ncld.org/)

National Resources for Parents of Children and Youth With Disabilities (www.washington.edu/doit/Brochures/Parents/naparent.html)

Support for Families of Children With Disabilities (www.supportforfamilies.org/internetguide/)

Resource D

Evidence-Based Interventions, Programs, and Manuals

Blueprints for Violence Prevention: Model Programs. This resource from the *Center for the Study and Prevention of Violence, Institute of Behavioral Science, University of Colorado Boulder* highlights model intervention programs that prevent violence. This website provides a brief summary of each intervention program, a video segment describing each program, and contact information to get more information about the program. A strong research design, sustained effect, and multiple site replication of the evidence-based violence deterrent effects is represented in these "Model" programs. *(http://www.colorado.edu/cspv/blueprints/modelprograms.html)*

Collaborative for Academic, Social, and Emotional Learning (CASEL): 2013 CASEL Guide. This resource identifies well-designed, evidence-based social and emotional learning (SEL) programs that have a strong likelihood of broad dissemination in schools. The *CASEL* Guide also shares best practices for district and school teams on how to select and implement SEL programs. *(http://casel.org/guide/)*

Empirically Supported Interventions in School Mental Health. The Center for School Mental Health Assistance (2002; CSMHA) provides a list of evidence-based treatments that can be adapted for use in schools. *(http://csmh.umaryland.edu/Resources/ResourcePackets/files/empirically supported.pdf)*

Evidence-Based Mental Health Treatment for Children and Adolescents by APA Division 53. This website presents mental health treatments that have the strongest scientific support and are most likely to work. The specific, manualized treatment programs are organized by mental health disorders (e.g., depression, ADHD) for professionals. In addition, a section for parents provides a general overview of different types of psychotherapy (e.g., cognitive-behavior therapy, family therapy). (*http://www.effective childtherapy.com*)

National Center for Mental Health Promotion and Youth Violence Prevention. The goal of this website is to provide technical assistance (TA) and training to school districts and communities that receive grants from the U.S. Departments of Education and Justice, and Substance Abuse and Mental Health Services Administration (SAMHSA). Products and services that help to plan, implement, evaluate, and sustain activities that foster resilience, promote mental health, and prevent youth violence and mental and behavioral disorders are featured. *(http://www.promoteprevent.org/about/ tacenter)*

National Child Traumatic Stress Network Empirically Supported Treatments and Promising Practices. This website presents facts pertaining to clinical treatment and trauma-informed service approaches implemented by National Child Traumatic Stress Network centers. The goal of these interventions is to reduce the impact of exposure to traumatic events on children and adolescents. *(http://www.nctsn.org/resources/topics/treatments-that-work/promising-practices)*

Promising Practices Network on Children, Families, and Communities: What Works for Children and Families. This website presents programs that have been documented as having ratings meeting the criteria for a "Proven" or "Promising" approach to improve the lives of children and families. Research information pertaining to children's well-being, academic success, and economic security are featured. The purpose of this website is to promote the successful implementation of best practices and model programs. *(http://www.promisingpractices.net/default.asp)*

SAMHSA's National Registry of Evidence-Based Programs and Practices. The National Registry of Evidence-based Programs and Practices (NREPP) is a searchable online registry of mental health and substance abuse interventions that have been reviewed for evidence of effectiveness. This registry helps identify scientifically based approaches to preventing and treating mental disorders. *(http://www.nrepp.samhsa.gov/)*

School Psychiatry Program and MADI Resource Center; Massachusetts General Hospital. This website was created for parents, educators, and clinicians working to support children and adolescents with mental health conditions. The site provides general school-based intervention strategies when working with those diagnosed with depression, bipolar disorder, attention deficit/hyperactivity disorder, autism spectrum disorders, and anxiety disorders, including panic disorder and obsessive-compulsive disorder. *(www .schoolpsychiatry.org)*

What Works Clearinghouse (WWC). As an initiative of the U.S. Department of Education's Institute of Education Sciences (IES), the What Works Clearinghouse (WWC) was created in 2002 to be a central and trusted source of scientific evidence for what works in education. WWC reviews evidence for student behavior interventions including programs, curricula, and practices whose purpose is to foster positive behavioral outcomes. *(http://ies .ed.gov/ncee/wwc/)*

Resource E

ABC Observation Form

Student: _____ Date: _____ Setting: _____

Observer: _____ Reason for Observation: _____

Setting Event	Antecedent	Behavior	Consequence
What was happening when behavior occurred?	What happened right before behavior?	What did student do?	What was result of behavior?

Function of
Behavior: _____

Resource F

Daily Behavior Rating Form (Teacher)

Student Name:							
Date:							
Target Behavior:							

Period	Behavior Rating (Teacher)					Comments	Teacher Initials
	Excellent				Poor		
1	5	4	3	2	1		
2	5	4	3	2	1		
3	5	4	3	2	1		
4	5	4	3	2	1		
5	5	4	3	2	1		
6	5	4	3	2	1		
7	5	4	3	2	1		

Resource G

Counselor Self-Evaluation Survey

Instructions: Rate yourself on each of the following items based on what you perceive as your *relative strengths and weaknesses* as a counselor. This is not to be a comparison rating with other counselors, but rather a rating of one's own relative strengths and weaknesses. The purpose of this survey is to facilitate self-reflection and self-awareness to identify personal strengths as well as areas that can be targeted for additional growth. After completing, follow the scoring instructions at the end of the survey.

Enter number in blank: 1 = Significant weakness for me

2 = Relative weakness for me

3 = Relative strength for me

4 = Significant strength for me

_____ 1. I am knowledgeable in the code of ethics of my credentialing/ licensing agency as well as state and federal laws applicable to the provision of mental health services.

_____ 2. I regularly plan counseling sessions. For example, I plan activities and lessons and may use curricula, manuals, or books to assist me.

_____ 3. During assessment, I explore the potential impact of setting variables (e.g., classroom, home, peers, community, events) on the client's behavior.

_____ 4. I seek clients' input (or team members' input when client is a young child) to assist in developing relevant counseling goals.

_____ 5. I am generally optimistic about the usefulness of counseling.

_____ 6. I have supportive relationships outside of work.

_____ 7. I stay apprised of the research and recommendations for evidence-based practices.

_____ 8. I am knowledgeable regarding diagnostic considerations, such as formal diagnostic criteria (DSM and special education definitions), differential diagnoses, and comorbidities.

_____ 9. I seek opportunities for professional growth through workshops, conferences, and other learning opportunities.

_____ 10. I am accepting and nonjudgmental with clients.

_____ 11. I live a healthy lifestyle (e.g., sleep, diet, exercise, manage health care needs).

_____ 12. I measure clients' present levels of performance to establish a baseline.

_____ 13. I implement evidence-based interventions in counseling.

_____ 14. I can explain how my theoretical orientation guides my counseling.

_____ 15. I provide clear direction and guidance regarding the counseling process with clients. For example, I clearly explain and clarify the goals and expectations for counseling.

_____ 16. I am genuine and authentic in my interactions with clients. I am free to be myself within the appropriate boundaries of the therapeutic relationship.

_____ 17. I am flexible with clients and recognize what's really important in the moment. I am able to shift gears and address the felt needs of the client even when it might take us away from the planned session.

_____ 18. I share relevant and useful strategies with teachers/school personnel to promote the generalization of skills students learn in counseling to the natural setting.

_____ 19. I seek help when I'm experiencing personal or professional problems.

_____ 20. I behave professionally in my work setting. I am careful not to engage in inappropriate types of behaviors that may negatively impact my reputation or erode trust with clients or coworkers.

_____ 21. I use (or implement) counseling techniques skillfully.

_____ 22. I instill hope in my clients.

_____ 23. I have a healthy sense of humor and try not to take myself too seriously.

_____ 24. I facilitate collaboration between multiple settings. For example, I provide information to parents regarding resources in the school and/or community and offer assistance in establishing connections when needed.

_____ 25. I am knowledgeable in (and carefully consider) the potential influence of cultural variables in assessment and treatment.

_____ 26. I use multiple methods to measure clients' progress.

_____ 27. I can implement a wide repertoire of well-developed counseling techniques and methods.

_____ 28. I have a solid understanding of a variety of seminal theoretical orientations to guide my understanding and practice of psychological counseling.

_____ 29. I am self-aware in my interactions with clients. I seek to understand how my attitudes and behaviors may influence clients.

_____ 30. I develop clear and measurable counseling goals.

_____ 31. I know which theoretical orientations are most appropriate to guide my counseling based on the client's context.

_____ 32. I often genuinely experience eager anticipation regarding a client's potential progress.

_____ 33. I have good timing and pacing in counseling. For example, I am good at gauging the amount of time to focus on topics or activities, I am in sync with my clients, I know appropriate times to transition to something new or slow down the process, etc.

_____ 34. I am effective in keeping counseling sessions focused and "on track."

_____ 35. I am knowledgeable in the various aspects of child and adolescent development.

_____ 36. I regularly use basic counseling skills during sessions (e.g., active listening, use of body language, paraphrasing, reflecting meaning or feeling, etc.).

_____ 37. When collaborating/consulting with others, I consistently follow up to provide clarification, give assistance, problem solve, and monitor progress.

_____ 38. I am knowledgeable about how neurobiological processes can impact clients' behaviors.

_____ 39. I enjoy hobbies and interests outside of work.

_____ 40. I am friendly and upbeat with clients.

_____ 41. I involve myself in both personal and professional growth activities.

_____ 42. I collect data to measure clients' progress on goals.

_____ 43. During team problem solving, I listen to other team members carefully and demonstrate that I value their input.

_____ 44. I set short-term and long-term professional goals for myself.

_____ 45. I enjoy my current work.

_____ 46. I seek consultation from professional colleagues and/or supervisors when I need guidance or assistance.

_____ 47. I am effective in promoting the implementation of well-designed classroom interventions through designing, explaining, demonstrating, organizing, and communicating.

_____ 48. In my use of evidence-based interventions I gather data and monitor outcomes. I conduct my own formal/informal research as a scientist-practitioner.

_____ 49. I seek to be well informed regarding schoolwide and classroom expectations for students as well as the expectations for teachers and school staff to assist me in designing ecologically valid as well as "doable" interventions.

_____ 50. I demonstrate care and warmth with clients in counseling.

Scoring: Add up the scores from the items that comprise each domain for a total score. To get the total score for five of the domains *add up the total score then divide by 2 (Applied Counseling Skills; Assessment and Case Conceptualization; Collaboration and Generalization; Emotional Health and Self-Care; Therapeutic Relationship).*

Total

_____ Applied Counseling Skills (Appl): *13, 17, 21, 27, 33, 36 / 2 =

_____ Assessment and Case Conceptualization (A/CC): *3, 8, 25, 31, 35, 38 / 2 =

_____ Collaboration and Generalization (C/G): ***18, 24, 37, 43, 47, 49** **/ 2 =**

_____ Developing Goals (DG): 4, 12, 30

_____ Emotional Health and Self-Care (Emo): ***6, 11, 19, 23, 39, 45 /** **2 =**

_____ Ethics, Professionalism, and Judgment (Eth): 1, 20, 46

_____ Evidence-Based Practice (EBP): 7, 13, 48

_____ Expectation of Progress (EP): 5, 22, 32

_____ Measuring Outcomes (MO): 12, 26, 42

_____ Professional Growth (PG): 9, 41, 44

_____ Theoretical Orientation (ThO): 14, 28, 31

_____ Therapeutic Relationship (ThR): ***10, 16, 17, 29, 40, 50 / 2 =**

_____ Therapeutic Structure and Process (ThStr): 2, 15, 34

Interpretation: Transfer total scores to Score Profile to view your relative areas of strength and weakness across domains. Place an "X" in the corresponding box on the Score Profile. For further analysis, examine individual items within the domains.

Score Profile

Score	Appl	A/CC	C/G	DG	Emo	Eth	EBP	EP	MO	PG	ThO	ThR	ThStr
12													
11													
10													
9													
8													
7													
6													
5													
4													
3													

3 Greatest Strengths	3 Weakest Areas
1. _____	1. _____
2. _____	2. _____
3. _____	3. _____

REFLECTION QUESTIONS

1. How can I maximize or capitalize on my strength areas in counseling?

2. What are some specific steps I can take to make growth in my weakest areas?

Resource H

*Personal and Professional
Growth Plan Form*

*Provision of School-Based
Counseling or Therapy*

Name: _____   **Date:** _____

A. <u>Self-Assessment</u> (Use results from Counselor Self-Evaluation Survey in Resource G)

    My personal strength areas as a counselor/therapist:

    1.

    2.

    3.

    Weakest areas as a counselor/therapist:

    1.

    2.

    3.

B. <u>Planning for Goal Setting</u> (Consider the following questions)

    1.   What else might I consider in assessing my strengths and weaknesses as a counselor?

    2.   Am I open to feedback from others?

    3.   What types of blind spots might I be susceptible to?

    4.   Am I too self-critical of myself as a counselor?

5. What types of personal and professional growth activities benefit me most?

6. Am I developing goals that are meaningful, relevant, challenging, attainable, specific, positive, time limited, and measureable?

C. <u>Goals</u>

Targeted Area 1: _____

Goals	Strategies/ Activities	Methods for Measuring Outcome	Completion Date

Targeted Area 2: _____

Goals	Strategies/ Activities	Methods for Measuring Outcome	Completion Date

Targeted Area 3: _____

Goals	Strategies/ Activities	Methods for Measuring Outcome	Completion Date

References

Adelman, H. S., & Taylor, L. (2010). *Mental health in schools: Engaging learners, preventing problems, and improving schools.* Thousand Oaks, CA: Corwin.

Alberto, P. A., & Troutman, A. C. (1999). *Applied behavior analysis for teachers.* Upper Saddle River, NJ: Prentice Hall.

American Academy of Pediatrics. (2004). School-based mental health services. *Pediatrics, 113,* 1839–1845.

American Psychological Association (APA). (2006). *Task force report of the working group on psychotropic medication for children and adolescents: Psychopharmacological, psychosocial, and combined interventions for childhood disorders: Evidence base, contextual factors, and future directions.* Washington, DC: Author. Retrieved from http://www.apa.org/pi/families/resources/child-medications.pdf

American School Counselor Association (ASCA). (2003). *The ASCA national model: A framework for school counseling programs.* Alexandria, VA: Author.

American School Counselor Association (ASCA). (2005). *The ASCA national model: A framework for school counseling programs* (2nd ed.). Alexandria, VA: Author.

American School Counselor Association (ASCA). (2008). *The professional school counselor and response to intervention position statement.* Retrieved from http://asca2timberlakepublishing.com//files/PS_Intervention.pdf

Appelbaum, M. (2009). *One stop guide to implementing RTI: Academic and behavioral interventions, K–12.* Thousand Oaks, CA: Corwin.

Asay, T. P., & Lambert, M. J. (1999). The empirical case for the common factors in therapy: Qualitative findings. In M. A. Hubble, B. L. Duncan, & S. D. Miller (Eds.), *The heart and soul of change: What works in therapy* (pp. 33–56). Washington, DC: American Psychological Association.

Atkins, M. S., Hoagwood, K. E., Kutash, K., & Seidman, E. (2010). Toward the integration of education and mental health in schools. *Administration and Policy in Mental Health and Mental Health Services Research, 37,* 40–47.

Baron-Cohen, S. (2000). Is Asperger syndrome/high-functioning autism necessarily a disability? *Development and Psychopathology, 12,* 489–500.

Bateman, B. D., & Herr, C. M. (2006). *Writing measurable IEP goals and objectives.* Verona, WI: Attainment Company.

Bear, G. (2008). School-wide approaches to behavioral problems. In B. Doll & J. Cummings (Eds.), *Transforming school mental health services: Population-based approaches to promoting the competency and wellness of children* (pp. 103–141). Thousand Oaks, CA: Corwin.

Beets, M. W., Flay, B. R., Vuchinich, S. Snyder, F. J., Acock, A., Li, K.-K., . . . Durlak, J. (2009). Use of a social and character development program to prevent substance use, violent behaviors, and sexual activity among elementary-school students in Hawaii. *American Journal of Public Health, 99,* 1438–1445.

Benard, B. (1991). *Fostering resiliency in kids: Protective factors in the family, school, and community.* Portland, OR: Northwest Regional Educational Laboratory.

Bennett-Levy, J. (2006). Therapist skills: A cognitive model of their acquisition and refinement. *Behavioural and Cognitive Psychotherapy, 34,* 57–78.

Bertalanffy, L. von. (1968). *General system theory: Essays on its foundation and development* (Rev. ed.). New York, NY: George Braziller.

Binder, J. L. (1993). Is it time to improve psychotherapy training? *Clinical Psychology Review, 13,* 301–318.

Bransford, J. D., & Stein, B. S. (1984). *The IDEAL problem solver: A guide for improving thinking, learning, and creativity.* New York, NY: Freeman.

Brody, A. L., Sanjaya, S., Stoessel, P., Gillies, L. A., Fairbanks, L. A., Alborzian, S., et al. (2001). Regional brain metabolic changes in patients with major depression treated with either paroxetine or interpersonal therapy. *Archives of General Psychiatry, 58,* 631–640.

Bronfenbrenner, U. (Ed.). (2005). *On making human beings human: Biological perspectives on human development.* Thousand Oaks, CA: Sage.

Brown-Chidsey, R., & Steege, M. W. (2010). *Response to intervention: Principles and strategies for effective practice* (2nd ed.) New York, NY: Guilford.

Burns, D., (1999). *The feeling good handbook.* (Revised edition). New York, NY: Penguin.

Carey, J. C., Dimmitt, C., Hatch, T. A., Lapan, R. T., & Whiston, S. C. (2008). Report of the national panel for evidence-based school counseling: Outcome research coding protocol and evaluation on student success skills and second step. *Professional School Counseling, 11,* 197–206.

Carlson, J. S., Demaray, M. K., & Hunter-Oehmke, S. (2006). A survey of school psychologists' knowledge and training in child psychopharmacology. *Psychology in the Schools, 43,* 623–633.

Carr, A. (2009). The effectiveness of family therapy and systemic interventions for child-focused problems. Journal of Family Therapy, *31,* 3–45.

Casey, A., Skiba, R., & Algozzine, B. (1988). Developing effective behavioral interventions. In J. L. Graden, J. E. Zins, & M. J. Curtis (Eds.), *Alternative educational delivery systems: Enhancing instructional options for all students* (pp. 413–430). Washington, DC: National Association of School Psychologists.

Center for Child and Family Policy. (n.d.). *Evaluation of school-based child and family support teams initiative (100 Schools Project).* Retrieved from http://childandfamilypolicy.duke.edu/project_detail.php?id=36

Child and Family Center. (n.d.). *Ecological approach to family intervention and treatment (EcoFIT) integrated with PBS: An effectiveness trial in middle schools.* Retrieved from http://cfc.uoregon.edu/projects-ecofit.htm

Child with a disability, 34 C.F.R. § 300.8 (2007).

Christ, T. J. (2008). Best practices in problem analysis. In A. Thomas & J. Grimes (Eds.), *Best practices in school psychology* (5th ed., pp. 159–176). Bethesda, MD: National Association of School Psychologists.

Christenson, S. L., Whitehouse, E. M., & VanGetson, G. R. (2008). Partnering with families to enhance students' mental health. In B. Doll & J. A. Cummings (Eds.), *Transforming school mental health services* (pp. 69–101).Thousand Oaks, CA: Corwin & National Association of School Psychologists.

Cicchetti, D., & Barnett, D. (1991). Attachment organization in maltreated pre-schoolers. *Development and Psychopathology, 3,* 397–411.

Cipani, E., & Schock, K. M. (2010). *Functional behavioral assessment, diagnosis, and treatment: A complete system for education and mental health settings.* New York, NY: Springer.

Cognitive Behavioral Intervention for Trauma in Schools. (n.d.). *CBITS at-a-Glance.* Retrieved from http://cbitsprogram.org/

Consortium for Citizens with Disabilities. (2006). *Principles for the reauthorization of No Child Left Behind.* Retrieved from http://www.c-c-d.org/task_forces/education/NCLB_Principles.pdf

Corey, G. (2009). *Theory and practice of counseling and psychotherapy* (8th ed.). Pacific Grove, CA: Brooks/Cole.

Crone, D. A., & Horner, R. H. (2003). *Building positive behavior support systems in schools: Functional behavioral assessment.* New York, NY: Guilford.

Crone, D. A., Horner, R. H., & Hawken, L. S. (2004). *Responding to problem behavior in schools: The behavior education program.* New York, NY: Guilford.

Definition of Individualized Education Program, 34 C.F.R. §300.320(a)(4) (2007).

DeLucia-Waack, J. (2006). *Leading psychoeducational groups for children and adolescents.* Thousand Oaks, CA: Sage.

Deno, S. L. (2005). Problem-solving assessment. In R. Brown-Chidsey (Ed.), *Assessment for intervention: A problem-solving approach* (pp. 10–40). New York, NY: Guilford.

Doll, B., & Cummings, J. (2008). *Transforming school mental health services: Population-based approaches to promoting the competency and wellness of children.* Thousand Oaks, CA: Corwin.

DuPaul, G. J., & Carlson, J. S. (2005). Child psychopharmacology: How school psychologists can contribute to effective outcomes. *School Psychology Quarterly, 20,* 206–221.

Durlak, J. A., Weissberg, R. P., Dymnicki, A. B., Taylor, R. D., & Schellinger, K. B. (2011). The impact of enhancing students' social and emotional learning: A meta-analysis of school-based universal interventions. *Child Development, 82,* 405–432.

Egan, G. (2009). *The skilled helper: A problem-management and opportunity-development approach to helping* (9th ed.). Pacific Grove, CA: Brooks/Cole.

Eggert, L. L., Nicholas, L. J., & Owen, L. (2004). *Reconnecting youth: Peer group approach to building life skills* (2nd ed.). Bloomington, IN: National Educational Service.

Ellickson, P. L., Bell, R. M., & Harrison, E. R. (1993). Changing adolescent propensities to use drugs: Results from Project ALERT. *Health Education Quarterly, 20,* 227–242.

empathy. (2012). In *Merriam-Webster.com.* Retrieved May 7, 2012, from http://www.merriam-webster.com/

Epstein, M., Atkins, M., Cullinan, D., Kutash, K., & Weaver, R. (2008). Reducing behavior problems in the elementary school classroom. Washington, DC: What Works Clearinghouse. Retrieved from http://www.ies.ed.gov/ncee/wwc

Erford, B. T., Eaves, S. T., Bryant, E. M., & Young, K. A. (2010). *Thirty-five techniques every counselor should know.* Upper Saddle River, NJ: Pearson.

Erskine, R. G. (n.d.). Beyond empathy: A therapy of contact-in-relationship. *Integrative Psychotherapy Articles.* Retrieved from http://www.integrativetherapy.com/en/articles.php?id=39

Erskine, R. G. (1998). Attunement and involvement: Therapeutic responses to relational needs. *International Journal of Psychotherapy, 3,* 235–244.

Erskine, R. G., Moursund, J. P., & Trautmann, R. L. (1999). *Beyond empathy: A theory of contact-in-relationship.* Philadelphia, PA: Brunner/Mazel.

Farmer, E., Burns B. J., Phillips, S. D., Angold, A., & Costello, E. J. (2003). Pathways into and through mental health services for children and adolescents. *Psychiatric Services, 54,* 60–66.

Fixsen, D. L., Blase, K. A., Duda, M. A., Naoom, S. F., & Van Dyke, M. (2010). Implementation of evidence-based treatments for children and adolescents: Research findings and their implications for the future. In J. R. Wiez & A. E. Kazdin (Eds.), *Evidence-based psychotherapies for children and adolescents.* New York, NY: Guilford.

Fixsen, D. L., Naoom, S. F., Blase, K., Friedman, R. M., & Wallace, F. (2005). Implementation research: A synthesis of the literature (p. 5). National Implementation Research Network, University of South Florida, Louis de la Parte Florida Mental Health Institute. Available online at http://nirn.fmhi.usf .edu/resources/publications/Monograph/

Fletcher, J. M., & Vaughn, S. (2009). Response to intervention: Preventing and remediating academic difficulties. *Child Development Perspectives, 3,* 30–37.

Fletcher, K. E. (2003). Childhood posttraumatic stress disorder. In E. J. Mash & R. A. Barkley (Eds.), *Child psychopathology* (2nd ed., pp. 330–371). New York, NY: Guilford.

Foster, S., Rollefson, M., Doksum, T., Noonan, D., Robinson, G., & Teich, J. (2005). *School mental health services in the United States, 2002–2003.* DHHS Pub. No. (SMA) 054068. Rockville, MD: Center for Mental Health Services, Substance Abuse and Mental Health Services Administration.

Franklin, C., Biever, J., Moore, K., Clemons, D., & Scamardo, M. (2001). The effectiveness of solution-focused therapy with children in a school setting. *Research on Social Work Practice, 11,* 411–434.

Franklin, C., Moore, K., & Hopson, L. (2008). Effectiveness of solution focused brief therapy in a school setting. *Children and Schools, 30,* 15–26.

Frye, H. N. (2005). How elementary school counselors can meet the needs of students with disabilities. *Professional School Counseling, 8,* 442–450.

Fuchs, D., & Fuchs, L. S. (1989). Exploring effective and efficient prereferral interventions: A component analysis of behavioral consultation. *School Psychology Review, 18,* 260–279.

Fuchs, D., & Fuchs, L. (2005). Operationalizing response-to-intervention (RTI) as a method of LD identification. Retrieved from http://www.tn.gov/education/ speced/doc/sefuopertifaq.pdf

Gadow, K. D. (1993). A school-based medication evaluation program. In J. L. Matson (Ed.), *Handbook of hyperactivity in children* (pp. 186–219). Needham Heights, MA: Allyn & Bacon.

Garbarino, J. (1995). *Raising children in a socially toxic environment.* San Francisco, CA: Jossey-Bass.

Gelso, C. J., & Hayes, J. A. (1998). *The psychotherapy relationship.* New York, NY: Wiley.

Goldapple, K., Segal, Z., Garson, C., Lau, M. Bieling, M., & Sidney, K. (2004). Modulation of cortical-limbic pathways in major depression: Treatment-specific effects of cognitive behavioral therapy. *Archives of General Psychiatry, 61,* 34–41.

Goldman, H. M. (2009). President Obama and mental health policy—the audacity to hope. *Journal of Mental Health, 18,* 193–197.

Gonet, M. M. (1994). *Counseling the adolescent substance abuser: School-based intervention and prevention.* Thousand Oaks, CA: Sage.

Gottfredson, D. C., & Wilson, D. B. (2003). Characteristics of effective school-based substance abuse prevention. *Prevention Science, 4,* 27–38.

Gottfredson, D. C., Wilson, D. B., & Najaka, S. S. (2002). The schools. In J. Q. Wilson & J. Petersilia (Eds.), *Crime: Public policies for crime control* (pp. 149–190). San Francisco, CA: ICS Press.

Greenberg, G., Ganshorn, K., & Danilkewic, A. (2001). Solution-focused therapy: A counseling model for busy family physicians. *Canadian Family Physician, 47,* 2289–2295.

Gresham, F. M., Sugai, G., & Horner, R. H. (2001). Interpreting outcomes of social skills training for students with high-incidence disabilities. *Exceptional Children, 67,* 331–344.

Hackney, H. L., & Cormier, L. S. (2001). *The professional counselor: A process guide to helping* (4th ed.). Boston, MA: Allyn & Bacon.

Hahn, R. A., Fuqua-Whitley, D. S., Lowy, J., et al. (2007). Effectiveness of universal school-based programs for the prevention of violence. *American Journal of Preventive Medicine, 33,* 114–129.

HaileMariam, A., Bradley-Johnson, S., & Johnson, M. C. (2002). Pediatricians' preferences for ADHD information from schools. *School Psychology Review, 31,* 94–105.

Hart, R., & Jacobi, M. (1992). *Gatekeeper to advocate.* New York, NY: College Board Press.

Hawken, L. S., Adolphson, S. L., MacLeod, K. S., & Schumann, J. (2009). Secondary-tier interventions and supports. In W. Sailor, G. Sugai, R. H. Horner, & G. Dunlap (Eds.), *Handbook of positive behavior support* (pp. 395–420). New York, NY: Springer.

Henggeler, S. W., Schoenwald, S. K., Borduin, C. M., Rowland, M. D., & Cunningham, P. B. (1998). *Multisystemic treatment of antisocial behavior in children and adolescents.* New York, NY: Guilford.

Heslop, P., & Macaulay, F. (2009) *Hidden pain? Self-injury and people with learning disabilities.* Bristol, UK: Bristol Crisis Service for Women.

Hoagwood, K., & Erwin, H. D. (1997). Effectiveness of school-based mental health services for children: A 10-year research review. *Journal of Child and Family Studies, 6,* 435–451.

Hoffman, R., & Kress, V. E. (2010). Adolescent non-suicidal self-injury. Recommendations for minimizing client and counselor risk and enhancing client care. *Journal of Mental Health Counseling, 32*(4), 342–353.

Horner, R., Sugai, G., Kincaid, D., George, H., Lewis, T., Eber, L., . . . Algozzine, B. (2012). *What does it cost to implement school-wide PBIS?* Retrieved from http://www.pbis.org/common/pbisresources/publications/20120802_WhatDoesItCostToImplementSWPBIS.pdf

Hubble, M., Duncan, B., & Miller, S. (Eds.) (1999). *The heart and soul of change: What works in therapy.* Washington, DC: American Psychological Association.

Hunley, S., & McNamara, K. M. (2010). *Tier 3 of the RTI Model: Problem solving through a case study approach.* Thousand Oaks, CA: Corwin.

Hyman, I. A., Wojtowicz, A., Lee, K. D., Haffner, M. E., Fiorello, C. A., Storlazzi, J. J., & Rosenfeld, J. (1998). School-based methylphenidate placebo protocols: Methodological and practical issues. *Journal of Learning Disabilities, 31,* 581–594.

Ialongo, N., Poduska, J., Werthamer, L., & Kellam, S. (2001). The distal impact of two first-grade preventive interventions on conduct problems and disorder in early adolescence. *Journal of Emotional and Behavioral Disorders, 9,* 146–160.

Innovative Programs. (n.d.). *Integrated mental health services in the schools.* Retrieved July 30, 2012, from http://www.thekimfoundation.org/html/edu_training/integrated-services.html

Institute of Educational Sciences. (n.d.). *Ecological approach to family intervention and treatment (Eco-FIT) integrated with PBS: An effectiveness trial in middle school.* Retrieved from http://ies.ed.gov/funding/grantsearch/details.asp?ID=774

IRIS Center. (2007). *What is the IQ-achievement discrepancy model?* National Association of State Directors of Special Education, U.S. Department of Education, Office of Special Education Programs. Retrieved from http://www.ideapartnership.org/documents/IRIS_DG_IQ-Discrep_RTI.pdf

Jans, L., Stoddard, S., & Kraus, L. (2004). *Chartbook on mental health and disability in the United States.* An InfoUse Report. Washington, DC: U.S. Department of Education, National Institute on Disability and Rehabilitation Research.

Jennings, L., & Skovholt, T. M. (1999). The cognitive, emotional, and relational characteristics of master therapists. *Journal of Counseling Psychology, 46,* 3–11.

Jørgensen, C. R. (2004). Active ingredients in individual psychotherapy: Searching for common factors. *Psychoanalytic Psychology, 21,* 516–540.

Karl, A., Schaefer, M., Malta, L. S., Dörfel, D., Rohleder, N., & Werner, A. (2006). A meta-analysis of structural brain abnormalities in PTSD. *Neuroscience and Biobehavioral Reviews, 30,* 1004–1031.

Karver, M. S., Handelsman, J. B., Fields, S., & Bickman, L. (2005). A theoretical model of common process factors in youth and family therapy. *Mental Health Services Research, 7,* 35–51.

Karver, M. S., Handelsman, J. B., Fields, S., & Bickman, L. (2006). Meta-analysis of therapeutic relationship variables in youth and family therapy: The evidence for different relationship variables in the child and adolescent treatment outcome literature. *Clinical Psychology Review, 26,* 50–65.

Kavale, K. A., & Forness, S. R. (1999). *Efficacy of special education and related services.* Washington, DC: American Association on Mental Retardation.

Kazdin, A. E. (1982). *Single-case research designs: Methods for clinical and applied settings.* New York, NY: Oxford University Press.

Kazdin, A. (1997). Practitioner review: Psychosocial treatments for conduct disorder in children. *Journal of Child Psychology and Psychiatry, 38,* 161–178.

Kelleher, K., McInerny, T., Gardner, W., Childs, G., Wasserman, R., Gardner, W., . . . Wasserman, R. (2000). Increasing identification of psychosocial problems: 1979–1996. *Pediatrics, 105,* 1313–1321.

Kelly, M., Kim, J., & Franklin, C. (2008). *Solution-focused brief therapy in schools: A 360-degree view of research and practice.* Oxford, UK: Oxford University Press.

Kennedy, S. H., Konarski, J. Z., Segal, Z. V., Lau, M. A., Bieling, P. J., et al. (2007). Differences in brain glucose metabolism between responders to CBT and venlafaxine in a 16-week randomized controlled trial. *American Journal of Psychiatry, 164,* 778–788.

Kim, W. J. (2003). Child and adolescent psychiatry workforce: A critical shortage and national challenge. *Academic Psychiatry, 27,* 277–282.

Kratochwill, T. R., & Bergan, J. (1990). *Behavioral consultation in applied settings: An individual guide.* New York, NY: Plenum.

Kress, V. E., & Hoffman, R. (2008). Non-suicidal self-injury and motivational interviewing: Enhancing readiness for change. *Journal of Mental Health Counseling, 30,* 311–329.

Kruger, J., & Dunning, D. (1999). Unskilled and unaware of it: How difficulties in recognizing one's own incompetence lead to inflated self-assessments. *Journal of Personality and Social Psychology, 77,* 1121–1134.

Kubiszyn, T. (1994). Pediatric psychopharmacology and prescription privileges: Implications and opportunities for school psychology. *School Psychology Quarterly, 9,* 26–40.

Kubiszyn, T. (2011). Pediatric psychopharmacology. In M. Bray & T. Kehle (Eds.), *The Oxford handbook of school psychology* (pp. 696–727). New York, NY: Oxford University Press.

Kutash, K., Duchnowski, A. J., & Lynn, N. (2006). *School-based mental health: An empirical guide for decision makers.* Tampa, FL: University of South Florida, The Louis de la Parte Florida Mental Health Institute, Department of Child and Family Studies, Research and Training Center for Children's Mental Health.

LaFountain, R. M., & Garner, N. E. (1996). Solution focused counseling groups: The results are in. *Journal for Specialists in Group Work, 21,* 128–143.

Lambert, M. J. (2003). Psychotherapy outcome research: Implications for integrative and eclectic therapists. In C. Norcross & M. Goldfried (Eds.), *Handbook of psychotherapy integration* (pp. 94–129). New York, NY: Basic Books.

Lambert, M. J., & Barley, D. E. (2002). Research summary on the therapeutic relationship and psychotherapy outcome. In J. C. Norcross (Ed.), *Psychotherapy relationships that work: Therapist contributions and responsiveness to patients* (pp. 17–32). Oxford, England: Oxford University Press.

Lane, K. L., Kalberg, J. R., & Menzies, H. M. (2009). *Developing school-wide programs to prevent and manage problem behavior: A step-by-step approach.* New York, NY: Guilford.

Langer, D. A., McLeod, B. D., & Weisz, J. R. (2011). Do treatment manuals undermine youth-therapist alliance in community clinical practice? *Journal of Consulting and Clinical Psychology, 79,* 427–432.

Larson, J., & Lochman, J. E. (2004). *Helping schoolchildren cope with anger: A cognitive-behavioral intervention.* New York, NY: Guilford.

Lazarus, A. A. (1976). *Multimodal behavior therapy.* New York, NY: Springer.

Lehto, S. M., Tolmunen, T., Joensuu, M., et al. (2008). Changes in midbrain serotonin transporter availability in atypically depressed subjects after one year of psychotherapy. *Progress in Neuropsychopharmacology and Biological Psychiatry, 32,* 229–237.

Levinson, E. M. (1993). *Transdisciplinary vocational assessment: Issues in school-based programs.* Brandon, VT: Clinical Psychology Publishing.

Levinson, E. M. (2004). Introduction to transition assessment. In E. M. Levinson (Ed.), *Transition from school to post-school life for individuals with disabilities: Assessment from an educational and school psychological perspective* (pp. 3–35). Springfield, IL: Charles C. Thomas.

Levinson, E. M. (2008). Best practices in school-based career assessment and school-to-work transition for students with disabilities. In A. Thomas & J. Grimes

(Eds.), *Best practices in school psychology* (5th ed., pp. 1563–1580). Bethesda, MD: National Association of School Psychologists.

Liggan, D. Y., & Kay, J. (1999). Some neurobiological aspects of psychotherapy. *Journal of Psychotherapy Practice and Research, 8,* 103–114.

Littrell, J. M., Malia, J. A., & Vanderwood, M. (1995). Single-session brief counseling in a high school. *Journal of Counseling and Development, 73,* 451–458.

Lochman, J. E., & Wells, K. C. (1996). A social-cognitive intervention with aggressive children: Prevention effects and contextual implementation issues. In R. DeV Peters & R. J. McMahon (Eds.), *Prevention and early intervention: Childhood disorders, substance use, and delinquency* (pp. 111–143). Thousand Oaks, CA: Sage.

Margolin, S. (1996). *Complete group counseling program for children of divorce: Ready-to-use plans & materials for small & large groups, grades 1–6.* San Francisco, CA: Jossey-Bass.

Marshak, L. E., Dandeneau, C. J., Prezant, F. P., & L'Amoreaux, N. A. (2010). *The school counselor's guide to helping students with disabilities.* San Francisco, CA: Jossey-Bass.

Martella, R. C., Nelson, J, R., Marchand-Martella, N. E., & O'Reilly, M. (2012). *Comprehensive behavior management: Individualized, classroom, and school-wide approaches* (2nd ed.). Thousand Oaks, CA: Sage.

Mayer, M., Van Acker, R., Lochman, J., & Gresham, F. (2009). *Cognitive-behavioral interventions for emotional and behavioral disorders: School-based practice.* New York, NY: Guilford.

McDougal, J., Bardos, A. N., & Meier, S. (2011). The Behavior Intervention Monitoring Assessment System (BIMAS). Toronto, Canada: MHS.

McGrath, R. E., Berman, S., LeVine, E., Mantell, K., Rom-Rymer, B., Sammons, M., & Quillin, J. (2011). Practice guidelines regarding psychologists' involvement in pharmacological issues. *American Psychologist, 66,* 835–849.

McKevitt, B. C., & Braaksma, A. D. (2008). Best practices in developing a positive behavior support system at the school level. In A. Thomas & J. Grimes (Eds.), *Best practices in school psychology* (5th ed., pp. 735–747). Bethesda, MD: National Association of School Psychologists.

Mellard, D. F., & Johnson, E. (2008). *RTI: A practitioner's guide to implementing response to intervention.* Thousand Oaks, CA: Corwin.

Mennuti, R., Christner, R., & Freeman, C. (2012). *Cognitive-behavioral interventions in educational settings: A handbook for practice* (2nd ed.). New York, NY: Routledge.

Merikangas, K., He, J., Burstein, M., Swanson, S., Avenevoli, S., Cui, L., . . . Swendsen, J. (2010). Lifetime prevalence of mental disorders in U.S. adolescents: Results from the National Comorbidity Survey Replication–Adolescent Supplement (NCS-A). *Journal of the American Academy of Child & Adolescent Psychiatry, 49,* 980–989.

Michigan Department of Education. (2011). *Dropout rates: Michigan's state performance plan, indicator 2.* Annual Performance Report 2005–06. Michigan Department of Education Office of Special Education and Early Intervention Services. Retrieved from http://www.cenmi.org/LinkClick.aspx?fileticket=GtJNLIuoA0%3D&tabid=105&mid=544

Miller, W. R., & Rollnick, S. (2002). *Motivational interviewing: Preparing people for change* (2nd ed.). New York, NY: Guilford.

Miltenberger, R. G. (2008). *Behavior modification: Principles and procedures* (4th ed.). Belmont, CA: Wadsworth/Thomson Learning.

Mobley, J., & Fort, S. (2007). *Planning psychoeducational groups for schools.* Retrieved from http://counselingoutfitters.com/vistas/vistas07/Mobley.pdf

Murphy, J. J. (2008). *Solution-focused counseling in schools.* Based on a program presented at the ACA Annual Conference & Exhibition, Honolulu, HI. Retrieved from http://counselingoutfitters.com/vistas/vistas08/Murphy.htm

National Alliance on Mental Illness. (2011). *Facts on children's mental health in America.* Retrieved from http://www.nami.org/Template.cfm?Section=federal_ and_state_policy_legislation&template=/ContentManagement/ContentDisplay .cfm&ContentID=43804

National Association of School Psychologists. (2009). *Appropriate behavioral, social, and emotional supports to meet the needs of all students* [Position statement]. Bethesda, MD: Author. Retrieved from http://www.nasponline.org/ about_nasp/positionpapers/appropriatebehavioralsupports.pdf

National Association of State Directors of Special Education (NASDSE). (2007). *Response to intervention: Research for practice.* Retrieved from http://www .nasdse.org/Portals/0/Documents/RtI_Bibliography2.pdf

National Center on Response to Intervention (NCRTI). (2010, March). *Essential components of RTI—A closer look at response to intervention.* U.S. Department of Education, Office of Special Education Programs. Washington, DC. Public Law 107–110, 115 Stat. 1425, enacted January 8, 2002.

National Education Association. (2012). *Positive behavioral interventions and supports: A multi-tiered framework that works for every student* [Policy brief]. Washington, DC: NEA Education Policy and Practice Department. Retrieved from http://www.nea.org/assets/docs/PB41positivebehavioralinterventions2012 .pdf

Nicholson, H., Foote, C., & Grigerick, S. (2009). Deleterious effects of psychotherapy and counseling in the schools. *Psychology in the Schools, 46,* 232–237.

Norcross, J. C., & Beutler, L. E. (2011). Integrative psychotherapies. In R. J. Corsini & D. Wedding (Eds.), *Current psychotherapies* (9th ed.). Belmont, CA: Brooks/ Cole Cengage.

North Carolina Department of Health and Human Services. (n.d.). Child and Family Support Teams: A joint project of NC DHHS and the NC Department of Public Instruction. Retrieved from http://www.ncdhhs.gov/childand familyteams/

O'Neill, R. E., Horner, R. H., Albin, R. W., Sprague, J. R., Storey, K., & Newton, J. S. (1997). *Functional assessment and program development for problem behavior: A practical handbook.* Pacific Grove, CA: Brooks/Cole.

Pentz, M. A., Cormack, C, Flay, B. R., Hansen, W. B., & Johnson, C. A. (1986). Balancing program and research integrity in community drug abuse prevention: Project STAR approach. *Journal of School Health, 56,* 389–393.

Plionis, E. M. (2007). *Competency in generalist practice: A guide to theory and evidence-based decision making.* New York, NY: Oxford University Press.

Ponterotto, J. G. (1985). A counselor's guide to psychopharmacology. *Journal of Counseling and Development, 64,* 109–115.

Positive Family Support. (n.d.). Positive family support for middle schools. *Psychiatric Research, 41,* 837–847. Retrieved June 12, 2012, from https:// research.ori.org/pfs/docs/PFS_FAQs_2009.pdf

Rappaport, N. (2001). Psychiatric consultation to school-based health centers: Lessons learned in an emerging field. *Journal of the American Academy of Child and Adolescent Psychiatry, 40,* 1473–1475.

Reichow, B., & Volkmar, F. R. (2010). Social skills interventions for individuals with autism: Evaluation for evidence-based practices within a best evidence synthesis framework. *Journal of Autism and Developmental Disorders, 40,* 149–166.

Reschly, D. J. (2008). School psychology paradigm shift and beyond. In A. Thomas & J. Grimes (Eds.), *Best practices in school psychology* (5th ed., pp. 3–16). Bethesda, MD: National Association of School Psychologists.

Riley-Tillman, C. T., & Burns, M. K. (2009). *Evaluating educational interventions: Single-case design for measuring response to intervention.* New York, NY: Guilford.

Roberts, H. J., Floress, M. T., & Ellis, C. R. (2009). Training school psychologists in psychopharmacology consultation. *Psychology in the Schools, 46,* 827–835.

Rogers, C.R. (1961). *On becoming a person.* Boston, MA: Houghton Mifflin.

Rollnick, S., & Miller, W. R. (1995). What is motivational interviewing? *Behavioural and Cognitive Psychotherapy, 23,* 325–334.

Rosenfeld, G. W. (2009). *Beyond evidence-based psychotherapy: Fostering the eight sources of change in child and adolescent treatment.* New York, NY: Routledge.

SAMHSA's National Registry of Evidence-based Programs and Practices. (2007). *Motivational interviewing.* Retrieved from http://www.nrepp.samhsa.gov/ViewIntervention.aspx?id=130

Schear, T., & Warhuus, L. (2007, January). *Berkeley integrated resources initiative–Schools mental health partnership: Strategic plan.* Retrieved from http://berkeleyschools.net/uploads/biri/BIRI_Schools_Mental_Health%20.pdf

Schloss, P. J., & Smith, M. A. (1994). *Applied behavioral analysis in the classroom.* Needham Heights, MA: Allyn & Bacon.

Schnell, K., & Herpertz, S. C. (2007). Effects of dialectic-behavioral-therapy on the neural correlates of affective hyperarousal in borderline personality disorder. *Journal of Psychiatric Research, 41*(10), 837–847.

Shahidullah, J. D., & Carlson, J. S. (2012). Training considerations for pediatric psychopharmacology in RxP. *The Tablet: Newsletter of Division 55 of the American Psychological Association, 13,* 6–18.

Shahidullah, J. D., & Carlson, J. S. (2013). *A national survey of school psychologists' roles and training in psychopharmacology.* Poster presented at the National Association of School Psychologists (NASP) Conference, Seattle, WA.

Shirk, S., & Karver, M. (2003). Prediction of treatment outcome from relationship variables in child and adolescent therapy: A meta-analytic review. *Journal of Consulting and Clinical Psychology, 71,* 462–471.

Siegel, L. S. (1988). Evidence that IQ scores are irrelevant to the definition and analysis of reading disability. *Canadian Journal of Psychology, 42,* 201–215. doi: 10.1037/h0084184

Siegle, G. J., Carter, C. S., & Thase, M. E. (2006). Use of fMRI to predict recovery from unipolar depression with cognitive behavior therapy. *American Journal of Psychiatry, 163,* 735–738.

Simonsen, B., Eber, L., Black, A., Sugai, G., Lewandowski, H., Sims, B., & Myers, D. (2012). Illinois statewide positive behavioral interventions and supports evolution and impact on student outcomes across years. *Journal of Positive Behavior Interventions, 14,* 5–16.

Smart, J. F., & Smart, D. W. (1997). The racial/ethnic demography of disability. *Journal of Rehabilitation, 63,* 9–15.

Smith, A. C., & Smith, D. I. (2001). *Emergency and transitional shelter population: 2000* (Census 2000 special reports). Washington, DC: U.S. Department of Commerce. Available: www.census.gov/prod/2001pubs/censr01-2.pdf

Speece, D. L., Molloy, D. E., & Case, L. P. (2003). Starting at the beginning for learning disabilities identification: Response to instruction in general education. *Advances in Learning and Behavioral Disabilities, 16,* 37–50.

Sprenkle, D., & Blow, A. (2004). Common factors and our sacred models. *Journal of Marital and Family Therapy, 30,* 113–130.

Steege, M. W., & Watson, T. S. (2008). Best practices in functional behavioral assessment. In A. Thomas & J. Grimes (Eds.), *Best practices in school psychology* (5th ed., pp. 337–348). Bethesda, MD: National Association of School Psychologists.

Steege, M. W., & Watson, T. S. (2009). *Conducting school-based functional behavioral assessments: A practitioner's guide* (2nd ed.). New York, NY: Guilford.

Stormont, M., Lewis, T. J., Beckner, R., & Johnson, N. W. (2008). *Implementing positive behavior support systems in early childhood and elementary settings* (p. 123). Thousand Oaks, CA: Corwin.

Stormshak, E. A., Connell, A. M., Véronneau, M., Myers, M. W., Dishion, T. J., Kavanagh, K., et al. (2011). An ecological approach to promoting early adolescent mental health and social adaptation: Family-centered intervention in public middle schools. *Child Development, 82,* 209–225.

Sugai, G., Horner, R., & McIntosh, K. (2008). Best practices in developing a broad-scale system of school wide positive behavior support. In A. Thomas & J. Grimes (Eds.), *Best practices in school psychology* (5th ed., pp. 17–36). Bethesda, MD: National Association of School Psychologists.

Sugai, G., Lewis-Palmer, T., Todd, A., & Horner, R. (2001). *School-wide evaluation tool version 2.1.* Educational & Community Supports, University of Oregon.

Sussman, S., Dent, C. W., & Stacy, A. W. (2002). Project Towards No Drug Abuse: A review of the findings and future directions. *American Journal of Health Behavior, 26,* 354–365.

Teicher, M. D. (2000). Wounds that time won't heal: The neurobiology of child abuse. *Cerebrum: The Dana Forum on Brain Science, 2,* 50–67.

Teyber, E., & McClure, F. H. (2011). *Interpersonal process in psychotherapy: An integrative model* (6th ed.). Pacific Grove, CA: Brooks/Cole.

Thomas C. R., & Holzer, C. E. (2006). The continuing shortage of child and adolescent psychiatrists. *Journal of the American Academy of Child & Adolescent Psychiatry, 45,* 1023–1031.

Thompson, R., & Littrell, J. M. (1998). Brief counseling for students with learning disabilities. *Professional School Counseling, 2,* 60–67.

Tilly, D. W. (2008). The evolution of school psychology to science-based practice: Problem solving and the three-tiered model. In A. Thomas & J. Grimes (Eds.), *Best practices in school psychology* (5th ed., pp. 17–36). Bethesda, MD: National Association of School Psychologists.

Tobler, N. S., & Stratton, H. H. (1997). Effectiveness of school-based drug prevention programs: A meta-analysis of the research. *The Journal of Primary Prevention, 18,* 71–128.

Trepper, T. S., McCollum, E. E., De Jong, P., Korman, H., Gingerich, W., & Franklin, C. (2008). *Solution focused therapy treatment manual for working with individuals* (pp. 1–16). Retrieved from http://www.sfbta.org/Research.pdf

Trolley, B. C., Haas, H. S., & Patti, D. C. (2009). *The school counselor's guide to special education.* Thousand Oaks, CA: Corwin.

Twachtman-Cullen, D., & Twachtman-Bassett, J. (2011). *The IEP from A to Z: How to create meaningful and measurable goals and objectives.* San Francisco, CA: Jossey-Bass.

U.S. Department of Education. (2004). Individuals with Disabilities Improvement Act of 2004, Pub. L. 108–466. Federal Register, 70, 35802–35803.

U.S. Government Accounting Office. (2003, July). Special education: Federal actions can assist states in improving postsecondary outcomes for youth. (Publication No. GAO-03–773). Retrieved from GAO Reports Main Page via GPO Access database: http://www.gao.gov/assets/240/238677.pdf

VanDerHeyden, A. M., & Witt, J. C. (2008). Best practices in can't do/won't do assessment. In A. Thomas & J. Grimes (Eds.), *Best practices in school psychology* (5th ed., pp. 131–140). Bethesda, MD: National Association of School Psychologists.

Volpe, R. J., Heick, P. F., & Gureasko-Moore, D. (2005). An agile behavioral model for monitoring the effects of stimulant medication in school settings. *Psychology in the Schools, 42,* 509–523.

Walters, S. T., Clark, M. D., Gingerich, R., & Meltzer, M. L. (2007, June). *A guide for probation and parole: Motivating offenders to change.* U.S. Department of Justice, National Institute of Corrections. Retrieved from http://static.nicic.gov/Library/022253.pdf

Wampold, B. E. (2001). *The great psychotherapy debate: Models, methods and findings.* Mahwah, NJ: Lawrence Erlbaum.

Werner, E., & Smith, R. (1992). *Overcoming the odds: High-risk children from birth to adulthood.* New York, NY: Cornell University Press.

Wheeler, J. J., & Richey, D. D. (2010). *Behavior management: Principles and practices of positive behavior supports* (2nd ed.). Columbus, OH: Pearson.

Whiston, S. C., & Quinby, R. F. (2009). Review of school counseling outcome research. *Psychology in the Schools, 46,* 267–272.

White, S. W., Keonig, K., & Scahill, L. (2007). Social skills development in children with autism spectrum disorders: A review of the intervention literature. *Journal of Autism and Developmental Disorders, 37,* 1858–1868.

Wilson, S. J., Lipsey, M. W., & Derzon, J. H. (2003). The effects of school-based intervention programs on aggressive and disruptive behavior: A meta-analysis. *Journal of Consulting and Clinical Psychology, 71,* 136–149.

Wilson, S. J., & Lipsey, M. W. (2005, May). *The effectiveness of school-based violence prevention programs for reducing disruptive and aggressive behavior.* Revised Report for the National Institute of Justice School Violence Prevention Research Planning Meeting (1–26). Retrieved from https://www.ncjrs.gov/pdffiles1/nij/grants/211376.pdf

Winner, M. G. (2010, November 15). *Latest research on social skills interventions.* Retrieved July 18, 2012, from http://www.socialthinking.com/what-is-social-thinking/michelles-blog/408-latest-research-on-socials-skills-interventions

Wood, C., & Hinkelman, L. (2008). Substance abuse. In H. L. K. Coleman & C. Yeh (Eds.), *Handbook of school counseling* (pp. 717–736). New York, NY: Routledge.

Ysseldyke, J., Burns, M., Dawson, P., Kelley, B., Morrison, D., Ortiz, S., . . . Telzrow, C. (2006). School psychology: A blueprint for training and practice III. In A. Thomas & J. Grimes (Eds.), *Best practices in school psychology* (5th ed., pp. 37–70). Bethesda, MD: National Association of School Psychologists.

Zalaquett, C. P., Fuerth, K. M., Stein, C., Ivey, A. E., & Ivey, M. B. (2008). Reframing the *DSM-IV-TR* from a multicultural/social justice perspective. *Journal of Counseling & Development, 86,* 364–371.

Zinn, B. (1996). The relationship of ego development and the counseling effectiveness of counselor trainees. *Dissertation Abstracts International, 56,* 12B. (UMI No. 95011–161).

Zirpoli, T. J., & Melloy, K. J. (1993). *Behavior management: Applications for teachers and parents.* New York, NY: Macmillan.

Zubin, J., & Spring, B. (1977). Vulnerability: A new view of schizophrenia. *Journal of Abnormal Psychology, 86,* 103–126.

Zyromski, B., & Edwards-Joseph, A. E. (2008). Utilizing cognitive behavioral interventions to positively impact academic achievement in middle school students. *The Journal of School Counseling, 6.* Retrieved from http://www.jsc.montana.edu/articles/v6n15.pdf

Index

CORWIN

A SAGE Company

The Corwin logo—a raven striding across an open book—represents the union of courage and learning. Corwin is committed to improving education for all learners by publishing books and other professional development resources for those serving the field of PreK–12 education. By providing practical, hands-on materials, Corwin continues to carry out the promise of its motto: **"Helping Educators Do Their Work Better."**